Investigating ALIAS

INVESTIGATING CULT TV

Series Editor: Stacey Abbott

The *Investigating Cult TV* series is a fresh forum for discussion and debate about the changing nature of cult television. It sets out to reconsider cult television and its intricate networks of fandom by inviting authors to rethink how cult TV is conceived, produced, programmed and consumed. It will also challenge traditional distinctions between cult and quality television.

Offering an accessible path through the intricacies and pleasures of cult TV, the books in this series will interest scholars, students and fans alike. They will include close studies of individual contemporary television shows. They will also reconsider genres at the heart of cult programming, such as science fiction, horror and fantasy, as well as genres like teen TV, animation and reality TV when these have strong claims to cult status. Books will also examine themes or trends that are key to the past, present and future of cult television.

The first books in the **Investigating Cult TV** series:

Investigating **Farscape** by Jes Battis
Investigating **Alias** edited by Stacey Abbott and Simon Brown
Investigating **Charmed** edited by Stan Beeler and Karin Beeler

Ideas and submissions for **Investigating Cult TV** to
s.abbott@roehampton.ac.uk
p.brewster@blueyonder.co.uk

Investigating ALIAS

Secrets and Spies

edited by
Stacey Abbott and Simon Brown

I.B. TAURIS

LONDON · NEW YORK

Published in 2007 by I.B.Tauris & Co Ltd
6 Salem Road, London W2 4BU
175 Fifth Avenue, New York NY 10010
www.ibtauris.com

In the United States of America and Canada
distributed by Palgrave Macmillan, a division of St Martin's Press
175 Fifth Avenue, New York NY 10010

Investigating Cult TV Series
ISBN 978 1 84511 405 3

A full CIP record for this book is available from the British Library
A full CIP record is available from the Library of Congress

Library of Congress Catalog Card Number: available

Typeset in Palatino by JCS Publishing Services, www.jcs-publishing.co.uk
Printed and bound in India by Replika Press Pvt. Ltd

Contents

Acknowledgements

Undoubtedly our first vote of thanks should go to Sergio Angelini, who first drew our attention to this great show on Sky One (which we didn't get at the time) that he thought we would really like. After much indifference on our part, finally he bought and lent us the DVD's of Seasons One through Three, which we raced through in a matter of weeks. If it wasn't for his persistence, not only would this book not exist, we would probably never have seen *Alias* at all. Maybe he was right about *Babylon 5* too.

While Sergio provided us with initial access to the first three seasons (and watching Season Four was all our own work), we also want to thank Rachel De Grace and Danielle McBride, our Canadian cell, who diligently recorded and sent us every episode of Season Five. Without them we would have been barely halfway through the season before the book was due, and we are both grateful for their immense generosity, not just in terms of time, but also in spirit.

Editing this book has been an absolute pleasure, and the thanks for that must go to our contributors. Each has been consummately professional in terms of meeting deadlines and responding to our (frequent but polite) editorial comments. More importantly, they have brought insight, energy and enthusiasm to the project and each of them has made not just a major contribution to this book but to TV scholarship in general. Thank you to all at I.B.Tauris who have helped us take this book from its original inception to final publication, especially also to Jessica Cuthbert-Smith for her amazing editorial and design work. Thanks to ABC for providing the cover image and Coral Pettreti for clearing the copyright.

Most importantly, this book would not exist were it not for the support and encouragement of Philippa Brewster, who sees the value and worth in contemporary television and has tirelessly promoted its study. Philippa deserves to be recognised for the important and yet invisible part she has played in the emerging field of television studies.

On a more personal note, many of the ideas for this book have been discussed over long walks in the park with our dog, Max.

Thanks for the walks, little man. Finally, it seems appropriate when writing about a TV series that features so many strong women that we dedicate this book to the two strongest women we know: our mothers Joan Abbott and Sheila Brown. Their courage is inspiring. We thought they ought to know that.

Contributors

Stacey Abbott is Senior Lecturer in Film and Television Studies at Roehampton University. She has written on the horror genre, computer special effects in science fiction and *Buffy the Vampire Slayer*. She is the editor of *Reading Angel: The TV Spin-off with a Soul* (I.B.Tauris, 2005) and the author of *Celluloid Vampires* (The University of Texas Press, forthcoming).

Sergio Angelini translated the English language version of Virgilio Tosi's *Cinema Before Cinema* (BUFVC, 2005), edited *The Researcher's Guide* (BUFVC, 2006) and has contributed dozens of entries to *Dizionario dei Registi del Cinema Mondiale* (Einaudi, 2005/06), *The Reference Guide to British and Irish Film Directors* (BFI, 2006) and the screenonline web resource. He is the television reviewer for *Sight & Sound* magazine.

Dyrk Ashton is an Assistant Professor of Film at the University of Toledo, where he teaches Film Studies and Production. He worked professionally in the 'biz' until finding his true calling as a film scholar through his PhD in Film Studies with an extensive concentration in American Culture Studies, Popular Culture and Philosophy.

Elizabeth Barnes is Associate professor of English and American Studies at the College of William and Mary. She is author *States of Sympathy: Seduction and Democracy in the American Novel* (Columbia University Press, 1997) and editor of *Incest and the Literary Imagination* (University Press of Florida, 2002). She is currently finishing a book-length project on love and violence in nineteenth-century American culture titled, *The Whipping Boy of Love: Substitution and Sentiment in the American Imagination*.

Linda Baughman is an assistant professor of Communication Studies at Christopher Newport University. Her work examines sex and sexuality from a critical/cultural theoretical perspective, and includes essays on the 1930s birth control activist Mary Ware Dennett and the 1957 Supreme Court case, *Roth v. U.S.*

Simon Brown is Senior Lecturer in Film Studies at Kingston University. A specialist in early cinema history, he has published on such diverse topics as early erotic cinema, the Titanic and the economic development of the film industry in London. He is currently completing his PhD thesis on the British filmmaking pioneer Cecil Hepworth.

Deborah Finding is a PhD student at the Gender Institute at the London School of Economics. Her research is concerned with sexual violence narratives in popular music and draws on her professional work with survivors of violence. She has a BA and an MA from the University of Cambridge.

Tricia Jenkins is an American Studies Doctoral Candidate at Michigan State University, where she is writing a dissertation on the evolution of the female spy in American television. Her published articles have appeared in the Journal of Popular Culture, the Journal of American Culture, and Popular Music and Society.

David Lavery holds a chair in Film and Television at Brunel University, London. He is the author of over 100 published essays and reviews and author/editor/co-editor of eleven books, including *Reading Deadwood: A Western to Swear By* (I.B.Tauris, 2006) and *Reading The Sopranos: Hit TV from HBO* (I.B.Tauris, 2006) in the Reading Contemporary Television Series. He co-edits the e-journal *Slayage: The Online International Journal of Buffy Studies*, and is one of the founding editors of the new journal *Critical Studies in Television: Scholarly Studies of Small Screen Fictions*.

Alice MacLachlan is a PhD student at Boston University and a Junior Visiting Fellow at the Institute for Human Sciences (Vienna). She holds degrees in Philosophy from the University of Cambridge and from Queen's University (Canada). Her research interests include topics in moral philosophy and feminist theory.

Michaela D.E. Meyer is an Assistant Professor of Communication Studies at Christopher Newport University. She received her PhD in

Communication Studies and a Certificate in Women's Studies from Ohio University. Meyer's work publications about the representation of women on television include essays on *Charmed*, *Law & Order* and *Dawson's Creek*.

Henrik Örnebring is Senior Lecturer in Television Studies at Roehampton University. His research interests include genre history and theory, television history, and journalism studies. He has published articles on these subjects in *European Journal of Communication* and *Journalism Studies*, and has recently contributed to *Re-viewing Television History: Critical Issues in Television Historiography* (I.B.Tauris, forthcoming).

Denzell Richards is a Visiting Lecturer in Film Studies at Roehampton University, where he is working on a doctoral thesis researching audience relationship to DVD.

Hillary Robson is a recent graduate from Middle Tennessee State University with a Masters degree in English. Her major areas of interest include fandom, popular culture and television studies. Future projects include contributing to a forthcoming encyclopedia on the television series *Lost*, a composition series textbook and an edited collection on *Grey's Anatomy*.

Sharon Sutherland is Clinical Instructor in Dispute Resolution at the University of British Columbia Faculty of Law where she teaches mediation, advocacy and contract law. Sharon practises as a child protection mediator and is leading the development of a child protection mediation practicum programme for British Columbia.

Sarah Swan is a practising lawyer. She has collaborated with Sharon Sutherland on a variety of law and popular culture topics, including essays on *Angel*, women lawyers on television and 24.

Jennifer R. Young earned her PhD in American Literature from Howard University and is currently an Assistant Professor at Hope College. Her scholarship interests include cultural criticism, African-American literature (pre 1865) and comparative literature which links contemporary artists and cultures to early Black writers and artists of the eighteenth century.

Paul Zinder is a Professor of Media Studies and Production at The American University of Rome, Italy. He is also an award winning film and video maker, whose work has screened internationally. He was born in Baltimore, Maryland.

Cast List

Principal Characters

Jennifer Garner	Sydney Bristow
Ron Rifkin	Arvin Sloane
Michael Vartan	Michael Vaughn
Victor Garber	Jack Bristow
Carl Lumbly	Marcus Dixon
Kevin Weisman	Marshall Flinkman

Supporting and/or Recurring Characters

Amy Acker	Kelly Peyton
David Anders	Julian Sark
Bradley Cooper	Will Tippen
Merrin Dungey	Francie/Allison Doren
Melissa George	Lauren Reed
Balthazar Getty	Thomas Grace
Greg Grunberg	Eric Weiss
Mia Maestro	Nadia Santos
Lena Olin	Irina Derevko
Terry O'Quinn	Director Kendall
Rachel Nichols	Rachel Gibson
Elodie Bouchez	Renée Rienne
Patricia Wettig	Dr Judy Barnett

For our mothers, Joan and Sheila

Preface

Five Incredible Years

David Lavery

'Thank you for five incredible years'.
Placard at the end of 'All the Time in the World',
the final episode of *Alias*

incredible
adjective 1 impossible or hard to believe. **2** informal extraordinarily
good.

Oxford English Dictionary

'Incredible' is an incredibly ambiguous word. The producers of the
recently deceased *Alias*, an ABC television spy drama that ended its
five-year, never-quite-successful-in-the-ratings run in May 2006,
were, of course, thinking of the *Oxford English Dictionary*'s (informal)
second definition – 'extraordinarily good' – when they posted their
now obligatory tip-of-the-hat-to-the-fans closing title.

The finales of popular television series – of a *M*A*S*H* or *Seinfeld*
or *Friends* – often engender 'cultural spectacles' (Morreale 2003), and
the endings of most long-running episodic series, with their perma-
nent closure of complex narratives, ordinarily result in at least an
attendant sense of the dramatic. But *Alias*' return to the air on 19
April, after a four-month 'maternity leave' in a season of bad ratings,[1] resulted in little fanfare, and the airing of the 104th and 105th
episodes on 22 May 2006 went virtually unnoticed. As Colin Mahan
(2006) would note the day after the end, '*Alias* left the air forever last
night, but audiences denied knowing it existed. Instead of giving the
show a normal send-off, ABC moved the finale to Monday and pitted it against the season finales of *24* and TV's number-one sitcom,
Two and a Half Men. Even Sydney Bristow couldn't get out of that
kind of fix'.

Recapping the final episode of *Alias* on the ever-snarky Television Without Pity website, 'Erin' would seem to have been reverting to the original meaning of 'incredible': 'impossible or hard to believe'. Snidely observant, Erin describes the setup for a sequence in which five years of Rambaldi mythology (and a thirty-year quest by criminal mastermind Arvin Sloane) comes to a climax:

> Mongolia. Somebody get me a sherpa and a flagon of yak's milk and get me the hell out of here. At a large encampment in the middle of Palm Desert, Sloane arrives in a Humvee. He gets out and meets with a man speaking Russian. The man says he thinks they've 'found it', and Sloane walks with him into a bunker that has the Rambaldi eye symbol <O> on it.

But then her incredulity gets the best of her and she loses it:

> Well, that [a Rambaldi symbol in Mongolia] can't be good. Or maybe it's awesome. Anything that moves this plot along is fine by me. The closer we are to *this mess* ending the better. Oh, what? Like YOU don't feel the same? Please. Even the ACTORS think this show should've ended, like, two seasons ago. And they actually LOVE it. *And Jaybrams CLEARLY thought it should have ended ages ago because he left back when shit still made sense*, and he's barely returned long enough to have a piece of cheesecake down in the damn commissary. *This shit is over, dudes. OVER.* (my italics)

Well the shit (aka *Alias'* no longer credible writing[2]) may have been 'over' (aka 'outstayed its welcome', 'continued its narrative too long', 'didn't know when to quit'), but the episode was not.

Much had already transpired: Sydney rappelled off a skyscraper in a pretend Sydney, managing, incredibly, to snap photos of The Twelve on the way down! (and perhaps inspiring the leap of faith of Ethan Hunt (Tom Cruise) in a real Shanghai in Jaybrams' *Mission: Impossible III*); Marshall Flinkman's revealing photoshoot in a Bangkok sauna; Marshall and Rachel's kidnapping; dizzying planet-hops to Rome, Ixtopia, London, Mount Subasio, etc. that made even 24's instantaneous crisscrossing of Los Angeles seem languid; the destruction of APO (and a good portion of downtown LA) by a Sark-planted explosion; numerous flashbacks to Syd's childhood; Peyton's Uzi-in-each-hand slaughter of The Twelve (or was it the Circle of the Black Thorn?).[3]

And much was yet to come. The satellites ('stars') had not yet fallen from the sky; the planned launch (by Irina Derevko) of stolen

Russian ICBMs toward London and Washington had not yet been activated (and then prevented). Jack had not yet been shot in the chest by Sloane or Sloane gunned down by Sydney, nor had Vaughn shot Sark in the leg, or Rachel revealed the secret (snakes) to getting answers out of Peyton. Sloane had not yet become immortal. Sydney had not battled to the death with her mother. Irina had not, like all good movie supervillains, plummeted to her death from a high place. Nor had Jack set off the explosion that would bury his friend-turned-nemesis Sloane, doomed to live forever-interred, or uttered his candidate-for-the-Last Words Hall of Fame exit line: 'You beat death Arvin, but you couldn't beat me.' Sloane was still to be abandoned to eternal loneliness by the ghost/hallucination of Nadia, the daughter he had murdered. Nor was 'All the Time in the World' over until Dixon visited an obviously content Sydney and Vaughn and children at their beach home, living, but not spying, happily ever after.

Still, TelevisionWithoutPity.com's ire is hardly *sui generis* nor without some justification. After a strong and promising start, creator J.J. Abrams' series about a dysfunctional spy family had, by almost any measure, indeed become 'a mess', if not shit. Yes, following his modus operandi – during its inaugural season, he would later abandon the most successful of his progeny, the international hit *Lost*, as well – 'Jaybrams' had left the spy business long before his creation Sydney Bristow would, back when *Alias* made very good sense indeed.[4]

Before *Alias*, the Mount Holyoke film studies major Abrams had authored/co-authored a variety of feature films[5] and created the television series *Felicity* (1998–2002). *Alias*, he has suggested, was the result of wanting to do 'something with dramatic stakes a few notches higher than the romantic turmoil of a college coed' (Dilmore 2005: 22).[6] '[My] favorite kind of story', genre fan Abrams insists,[7] is 'something that's *just left of real* but done with the commitment and the respect for characters and the audience that any well-told drama would apply. When that happens, you've got something special' (my italics; Dilmore 2005: 24).

Although admitting he's uncertain '[w]hether it's smart or successful storytelling', he confesses to being driven by the need to add a 'hyper-real' element (Gross 2005: 36). Under his guidance *Alias* developed a series-long 'mythology' involving the Renaissance genius Milo Rambaldi;[8] and in Abrams' (and co-creator Damon

Lindelof's) hands, *Lost* become much more than the originally proposed low concept 'plane crashes on a desert island'.[9] 'Well begun is
half done' (according to Aristotle – an old cliché), but as the second
Iraq War and many a failed or never-having-lived-up-to-their-
potential television series attest, half done ≠ well done.

Given her anger bred of disappointment and betrayal (an emotion not uncommon among *Alias* aficionados, as Hillary Robson
chronicles in her history of the evolution and dissolution of *Alias*
Fandom in this volume), Erin may well not be anxious to read this
exemplary collection of investigations into nearly every corner of
the *Alias*verse. Her loss. You, however, will find a wide variety of
ingenious maps by which to navigate such topoi as narrative, myth,
heroism, body image, family dynamics, race, ethics, epistemology
and fandom/fanfic. If the essential function of all criticism is to send
the reader back to the text renewed, reinvigorated for a fresh exploration with enhanced perception, this book is indispensable.

At the inception of *Buffy* Studies half a decade ago, no one
dreamed that a television series to which *Alias* is compared in these
pages (in Elizabeth Barnes' essay) would in a few short years inspire
hundreds of essays and at least eighteen books. *Alias* is not likely to
have an afterlife as rich as *Buffy*'s, but even if it does not continue in
the years ahead to garner critical scrutiny, even if five seasons of
Alias DVDs come to lie buried in a Rambaldish crypt, it will always
have this comprehensive, pluralistic, ingenious book to remind us of
its moment in the small-screen sun and our while-it-lasted
fascination.

Introduction

'Serious Spy Stuff':
The Cult Pleasures of *Alias*[1]

Simon Brown and Stacey Abbott

Since its premiere, *Alias* has been a critical darling and cult favorite but never found a mainstream audience. What kept it from being axed, more than anything, was that ABC couldn't afford to chop it. The network was doing too poorly, which meant it had to hold onto any show with any promise. But all that changed . . . with the huge success of *Lost* and *Desperate Housewives*. With two solid hits, it's in a far better position to slash shows that aren't performing.

(Tallerico 2005)

To begin, as the narrative of *Alias* did itself, with an admission of truth, we loved Season Three. We came to *Alias* late in the day at a friend's recommendation and spent a feverish period of several weeks catching up with three seasons on DVD, and as far as we were concerned, it just kept getting better and better. When we emerged, exhausted, having climbed over the dead body of Lauren and the shattered wasteland of Vaughn's marriage and his and Sydney's relationship we were staggered to find out that the majority of *Alias* fans, and even the show's creator J.J. Abrams, had little time for Season Three. What is even more surprising perhaps, is that the articles in this book almost all agree on one thing: Season Three was the most important and the most interesting in the development of the show, a development that, more than any other contemporary TV show, wore its industrial context and its audience relations right there on its sleeve for all to see.

Season Three offers a good starting point to consider this, since the season began with Sydney's desperate hunt to track down her missing time, complicated further by the introduction of Vaughn's phenomenally unpopular wife, Lauren Reed. Series creator J.J.

Abrams was outspoken about his unhappiness with the direction the show was taking while he was elsewhere preparing *Lost*, an unhappiness shared by the fans, which resulted in a startling mid-season U-turn in which the entire narrative around Sydney's missing years was resolved in a single episode ('Full Disclosure', 3:11) which was followed by the revelation that Lauren was in fact an operative for Season Three's big bad, The Covenant. This was not the first time such a dramatic turnround had taken place, of course. Mid-way through Season Two Abrams jettisoned the entire premise of the show up to that point, on the grounds that the show was basically too complicated for new or casual viewers. During the first season and a half, Sydney Bristow (Jennifer Garner) is an agent for SD-6, which most of its employees believe is a secret arm of the CIA but is, in fact, part of the Alliance, an evil terrorist organisation. Sydney discovers this in episode one 'Truth Be Told', and so becomes a double agent for the CIA, working with another double agent, her father, to bring down SD-6. Or, as Abrams himself puts it, 'it's a show with good guys pretending to be bad guys, many of the bad guys are pretending that they're good guys, and quite a few of the bad guys don't even know that they're bad guys' (quoted in Gross 2003: 47). Although Season One gained eleven Emmy nominations, massive hip credentials after a high-profile guest appearance by Quentin Tarantino, and certainly won the support of a beleaguered ABC, there were concerns about the show's ratings, with average audiences of 9.5 million and a ranking of only 65 out of 191. Abrams' streamlining strategy was designed to deal with this. 'Last year the show required some mental gymnastics', he said, 'We're trying to make it easier for new viewers to know what's going on' (quoted in Anon 2002: 21).

Decreased narrative complexity is, as Henrik Örnebring demonstrates in the first essay in this volume, visible throughout the progression of the series from season to season, and was further augmented by the breakdown of the season arc structure of the show in Season Four at the demands of the network for more one-off episodes to encourage the casual viewer. As writer Jesse Alexander points out, more stand-alone episodes was 'one of the mandates we had gotten from the network; that they were really concerned with the serialised nature of the show and the way that we told stories they felt that that was off-putting to a general audience'. (DVD audio commentary, 'Nocturne' S4:D2[2]). This was not just aimed at

Alias; the previous year the fifth season of Warner Brothers' *Angel* was likewise mandated to break from the season-length arc narratives it had been exploring the previous two years. Like *Angel*, the popularity of *Alias* was consistent year by year, but never really grew. Both shows retained a base of loyal viewers but failed to attract new ones in sufficient numbers. Hence both shows were allowed to finish their fifth seasons and reach the 100-episode watermark required for syndication in the USA before the plug was pulled.

Overall the popularity of *Alias* dropped. Season Two had an average 8.2 million viewers while Season Three maintained an average 9.7 million. Season Four began with 16 million for the opener but tailed off, while Season Five was placed only 90 out of 156, with an average of 6.7 million. ('Series 2005–6 Primetime Wrap' 2006). The problem faced by the show was that the more the basic premise changed to attract new viewers, the more its loyal audience suffered and disappeared. The demise of SD-6 in Season Two already caused rumbles of discontent, which turned into outright rebellion in Season Three, as Hillary Robson points out in this volume. The move to stand-alone episodes was equally unpopular. In one of the many *Alias* discussion boards, Season Four came out top in a poll of the worst season. One contributor noted that, 'I hated Season Four. The first 13 episodes were pointless. Not *Alias* style' (addyawesome 2006) while another added 'all the stand-alone eppys were boring' (rporche 2006) and a third that Season Four ranked lowest 'because the episodes were all self-contained' (aliasmycrack 2006). One fan, bitterbyrden (2006), complained, 'I'll never forgive JJ . . . for dumbing it down when ABC told him to'.

Clearly the result of these efforts to garner a wider mainstream audience for the series denies the fact that it was, from its inception, always a 'cult' show. *Alias* appeared in September 2001 alongside two other similar series, *The Agency* and *24*. While *The Agency* offered an authentic, and CIA-approved, examination of its agents, missions and codes of practice, *24* situated itself firmly within the 'constructed reality' camp, through its emphasis upon 'real' time and use of split-screen techniques to shift, big-brother style, between concurrent moments of interest while dealing with international terrorism in a homeland security context. *Alias* likewise dealt with international terrorism and espionage, but hidden within the folds of its narrative was a strong streak of the supernatural, in the guise of the mythical fifteenth-century prophet Milo Rambaldi, whose inventions and predictions held sway over the series' cast of super-spies and supervillains and, particularly, the show's heroine, Sydney Bristow. His omnipresence throughout the series' five-year run represented the same merging of conservative government institutions with the uncanny, the carnivalesque and the mystical that helped to popularise *The X-Files* – which by the time of *Alias'* arrival was well on the wane, making *Alias* its natural successor. Furthermore, the Rambaldi puzzle, alongside the gradual reveal of Sydney's complicated family history, Arvin Sloane's shifting loyalties and Irina Derevko's Machiavellian intrigues, offered audiences an intricate tapestry of missions, family secrets and political agendas to unravel as part of the viewing pleasure of the series. It is precisely this narrative complexity that incites the cult audience to immerse themselves within the series, as explained by Sara Gwenllian Jones and Roberta E. Pearson: ' "[c]ult television" has become a metagenre that caters to intense, interpretive audience practices' stemming from 'an imaginative involvement with the cult television narratives that afford fans enormous scope for further interpretation, specula-tion, and invention' (2004: xvi). Furthermore, as Örnebring points out, it is the series' devotion to its characters that drives the show even more than narrative and as such inspires the level of fan loyalty and time-consuming fan practices, as described by Hillary Robson and Tricia Jenkins, that is such an intrinsic element of cult TV. The corollary is equally true in that the seeming betrayal of established characters, such as Vaughn's marriage to Lauren so soon after Syd-ney's 'death', Vaughn's death at the beginning of Season Five and Irina's final attempt to kill Sydney in the series' finale 'All the Time in the World', inspires the cult TV audience's anger and frustration with a series, resulting in either their abandonment of the show or their appropriation of it through their own fan practices such as online discussion boards, fan fiction, slash fiction, fan art and inter-pretive music videos.[3] As Jones and Pearson point out: '[c]ult television's imaginary universes support an inexhaustible range of narrative possibilities, inviting, supporting, and rewarding close textual analysis, interpretation, and inventive reformulations' (2004: xii). The *Alias* universe offers such a limitless range of possibilities, attested to by the extreme fan responses, both negative and positive, that have been generated by the series. The fans' passionate expres-sions of adoration and anger throughout the show are a testament to *Alias'* cult status.

Another characteristic of cult TV is the manner in which such series 'provide the perfect vehicle for metaphorical explorations of social concerns' (Jones and Pearson 2004: xvii). In this *Alias* has much in common with its natural predecessor *Buffy the Vampire Slayer*, a series around which much interpretive discussion, by fans and scholars alike, has taken place. *Alias* shares with *Buffy*, as argued by Elizabeth Barnes in this volume, its representation of an ass-kicking, self-sacrificing, tortured heroine, and as such falls into a new tradition of series within cult television, seeking to redefine the action heroine within a post-feminist world. As Rhonda V. Wilcox points out, Buffy and Xena are simply 'among the most noteworthy of a proliferation of television series that highlight protagonists who might be called Athena's daughters: strong, intelligent, heroic warriors who defend the right as they see right' (2003: ix). Sydney is one of the most recent of such daughters. Like Buffy, she battles against both human and mystic threats against a backdrop of a more daunting struggle between a dysfunctional family, duty and a normal life, but while the narrative of *Buffy* followed her increasing challenge to patriarchal authority, from her initial break from the Watchers' Council to her reversal of the patriarchally imposed doctrine that there can only be One Slayer, Sydney struggles daily to assert her own agency from within a series of male-dominated espionage institutions (SD-6, the CIA and APO) as well as the spy genre itself. While Sydney does not overthrow such agencies, the series' juxtaposition of the conventions of the spy genre with melodrama offers a space for its heroine to regularly challenge and undermine them by offering a vision of the new heroine: a heroine strong enough in mind and body to confront her male superior, in the men's restroom, in order to challenge his competency when his political machinations compromise one of her missions:

Lindsey: What exactly is the purpose of this conversation?
Sydney: To let you know that I will take you to the mat every time you pull something like this. I am not impressed by the fact that you play golf with the President. What you did was moronic and borderline criminal.
Lindsey: Has it slipped your mind that I am the director of the National Security Council? I can pick up the phone and have you thrown into the same jail cell that your father just vacated. Hell! It's still warm.
Sydney: Do it. Give me an object lesson in the abuse of power. Show me how it's done.

Lindsey: If you're finished . . . this is the men's room.
Sydney: Who let you in? ('Succession', 3:2)

Here the narrative's position within this male-dominated environment enables Sydney to undermine patriarchy on its own terrain as
she challenges Lindsey's position as a politician and as a man. Furthermore, the series' overwhelming mosaic of female superspies who
surround Sydney – including her sister Nadia Santos, colleague
Rachel Gibson, nemesis Anna Espinosa, rival Lauren Reed, enemies
Allison Doren and Kelly Peyton, and most importantly the morally
ambiguous and dastardly unscrupulous Derevko sisters, Irina, Katya
and Elena – offer a range of images of powerful and imposing
women who by their very presence challenge patriarchal authority,
or as Frances Early and Kathleen Kennedy posit, disrupt 'the narrative tradition of the male just warrior' (2003: 3). More significantly, as
Wilcox argues, the strength of contemporary series featuring such
action heroines is that they do not require their characters to be 'mon-
olithically virtuous' and do not 'oversimplify complex issues' (2003:
x). When considered together, these women are neither 'monolithi-
cally' good nor evil, but rather present an exploration of the
complexities of female strength and power within an increasingly
morally ambiguous political world. In *Alias* we are presented with a
new action heroine not only for a post-feminist world but a post-9/11
world, as argued by Sharon Sutherland and Sarah Swan. Given that
that the series came on the air directly following the events of 11 September 2001 and is focused upon the theme of global terrorism, 9/11
is an obvious reference point for discussion. J.J. Abrams has throughout the series run sought to deny the series' relationship to the tragic
events of 9/11 by claiming that '[w]e were never doing a show about
real-life intelligence agencies or the actual terrorists they might be
pursuing', and director of photography Michael Bonvillain credited
the series' more fantastical elements as what separates it from 'real'
world terrorist events, '[t]he fact that we're more of a James Bondian
kind of fantasy and that she can sing, dance, and almost fly has made
it less comparable to 9/ll' (quoted in Gross 2002: 38). The fantastic
quality of this cult TV series has, however, enabled the show to
directly engage with and express the cultural climate of doubt, insecurity and the changing conceptions of 'right and wrong' that
dominates contemporary global society.

It is this fantastic quality that also forms the basis of the pleasures
of the show. The Rambaldi narrative with its endless series of inter-

locking puzzles leading only to further clues prefigures the global phenomenon of the *Da Vinci Code*, while the emphasis on Sydney's alias of the week and its accompanying fashion statement harks back to the camp of *The Avengers* and the sexy spy siren Emma Peel. In Season Four the credits were changed for the first time, removing the simple black and white rotating blocks and replacing them with a montage of Syd's more famous outfits. This dizzying parade of masquerades highlights both the fashion *and* the icon; Sydney is at the same time sexy model and action heroine. In each brief shot she is seen to be moving towards the camera with purpose, a mixture of catwalk strut and single-minded determination. Sydney the spy is both the observer and the observed, inviting the observation as part of the game. The pleasure comes from both watching her in a blue rubber dress, and knowing she can kick ass in it. The repetitive pleasure of the alias is mirrored by the series' constant obsession with fantastic technology and gadgetry, embodied in the opposite figures of Rambaldi and Marshall. Rambaldi's technology is a constant danger to Sydney, not just in the retrieval but in the make-up of the artefacts themselves. On the other hand Marshall Flinkman, a kind of 'Q' figure brought into briefings to dispense ludicrous spywear, becomes part of the security blanket surrounding Sydney. As he tells her, 'It's my job to keep you safe' ('The Abduction', 2:10).

What Marshall also brings to the *Alias*verse, perhaps the show's most secret pleasure, is his humour. Often perceived as a very serious show, and easy to mistake as such on a single viewing, it is through a cult reading of the show that the humour emerges. Marshall's regular intrusion into the drama with his awkward social skills and rambling, tangential observations provide welcome respites from the 'serious spy stuff', but again, it is through knowledge of the character that such humour comes to life. Likewise, when Jack dryly observes that his grand-daughter Isabelle is laughing at him because 'Apparently I'm funny' ('No Hard Feelings', 5:15), it is only those who know the character that get the joke.

It is this that designates *Alias* as a cult show. To fully appreciate it, you need to put time and effort into understanding its characters and appreciating its pleasures. It is necessary to put the work in to reap the rewards. This book is about exploring some of the rewards the show has to offer. To return to Jones and Pearson's claim, cult TV rewards 'close textual analysis, interpretation, and inventive reformulations' (2004: xii). If this is true, then this book is an extension of that cult experience as each of the contributors here rewards the reader by offering such analysis, interpretation and reformulation, not just of the series, but of those who watched it. *Alias* was cancelled about a month after work on this volume began, and while the narrative of the Bristows might be finished, this book forms part of their legacy and, like Rambaldi's prophecies, can help, we hope, to keep the followers of the Bristows loyal to the cause.

Part One

MISSIONS/
COUNTER MISSIONS

Narrative and *Alias*

1 The Show Must Go On...
And On:
Narrative and Seriality in *Alias*

Henrik Örnebring

Seriality, i.e. the narrative that continues from episode to episode, is becoming more and more important for understanding TV texts (Kozloff 1992: 92; Nelson 1997: 30ff; Hammond 2005: 80f). Through a case study of *Alias*, I will examine seriality as it currently appears in American 'quality TV' (AQT). The focus of my analysis is the role and function of seasonal narratives (the subplots that run across and sometimes between the seasons of a show), and I will seek to develop and critique the argument made by some scholars (notably Creeber 2004; Hammond 2005; Ndalianis 2005) that the increased seriality also means an increased narrative complexity.

The serial format and serial narratives have a long tradition and are not unique to television: serialised fiction, comics and television all make use of serial narratives. Ndalianis (2005: 85) identifies *delaying of closure* as a key feature of all serial narratives – through the use of cliffhangers and multiple parallel storylines not resolved within the scope of the individual serial instalment, consumers are encouraged to return for the next instalment, and the next, and so on. Hagedorn (1988) further argues that serials tend to become the dominant narrative form in periods where media competition (and therefore also the need to attract and retain audiences) is intense. This is also borne out by Nelson (1997: 69ff), who places the drive towards increased seriality in television within a context of increased competition and transnationalisation of the cultural economy.

AQT is by definition serial in character. Some key traits (as found in Thompson, 1996: 13ff) of the genre depend on seriality to function: for example series *memory* (i.e. episodes frequently refer back to earlier episodes and/or an extensive backstory) and *ensemble casts* (which allows for multiple viewpoints and multiple narratives centred on particular characters). AQT also attracts a particular audience. The increased competition from satellite and cable TV in the USA in the 1980s made the networks change tack, and instead of aiming for the mass audience they made it a conscious strategy to reach the most valuable audiences – well-educated, high-income young urbanites (Jancovich and Lyons 2003: 3). The seriality of AQT can thus be viewed as the result of a commercially motivated strategy to attract a particular audience segment that enjoys multi-layered, literary narratives, ensemble acting, complex backstory and serial 'memory' (again, see Thompson 1996 and Jancovich and Lyons 2003).

The industrial context is thus very important to an understanding of seriality. Some scholars of serial narrative on TV (like Jancovich and Lyons 2003; Allrath, Gymnich and Surkamp 2005; Ndalianis 2005) tend to focus very much on the text and largely ignore the conditions of textual production. Others (like Gitlin 1994; Nelson 1997; Thompson 2003) explicitly link serial narrative to a context of commercial TV production. This chapter is based on a textual analysis, but I will also attempt to bring a discussion of production conditions into the argument in order to provide a more nuanced and critical picture of narrative and seriality in modern American quality television.

ANALYTICAL FRAMEWORK

On the following pages, I present a series of diagrams illustrating the serial narrative in *Alias*, tracking the various subplots and how they develop across seasons. I have identified as subplots any element of the story that is framed within the discourse as a *conflict* moving towards a *resolution*. A rule of thumb is that I have classified as a subplot those parts of the text that can be summarised in a *question*. Subplots must be distinguished from *themes*, i.e. elements of discourse that recur within the narrative (frequently structured around character relationships) but are not represented as conflicts moving towards a resolution. For example, the relationship between

Sydney and her co-worker at SD-6, Marcus Dixon, does not start out as part of a subplot, i.e. there is no clearly identifiable conflict that moves towards a clearly identifiable resolution. The theme (the Dixon/Sydney relationship) turns into a subplot when Dixon starts suspecting that Sydney might be a double agent. The conflict of that subplot then moves towards a resolution containing the answer to the question: 'Will Dixon reveal Sydney as a double agent?' and possibly 'How will Dixon react to this revelation?'

The distinction between theme and plot lies in how possibilities for resolution are clearly posited within the discourse. For example, the question 'Will a reconciliation between Sydney and Jack ever occur?' (the question at the heart of the 'Sydney/Jack relationship' subplot in Season One) has two clear possible resolutions embedded in the discourse, these simply being 'Yes' and 'No'. On the other hand, while the relationship between Sydney and Dixon could be posed as a question along the lines of 'How will the relationship between Sydney and Dixon develop?', this question can be answered (and thus resolved) in an infinite number of ways *until* it is reframed as a question that can be answered unequivocally within the discourse ('Will Dixon reveal Sydney as a double agent?'), at which point it turns into a subplot.

I refer to the sum of the number of plots occurring within an episode as the *narrative density* of that episode. However, as I am mostly concerned with the serial narrative, I have not counted the *episode narrative*, i.e. the conflict introduced and resolved within the space of the single episode (frequently tied to one of Sydney's missions to steal something or prevent some disaster from occurring) towards the narrative density. We just need to keep in mind that in addition to all the plots across the series (i.e. the serial narrative), there is also, generally, a narrative presented and resolved within each individual episode.

I have also coded two narrative elements that belong more on the level of the single episode narrative than on the level of the serial narrative: the presence of *cliffhangers* and *in medias res* introductions. A cliffhanger is, of course, when an episode ends before the resolution of the episode narrative has occurred, and the resolution is instead presented in the beginning of the following episode (a typical feature of serial narratives, according to Ndalianis 2005: 85). *In medias res* means 'in the middle of the action' and refers to the narrative strategy of telling the story non-chronologically, beginning with

an (unexplained) action sequence (for example, Sydney fleeing from
some guards in a building), and then telling the rest of the story in
flashback (indicated by a title card saying '72 hours earlier' or something similar), culminating with the resolution of the sequence with
which the discourse began. I have included these elements in the
analysis as they contribute to the overall narrative complexity of the
series. As we shall see, the frequency of these elements varies across
seasons.

NARRATIVE AND SERIALITY IN *ALIAS*

The interweaving of multiple plot threads was long viewed as a particular characteristic of soap operas, but is now the norm in all AQT.
Ndalianis (2005), following Calabrese (1992), identifies contemporary serial television narratives as *neo-baroque* – the fifth of five basic
prototypes of television narrative. The five prototypes can be
viewed as different positions on the series/serial continuum: the first
prototype is founded on distinct episodes with no overall season
narrative (Ndalianis uses *I Love Lucy* as an example of this, despite
the fact that *I Love Lucy* actually had seasonal narratives), whereas
the fifth prototype, 'without a doubt the most dominant serial form
in television series today' (Ndalianis 2005: 95), is characterised by
multiple parallel narratives and an episode/seasonal structure that
blends elements of all previous prototypes. Ndalianis even uses
Alias as an example of neo-baroque television with its '. . . convoluted, multiple storylines that diverge and connect . . .' (2005: 97).
However, as we shall see, the narrative complexity of *Alias* is not
consistent when analysed across all five seasons.

Complexity and Narrative Density, Alias Seasons One to Five

In this section, I present a series of diagrams that describe the distribution and scope of the subplots in each season of *Alias*. This section
will by its nature be fairly descriptive, as I think it is important to set
out the descriptive conditions before I go into the analysis. Figure 1
shows the narrative structure of the first season of *Alias*.

Figure 1 shows the distribution of the sixteen subplots that I have
identified across the twenty-two episodes of the season. I have used
the term 'short conflict' to designate a number of distinct plots (five,
to be precise) that extend across two or more episodes but never run

parallel to each other. Short conflicts in Season One include the threat of Vaughn being removed as Sydney's handler (1:2–3), the invasion of SD-6 headquarters by McKenas Cole (1:12–13), Sydney being arrested by, and later fleeing from, the Department of Special Research (1:16–17), Sydney's ex-boyfriend Noah Hicks is revealed to be the assassin codenamed 'Snowman' (1:18–19) and the kidnap and subsequent freeing of Will (1:21–2).

Figure 1: *Season One, Episodes 1–22*

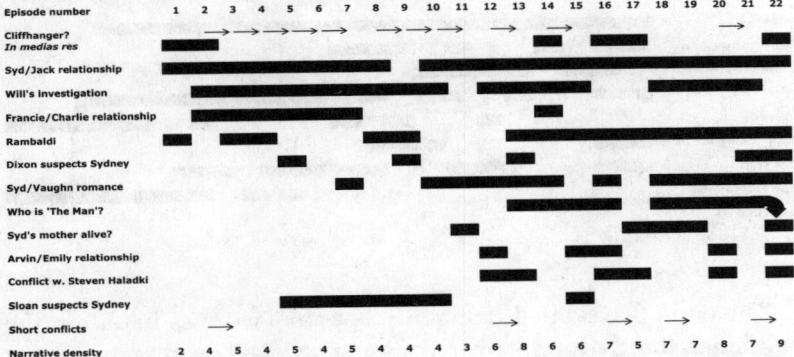

Figure 2: *Season Two, Episodes 1–22*

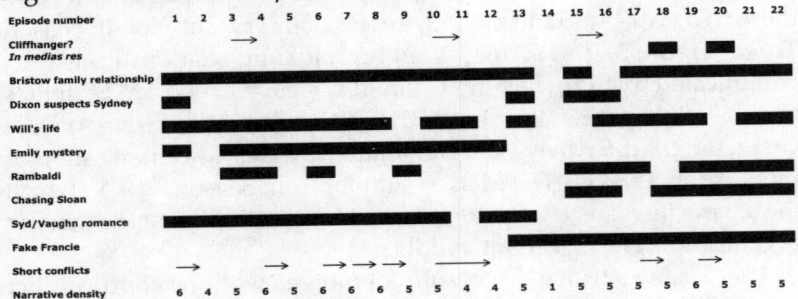

In the second season (Figure 2), the 'Bristow family relationship' is the dominant subplot, referring to the narrative centred on the triad of Sydney, Jack and Irina. The questions awaiting resolution in this subplot are approximately 'Can Irina be trusted?' and 'Will Sydney end up trusting her mother or her father?'. As to the short conflicts that are presented in this season, they are: Weiss being shot and then recovering, Jack framing Irina, Vaughn's disease, Sloane being kidnapped, the partnership with Sark, Ariana Kane's investigation into the blackmailing of Sloane (this subplot goes on for three episodes rather than the standard two), the kidnapping of the mathematician Caplan, and finally Will being framed by 'Fake Francie', imprisoned and then escaping.

Figure 3: *Season Three, Episodes 1–22*

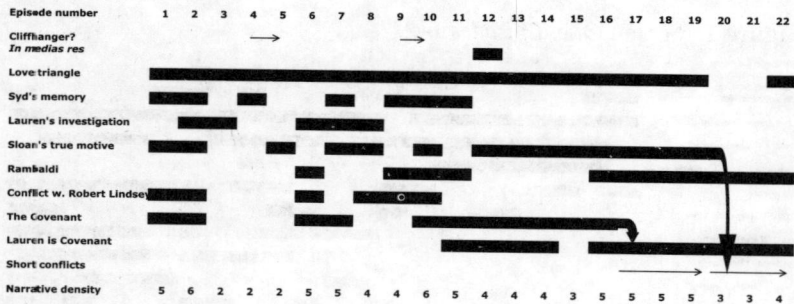

The end-of-season cliffhanger in Season Two was based on the revelation that Sydney has been missing believed dead for two years following a battle with the Francie double earlier in the episode. Sydney herself has no memory of what has happened to her during these two years, initiating the 'Sydney's memory' subplot. In Season Three (Figure 3), the Sydney-Vaughn romantic relationship is thus complicated by the fact that Vaughn has married in Sydney's absence (instigating the 'Love triangle' subplot, focusing on the character triad Sydney–Vaughn–Lauren). 'The Covenant' subplot mirrors the 'Who is "The Man"?' subplot from Season One, in which the characters are trying to find out about their new adversary organisation The Covenant and its goals.

The 'Sloane's true motive' subplot merges with the short conflict subplot relating to the character of Nadia in episode 3:20, when it is revealed that Sloane is Nadia's father and that he needs her to complete his work to fulfil Rambaldi's prophecies. In a similar fashion, 'The Covenant' subplot merges with the 'Lauren is Covenant' subplot in episode 3:17, when Lauren and Sark eliminate the leadership of their Covenant cell and assume control of it. The other short conflict begins with the decision to execute Sloane and ends when Jack helps him to survive the lethal injection.

Figure 4: *Season Four, Episodes 1–22*

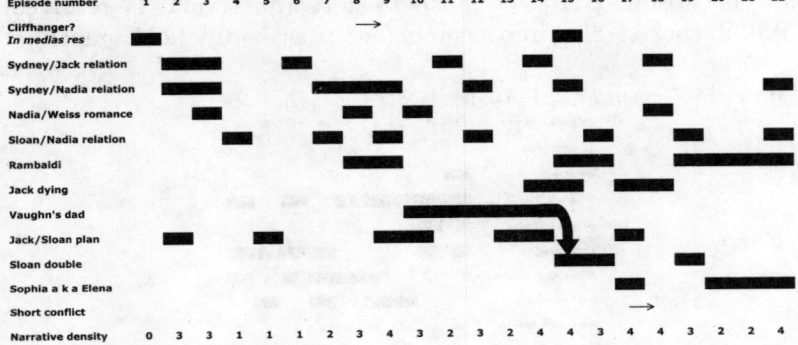

In Season Four (Figure 4), Sydney's conflict with her father is restarted with the revelation that Jack killed Sydney's mother ('Sydney/Jack relation'). Most subplots in Season Four are centred on character dyads: 'Sydney/Nadia relation' (question to be resolved: 'Will the sisters become enemies?'), the 'Nadia/Weiss romance', 'Sloane/Nadia relation' ('Will Sloane reconnect with his daughter and redeem himself?'), and 'Jack/Sloane plan' ('What is the purpose and nature of the secret plan Jack and Sloane have concocted together?'). Unlike previous seasons, the subplots in Season Four are introduced and resolved within the space of three or four non-consecutive episodes, making them somewhat similar to the short conflict subplots from previous seasons in terms of total episode length (i.e. the total number of episodes it takes to resolve the subplot). Finally the 'Vaughn's dad' subplot focuses on the search for Vaughn's father, previously believed dead. This subplot is resolved with the revelation that Vaughn's father is dead after all, and then merges with the 'Sloane double' subplot as it is revealed that the Sloane double is the man behind this deception. The 'short conflict' refers to the hunt for and eventual recovery of chemical warfare agent Hydrosek.

Any observations on Season Five (Figure 5) must be interpreted carefully, as at the time of writing only nine episodes had been broadcast before a lengthy hiatus. The major subplot in Season Five so far is 'Prophet Five' (very similar to 'The Man'/'The Covenant' subplots in that it introduces a new mystery adversarial organisation). Two subplots concern new characters on the show: the mystery of Renée's cryogenically preserved father (if it is indeed her father), 'Renée's father' subplot, and the gradual development of Rachel Gibson's character, 'Rachel's story' (question to be resolved: 'Will Rachel develop into a competent, trustworthy field agent?').

Figure 5:   *Season Five, Episodes 1–9*

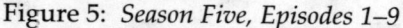
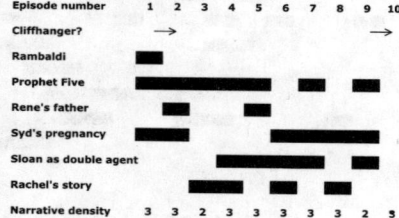

ANALYSIS: COMPLEXITY, BACKSTORY, CHARACTER

Three key themes emerge from the analysis of the seasonal narratives of *Alias*. These are: (1) a pattern of *decreasing narrative complexity* over the course of the series; (2) the importance of *backstory* to the construction of the serial narrative (highlighting the relationship between story and discourse within the narrative); and (3) the increasing importance of *character over plot*, and the related use of *character repositioning* as a way to deny narrative closure. The first theme will be described more extensively than the others, as that also incorporates reflections on the context of production.

Decreasing Narrative Complexity

Most aspects of narrative that could conceivably make the overall narrative more complex show a pattern of decrease across the seasons. Figure 6 shows the narrative density across the seasons as well as the total number of subplots in each season, whereas Figure 7 shows a pattern of decrease in cliffhangers and *in medias res* introductions across the run of the whole series.

These figures, along with the diagrams of subplots across each season presented previously, offer a more nuanced picture of the modern serial narrative than the one advanced by Ndalianis (2005) and Calabrese (1992). According to Ndalianis, the 'neo-baroque' narrative seems almost structure-free, where 'no stable, singular, linear framework dominates' and:

The shows are riddled with multiple narrative formations that stress polycentrism within the series itself. While one story may be introduced and resolved in a single episode, or across a series of episodes, other narrative situations may open up, extending the stories of multiple characters beyond a single episode and across the entire series.

(2005: 96)

Figure 6: *Narrative Complexity I*

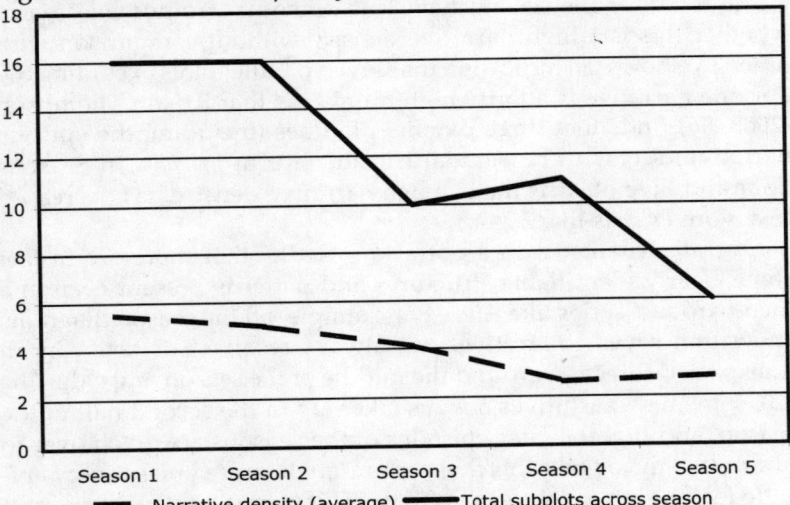

Season 1   Season 2   Season 3   Season 4   Season 5
▬▬ Narrative density (average) ▬▬Total subplots across season

Figure 7: *Narrative Complexity II*

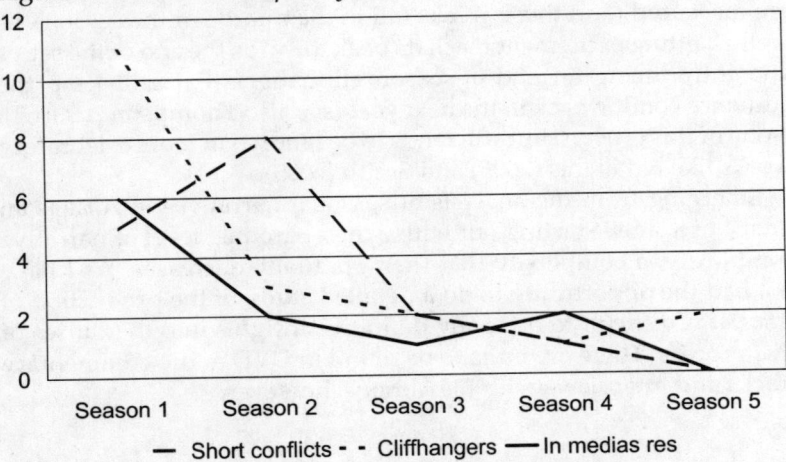

Season 1   Season 2   Season 3   Season 4   Season 5
▬ Short conflicts - - Cliffhangers ▬In medias res

This is partly true for *Alias*, of course – but we should note that the first and second seasons (or the first season and the first half of the second season, to be precise) are significantly more complex than the following seasons, and that the narratives of Season Four and (so far) Season Five are not even half as complex as in the first season. It is also notable that the second half of the first season is more complex than the first half – average narrative density for the first half is 4.2, and 7.0 for the second half. It is, of course, impossible to say whether this is a high narrative density without comparison with other TV shows; an indication that seven parallel plots excluding the episode narrative is a fairly high number is that Kristin Thompson (2003: 56) finds that three parallel plotlines (including the episode narrative) seems to be standard in the sitcom *Friends*. In Seasons Four and Five of *Alias* the average narrative density has decreased to a more *Friends*-like 2.7–2.8.

Overall, Ndalianis does not acknowledge that there are in fact some clearly identifiable structures and patterns present even in a 'neo-baroque' series like *Alias*. For example, all the season diagrams show that several narratives are always resolved or taken in an unexpected direction around the middle of the season (episodes 10–13), some new narratives always taken up in the second half of the season, and that the later episodes of the seasons are given over to one or two major subplots that are present in more or less every episode leading up to the season finale. This narrative structuring can of course be directly related to the fact that commercial TV demands attention-grabbing narratives during 'sweeps weeks' when ratings are measured (and those weeks fall in the middle of the season), as well as letting excitement reach its peak towards the end of the series and introducing an end-of-season cliffhanger that will keep the audience coming back in the next year (see also Thompson 2003: 62). None of this is news, but still tends to be ignored in more celebratory works like Ndalianis (2005) and Smith (2005).

Emerging from the analysis of seasonal narratives in *Alias* is an image of a show starting out with a 'neo-baroque' level of narrative complexity, a complexity that then gradually decreases. As I have not had the opportunity to do a detailed study of the production of *Alias*, it is difficult to offer any definitive insights into the causes of this process. There are hints to be found in DVD audio commentary tracks and interviews with J.J. Abrams, however.

The focal point for the gradual lessening of narrative complexity is 'Phase One' (2:13), in which SD-6, so far the major antagonist in the show, is brought down and Sydney and Jack's mission as double agents come to an end. On the audio commentary of this episode, J.J. Abrams states:

> So this idea of raiding SD-6 was kind of scary because it'd been a fixture of the show from the beginning. But it was something that ultimately was very confusing for a lot of people, in that it was a show about good guys working for the bad guys who had to pretend that they were bad good guys, some of the bad guys didn't know they were bad guys and other bad guys pretended they were good guys.

Abrams later continues:

> . . . and again, getting rid of SD-6 was more about trying to maintain the things we loved about the show, the relationships, the characters, and actually get rid of the stuff that made it hard for certain people to understand what the show was about.
>
> (J.J. Abrams, DVD audio commentary for 'Phase One', S2:D4)

A similar discussion of how the writers and producers of the show decide to end an ongoing subplot prematurely in order to reduce complexity for viewers is present on the DVD audio commentary track for 'Full Disclosure' (S3:D3). Abrams does not specify exactly who the 'people' who are finding *Alias* difficult to follow are – there is some ambiguity as to whether they are members of the audience or the network executives. It might be a bit of both, as another series of quotes from J.J. Abrams, taken from an online interview, shows: 'Abrams acknowledges that ABC had some concerns about first-time viewers grasping the show, but he says the network didn't force the change in direction.' Further on in the same interview, Abrams denies that the change in narrative can be described as a form of simplification:

> Abrams doesn't necessarily agree, however, with the shorthand description that the show has been 'simplified'.
> 'I think viewers are going to find that the premise of the show is definitely easier to understand', he says. 'But anyone who's watched the show post-takedown of the Alliance sees we're in no way making it simplistic or broad-stroked.'
>
> (J.J. Abrams interviewed by Porter, 2003)

Regardless of the exact reasons, we can clearly see that the decision to reduce the narrative complexity comes about in part because
of concern that the show did not draw as big an audience as it could.
Another indicator of this is that 'Phase One' and 'Double Agent'
(2:14) were originally scheduled to be broadcast in the reverse order
(i.e. 'Double Agent' first, then 'Phase One'). However, 'Phase One'
was rescheduled for the slot following the Superbowl – traditionally
viewed as a very good slot for attracting a large audience (again, this
can be heard in the DVD audio commentary for 'Phase One').

Backstory

The second theme is the importance of backstory, a theme that finds
support in previous literature (see Nelson 1997: 34 and Johnson
2005: 105). The importance of backstory can best be analysed using
the basic narratological distinction between *story* and *discourse*.
Story refers to the narrated events and participants in abstraction
from the text, reconstructed in their chronological order. Rimmon-
Kenan (2002: 6) makes a very simple but important point about story
and discourse (or text, in her usage): that the story is not directly
available to the reader. A key locus of meaning in the serial text then
becomes the gradual revelation of the *backstory*, i.e. the events of the
story that chronologically precede the narrative presented in the
text.

The *story* of *Alias* begins in the fifteenth century with the fictional
inventor and artist Milo Rambaldi, whose prophecies and discover-
ies come into fruition in the narrative 'now' of the series (i.e. the
early twenty-first century). Sydney Bristow and several other main
characters of the show (notably Arvin Sloane, Irina Derevko and
Nadia Santos) are connected to the prophecies and inventions of
Rambaldi, and the 'Rambaldi backstory' forms the backbone of the
narrative of the series as a whole. Similarly, the 'Bristow family
backstory' is also the source for many subplots across the seasons of
Alias.[1]

The *discourse* of *Alias*, on the other hand, for the most part follows
a chronological structure, starting with the dual revelations (to Sydney and to the audience) that SD-6, the organisation she has been
working for as a spy, is not part of the CIA (as she had previously
believed) and that her (at that time estranged) father works as a CIA
double agent inside SD-6. The chronological narrative structure is
sometimes broken up with the action of the episode starting *in*

medias res and then told in flashback, but by and large the text follows a chronological narrative structure, interspersed with
generous revelations about the narrative 'past', i.e. the backstory, as
well as foreshadowing future events (most notably in relation to
Rambaldi's prophecies).

Following Ndalianis, it is clear that the viewer of *Alias* is often
positioned like a puzzle solver (sometimes literally, considering the
frequent recurrence of actual puzzles and puzzle-like problems in
the narrative), working to make sense of how events in the narrative
'now' are related to the past and future of the narrative universe
(Ndalianis 2005: 96). The continuous revelation of more of the backstory fills the dual function of being a source of pleasure for a
knowing, 'quality TV' niche audience and an almost endless source
of narrative elements that can further delay narrative closure
through new revelations.

Character Over Plot and Character Repositioning

The third theme is the increased importance of *character over plot* and
the use of *character repositioning* to delay narrative closure. A somewhat surprising outcome of this detailed analysis of narrative is that
it seems to indicate that the structuring and resolution of narrative
and plot is rather unimportant to *Alias*. The series frequently
changes its own basic narrative premise, for example following
'Phase One' SD-6 is destroyed and Sydney and Jack are no longer
double agents within the organisation. The second half of Season
Two instead gets its narrative thrust from the hunt for Sloane and
the parallel culmination of one of Rambaldi's prophecies. In Season
Three the narrative thrust instead comes from the denying of the
Sydney–Vaughn romance built up over the previous seasons, as
well as the mystery of Sydney's missing memory. Again, just like in
Season Two this latter subplot/premise is resolved in the first half of
the season and gives way to the Rambaldi subplot and 'The Covenant'/'Lauren is Covenant' subplots in the second half of the season.
The fourth season again changes the narrative premise and focuses
much more on 'regular' spy story narratives that are resolved within
one single episode. This increased focus on the story contained
within a single episode is a significant change in character for the
series: while the actual number of subplots decreases in the second
half of Season Two, the focus in most of the subsequent episodes
until the end of Season Three is nonetheless on these ongoing sub-

plots. This goes on until the second half of the fourth season, where the hunt for the Sloane double (and later for Elena Derevko) and the mystery of another Rambaldi weapon provides most of the narrative drive.

All of this points to the essential interchangeability of plot: it does not really matter where the narrative thrust comes from or how the various subplots are interlinked, as long as the characters are given the opportunity to express their core traits. An important part of the narrative suspense in *Alias* is generated by the emergence of new character dyads and triads and changes in the relationships between characters, and the narratives are geared towards expressing this. The character focus also increases over the course of the series. The 'Sydney/Vaughn romance' is connected to several other subplots (the 'Sydney/Jack relationship' subplot, the 'Conflict with Steven Haladki' subplot, the Bristow family relationship subplot) and also with several other characters and character dyads (the 'Sydney/Vaughn romance' affects the Sydney/Jack and Sydney/Irina relationship dyads as well as the Vaughn/Steven Haladki and Vaughn/Weiss dyads, for example). Compare this with the much more focused subplots in Season Four, almost all of them dealing exclusively with one character dyad and with little interlinking with other character-dyad subplots (the 'Sloane/Nadia relation' subplot has little bearing on the 'Nadia/Weiss romance', and, perhaps more surprisingly, not on the 'Sydney/Nadia relation' subplot either). The series' narrative gradually becomes more geared towards repositioning characters in new dyads not necessarily interlinked with other character dyads and subplots.

The various strands of *Alias*' backstory also frequently interweave to create and change relationships between the characters. For example, the family backstory of Sydney is eventually connected to the family backstory of Vaughn when it is revealed that the KGB agent that killed Vaughn's father was in fact Irina Derevko, i.e. Sydney's mother. Characters are thus repositioned vis-à-vis each other through new backstory revelations.

This focus on character is a well-known characteristic of commercial television. It has long been the received wisdom that audiences come back for character, not plot (see Gitlin 1994: 63ff, for example) – another contextual factor that can explain the drop in narrative complexity over the seasons of *Alias*. The (perceived) primacy of character is further expressed through how the seasonal narrative(s) serve to highlight the key traits of the character. On the face of it, it would seem that seasonal narratives would be well suited to long-term character development, but the characters in *Alias* in fact develop very little in the traditional narratological sense of the word (Chatman 1978: 119ff). Instead, the seasonal narratives and the seriality of the show serve the purpose of what I call *character showcasing*, i.e. providing discursive opportunities not to develop and change the character but to let the character do 'what he/she does best'. The Rambaldi subplot provides an excuse for Sydney to don numerous disguises and to be troubled by her place in a larger destiny, as well as for Sloane to act duplicitously, but with flair. The Sydney–Jack relationship subplot and the Bristow family relationship subplot above all provide excuses for Jack to act in a non-emotional, rigid manner but interspersed with awkwardness or scary bursts of emotion. As I stated above, it is not a new discovery that commercial US TV regards character as paramount to the success of a series. Studies of the narrative intricacies of modern 'quality TV' often, however, get stuck on the narrative complexity (which is a very real feature of this type of TV, as I hope I have shown) but do not consider how narrative is linked to character and that character, ironically perhaps, is the stable basis for a set of interchangeable narratives. Nor do they appropriately consider that the narrative complexities of the seasonal serial format may not be present as much for their own sake (i.e. to provide an exciting plot or plots for the audience to follow) but to showcase characters and their traits, and that it is this showcasing that provides the main attraction for the audience – just as it has since the early days of TV.

CONCLUSION

This narrative analysis, while limited, does present a view of the relationship between character and narrative that marks a radical departure from traditional formalist analysis. The formalist conception of characters is as mere *actants*, i.e. characters are to be seen as functions of the plot (Chatman 1978: 111f). Formalism holds that character is a means rather than an end of the story. Chatman points out that this viewpoint clearly does not match audience experience, however: audiences may well be interested in characters for their own sake and not just as means to advance the plot. The contemporary serial narrative, as exemplified by *Alias*, seems to prove

Chatman right: 'quality TV' seriality does not position characters as functional actants in a narrative, but rather narrative becomes a vehicle for character realisation.

Much of current research on 'quality TV' and television narratives operates on the implicit assumption that 'quality TV' represents something essentially 'new' in television, particularly when it comes to narrative (as in Thompson 1996; Jancovich and Lyons 2003; Allrath, Gymnich and Surkamp 2005; Ndalianis 2005). The strength of these studies is that they do identify a clear trend and rightly draw the attention to an increased level of narrative complexity in serial television. Their weakness is that they do not emphasise the institutional context in which these narratives are created, which leads to a relative lack of recognition that even complex, multi-centred serial narratives have structures – structures that even seem rather stable from season to season. Viewed from this perspective, the similarities between 'quality TV' seriality and the television seriality of old are greater than the differences.

If we instead look to the works of Gitlin (1994), Nelson (1997) and Thompson (2003), we find a much stronger sense of history, where current developments in narrative are put into a context of commercial TV production that has not fundamentally changed since the 1950s. For all its narrative complexity, 'neo-baroque' TV is about characters, not narratives – at least from the point of view of the TV producers.

2 Endoscopic Spies
Mapping the Internal Landscape of *Alias*

Sergio Angelini

> Knowledge kills action; action requires the veil of illusion
> Friedrich Nietzsche (1967: 60)

Initially, the main narrative hook for *Alias* was what happened to American spy Sydney Bristow when she discovered that in fact she was really working for the enemy. The development of the next one and a half seasons saw episode plots run along parallel lines in which Sydney is frequently forced to undertake two simultaneous missions, one as part of her double agent cover working for the 'evil' SD-6 and a spoiling counter-mission for the 'good' CIA. This simple but clever reversal on the tired double agent cliché has proved a particularly fertile ground on which to present its main character in a huge variety of undercover characterisations (and wardrobe combinations) that also put her sense of identity under pressure.

As the series progressed, these foci became both narrower and more diverse, as a sense of emotional, temporal and physical liminality and instability was increasingly stepped up and applied to more and more members of the show's cast of characters. The mutability of the character arcs is always a factor in any long-running television series, but this was regularly taken to extremes in *Alias*. From the Season One finale onwards and with increasing and disturbing regularity, characters long thought dead turned out to be very much alive while others died and then returned, but frequently were revealed not to be the people we first thought they were.

In Season Two the decision was made to drastically revamp the format, so in the high-profile post-Super Bowl episode 'Phase One' (2:13) Sydney and her CIA handler Vaughn lead a mission into SD-6 headquarters and help smash it and most of the other 'Alliance' cells. Since then the show has increasingly reappraised its approach to all its characters, the prominence given to their personal lives and the extent to which their enemies, and employers, can manipulate them. In the third and fourth seasons of *Alias* especially, this sense of personal displacement and personal loss of identity and control, aligned to a quest narrative for some overarching 'ultimate truth', has moved increasingly inwards. David Cronenberg, director of such solipsistic and existential films as *Naked Lunch* (1991), *eXistenZ* (1999) and *Spider* (2002) tellingly appears in two Season Three episodes in which Sidney's mind is explored after her memories of the previous two years were wiped clean. Other examples of this interior exploration in the following season have seen Sloane confronted by a stranger claiming to be the true 'Sloane', at the same time that Sidney's cynical father Jack descended into an alternate reality following radiation poisoning.

Alias has used the smoke and mirrors that form the conceptual basis for the appeal of the spy genre and blended them with the demands of long-running American network television drama to produce a self-reflexive show in which representations of truth and reality are paramount and, crucially, not to be trusted. Beginning with its second season and throughout the two that followed, *Alias* has repeatedly explored the mind/body duality of Nietzsche's Apollonian and Dionysian conception of drama, a battle between the opposing forces of concrete reality against imaginative and emotional flights of fancy. To achieve this, the myth and archetype of the heroic quest, filtered through the espionage genre, has been repeatedly subjected to the irrationality of explanations, motivations and rationales based on pseudo-scientific precepts and quasi-religious mysticism and fervour.

This chapter aims to explore the ways that the quest narrative in *Alias* has been increasingly turned away from the external dynamism of traditional espionage narrative tropes towards a more distinctive internal exploration that truly sets it apart from other spy shows on television. While drawing on a number of precedents in the genre, especially the films, television shows and literature produced during the 1960s espionage boom, *Alias* has also used the pseudo-scientific conventions of the genre to explore imaginatively the inner lives of its characters Sydney, Jack and Sloane in new and stimulating ways.

'SOMETIMES IT'S HARD TO BE A WOMAN': FEMININITY INSIDE THE SPY GENRE

The emphasis on feelings and the consequent inward emotional journey undertaken by the characters in *Alias* can at least in part be ascribed to the unusual decision to have a woman in the lead role. In the past the spy genre showed little tolerance for the presentation of espionage as being anything other than a purely male purview. Although *The Avengers* was notable for its succession of dynamic female leads, these were always presented as amateur companions to spy professional John Steed, the undisputed senior partner in the relationship, as would later be the case with *Scarecrow and Mrs King*, a 1980s show that explicitly contrasted the domestic environment of its female title character with the international intrigue surrounding the world of the CIA agent codenamed 'Scarecrow'. The main examples of female spies on television were tellingly all brought centre stage as spin-offs from more traditionally male-led espionage shows – thus in the 1960s *The Man from U.N.C.L.E.* led to *The Girl from U.N.C.L.E.*, and the 1970s science-fiction/espionage hybrid *The Six Million Dollar Man* served as a launching pad for *The Bionic Woman*. More recently, the short-lived cyber thriller *VR5* and the cable series *La Femme Nikita* both focused on strong women used as pawns in convoluted spy games. *Nikita* especially seems to have had some influence on the development of *Alias* with its shifting identities for its characters and the overall focus on complex family relationships within espionage agencies, although only one episode ('Brainwash', 1:20) actually tried to get in the title character's head.

Sydney's own sense of self has frequently been undermined by her shifting relationships, not only with her parents but also with her friends, who not only act as a substitute for her very dysfunctional family, but who (in the first two seasons) also form part of her cover as a bank employee. Eventually her roommate Francie is assassinated and replaced with a murderous double Allison ('Phase One'). Sydney thinks she kills Allison (not unreasonably, having shot her in the chest several times), but Allison eventually returns from the dead ('The Nemesis', 3:6). Things have been even more tangled with her blood relatives. As the series has progressed, we first learnt that Sydney's long-thought-dead mother Laura was really a KGB mole named Irina Derevko sent to spy on Jack, Sydney's father, who it transpires is also a double agent (for the CIA). Typically it turns out that one of the main villains of Season One codenamed 'The Man' is actually a woman, the very much alive Irina. As a result of an affair with Sloane she gives birth to Nadia, Sydney's half-sister. Following the Season Three cliffhanger, we discover that Jack assassinated Irina ('Authorized Personnel Only, Part 2', 4:2) to protect Sydney. This later turns out to have been a set-up, Jack in fact killing Irina's double ('Search and Rescue', 4:21). Even Sydney's fiancé and fellow agent Vaughn (whose father was killed by Irina) turns out to be working under an assumed identity ('Prophet Five', 5:1). Vaughn, Jack and Sloane's own experiences mirror Sydney's parabolic emotional journey, each of them having also been made to look at their own lives and question their very foundations. First through Rambaldi and then through his bond with his daughter Nadia, Sloane has changed persona several times. We see him go from head of Alliance cell SD-6, to CIA informant while running a philanthropic European foundation, to leader of the genuine CIA black ops unit APO (Authorized Personnel Only). Throughout he has had to face the human cost of his actions as paid through deaths in his family, with his wife Emily dying and then resurrected on several occasions. Similarly, Jack apparently has Sloane killed only to resurrect him ('Hourglass', 3:19), has his own ex-wife Irina come back from the dead ('The Descent', 4:20) and goes from being a CIA double agent to being incarcerated by the CIA as a security risk ('The Two', 3:1). Even Vaughn is forced to go rogue for a time when he is led to believe that his father may in fact still be alive. This is eventually revealed to be a ruse perpetrated by the ersatz Sloane ('Pandora', 4:15). We later discover that Vaughn's real name is André Michaux and that his father was in fact part of Prophet Five ('Prophet Five'). What binds all these men together is Sydney, and it is her emotions that the viewer is primarily concerned with. This is not just because she is the star of the show, but also because she is depicted as being emotionally open, honest and therefore vulnerable and approachable to a much higher degree than the rest of the main cast of characters, whose shifting personae mean that they are invariably presented in a perpetually penumbral and equivocal light.

In Season Three Sydney's own body becomes the focus of acolytes in the gigantic Rambaldi conspiracy and in 'Full Disclosure' (3:11) we learn that one of her own eggs has been removed as they consider her to be the 'Chosen One', who will give birth to Rambaldi's child by using his DNA. Sydney later destroys the lab in which this is being engineered, but this subplot re-emerged with the real-life pregnancy of Jennifer Garner, which affected the entire direction of Season Five. This was also behind the decision to put the show on hiatus midway through that season while Garner had her baby[1] and recuperated before returning to work. The final pre-hiatus episode ('The Horizon', 5:9) shows Sydney drugged and strapped to a special machine being subjected to mental probes by her mother. The exploration of Sydney's mind and memory, as well as that of other characters, is a major facet of the series, which has undertaken the task through the use of three types of technology developed as projects with the codenames Christmas, Helix and Brainstorm.

PROJECT: CHRISTMAS

Amnesia recurs throughout *Alias*, and memory retrieval procedures are shown to be highly dangerous ('Prelude', 3:7). Psychoanalysis of one type or another has also featured heavily. Throughout Season Three Patricia Wettig played psychiatrist Dr Barnett, a counsellor for agents suffering from problems relating to, and caused by, their missions. The first indication that Sydney's own memories, and by extension her very personality, have been modified or conditioned relates to Project: Christmas, a CIA training programme to develop sleeper agents through indoctrination (a plot previously used most notably in Don Siegel's *Telefon* (1977)) to create 'next generation weapons'. This turns out to be cruel play on words, as it actually refers to the brainwashing of young children. A psychiatrist tells Sydney 'The best spies have certain traits, proficiency with numbers, three-dimensional thinking, creative problem solving. These abilities are all in evidence as early as five years old' ('The Indicator', 2:5). Thus the CIA, led by Jack, starts a programme to condition children to enhance such 'basic' spy skills as marksmanship and then erases the memory, with the potential of later reactivating these 'sleepers' when the children have reached adulthood. The subplot was first introduced in 'Snowman' (1:19) in which we learn that Irina was sent by the KGB to seduce Jack specifically to learn about this project. This story arc is then developed though an ingenious narrative proxy, with Sydney's friend Will investigating on Vaughn's behalf. We learn that millions of children round the world were given the test, nearly half attaining perfect scores. Through regression therapy ('The Indicator') Sydney is able to recover the lost memories of Project: Christmas. Sydney angrily confronts her father, unwilling to accept his explanations for his actions, dashing his (admittedly *sui generis*) parental aspirations and attempts to protect her future: 'You took away my choices in life. You programmed me to be a spy.'

Plots using hypnosis to control minds have been popular in the cinema ever since *The Cabinet of Dr Caligari* (1920), but in espionage fiction this became much more frequent with the dramatic possibilities offered by 'brainwashing', a term introduced by the Americans in the 1950s following the Korean War. In the 1960s it became a staple of the spy genre, from the scintillating black and white of John Frankenheimer's *The Manchurian Candidate* (1962) to the Techniscope swinging London psychedelia of *The Ipcress File* (1965). Even James Bond was subjected to it in Ian Fleming's novel *The Man with the Golden Gun* (1965), though this element has unsurprisingly been omitted for the more impregnable screen incarnations of the hero. More recently the psychological indoctrination of spies who later have their memories wiped as they try to leave their profession has been used as the basis for the Matt Damon-starring adaptations of Robert Ludlum's series about amnesiac secret agent Jason Bourne and the Geena Davis action film *The Long Kiss Goodnight* (1996). *Alias* has appropriated such elements both to explore the vulnerabilities of its characters and as part of its overall aesthetic strategy in its referencing of the look and motifs of the 1960s spy genre and then recasting, updating and recreating them for the neoconservative era.

Sydney seemingly loses control of her own identity with a massive bout of amnesia covering the two-year period that separates the stories of Seasons Two and Three. We later learn that she took on a new alias and became an assassin using the pseudonym 'Julia Thorne' after The Covenant believed they had successfully reprogrammed Sydney's personality. In a neat reversal typical of the series, it transpires that Sydney herself had her memory erased. In a scene (and plot development) reminiscent of *Total Recall* (1990), an adaptation of a Philip K. Dick story, Sydney learns of her past from a video she made of herself before the reprogramming. It is crucial to our understanding of Sydney as the series' primary forward mover that it be her own decision to blank out her memory. The

Möbius strip approach to character and plotting that this suggests, endlessly folding back on itself, is singularly well attuned to the specific demands of *Alias* in terms of story and character, but also riffs on the generic foundations of the spy genre as we have come to understand them. Intriguingly, the brainwashing she endures (which is highly reminiscent of *The Ipcress File*) has been overcome thanks to the fact that Jack subjected her in her childhood to Project: Christmas, giving her additional mental defences against psychological conditioning. In 'Full Disclosure' Kendall explains that the 'programme contained a fail-safe to protect its subject from being turned. Jack hardwired you to stand up to some pretty intense efforts at brainwashing.' The use of the term 'hardwired' is highly suggestive and slightly disturbing, equating Sydney's brain to a computer, her emotional responses potentially defended by protocols about which she knows nothing and which she is unable to control. In Jack's mind, of course, this is presented as just another kind of immunisation, a kind of supercharged MMR. Sydney is thus equated with a vessel – a synaptic *tabula rasa* – that is powerfully contrasted with the final revelation that not only was Sydney responsible for her own memory being wiped but that her own ovaries have been harvested to help fulfil one of Rambaldi's prophecies.

Alias has increasingly come to rely upon pseudo-science to explore facets of the genre hitherto left largely untapped, especially in the way it has used the conventions of the double and triple agent. This is taken literally and given a pseudo-scientific twist with Project: Helix, which in the appropriately titled episode 'Double Agent' (2:14) is described as 'a breakthrough in next-generation molecular gene therapy. It refers to a new procedure whereby a patient's face and body are reshaped to identically resemble someone else.' The use of doubles in espionage through plastic surgery or disguises led to such previous efforts as the deliriously titled *The Spy with my Face* (1965) and *The Double Man* (1967) with Yul Brynner playing CIA agent Dan Slater and his doppelganger Kalmar. Ironically, the plan to replace the spy fails when the KGB's brainwashed double is '. . . exposed by his inability to emulate Slater's inhumanity' (Murphy 1992: 318, n. 35). The most imaginative treatment of the doppelgänger theme until *Alias* can be found in the densely layered 'Schizoid Man' episode from Patrick McGoohan's groundbreaking television series *The Prisoner*, a postmodern and politically inclined critique of the same star's previous (and more traditional) spy show

Danger Man (also known in the USA as *Secret Agent*). McGoohan's 'Number 6' is subjected to behavioural conditioning to make him doubt his own identity. In the climax, he actually impersonates his own double in an attempt to escape from captivity. Doubling technology has taken the plots of *Alias* to an entirely new level of paranoia, emphasising the new ways it has developed to explore protagonists in affecting ways. With characters such as Francie/Allison and Irina coming back from the dead, and a crucial character given the provocative name of Lazarey, narrative closure can seemingly be put off indefinitely. When Sydney understandably cries 'She's supposed to be dead' when her old nemesis Anna Espinosa reappears, Jack's deadpan response, 'So are a lot of people' ('Echoes', 4:8) is even more understandable in the world of *Alias*. This is useful for the show's producers, of course, but is also a brilliant stratagem to test Sydney's resolve and make the scouring of *Alias'* characters' inner workings more challenging and at the same time more crucial. As plots also become more involuted and patterns constantly reassert themselves and mutate, a deepening and strengthening of the heroes and villains' characters have counterbalanced this, their identities relentlessly scrutinised, both scientifically and emotionally.

AMNESIA

In Season Three the series' trajectory took its cue from Sydney's amnesia and her loss of two years to move ever-more inwards from a narrative standpoint. The two linked episodes in the middle of Season Three ('Conscious', 3:9, and 'Remnants', 3:10) initiated the new approach with David Cronenberg as Dr Brezzel, a Timothy Leary-style hippy scientist inserting Sydney into her own dreams to recover her missing past and discover why she (apparently) murdered a man. Brezzel says at the beginning as he prepares to probe her mind: '. . . once you're aware that you're in the dream state, your objective will be to pick up the thread of your last memory in as much detail as you can'. In *Alias* dreams can be omens, keys to Rambaldi prophecies, psychological projections or remnants of memories deliberately removed. Sydney, however, refuses to explore the psyche (hers and those of others) in anything other than a spirit of scientific endeavour, using various technologies that can control the unconscious purely for empirical ends. When asked by Nadia if she believes that dreams can be portents, messages in disguise from Rambaldi, Sydney is adamant that she does not believe in Rambaldi's prophecies: 'No, but the people who do are dangerous. They're zealots who will stop at nothing to make their visions into reality' ('Echoes', 4:8). In Nietzschean terms the synthesis of the Apollonian and Dionysian tendencies is what we should aspire to, and Sydney is thus placed between the emotional frigidity of Jack and the technological monotheism of Marshall on one side and the passionate but inherently irrational followers of Rambaldi like Sloane and Irina on the other. As Heidegger's interpretation of Nietzsche postulated, '[t]he double ambiguity of truth and semblance, compels us to something that is neither one nor the other . . .' (1991: 132), a dichotomy that can only be resolved through action and the abolition of absolutes. Thus Sydney's ultimate role is to mediate these competing impulses within the drama, which of course is why both sides hunger for her, her body and her mind. At the press conference held by Anthony Blunt after he was revealed as being the so-called 'fourth man' planted by the KGB in British intelligence, he quoted E.M. Forster: 'If I had to choose between betraying my country and betraying my friend, I hope I should have the guts to betray my country' (cited by Angelini). This privileging of self over nation, loyalty to one's own sense of statehood within the extended family sphere of friendship and consanguinity before the obligation to abstract or impersonal notions of patriotism is what the internal struggle in Sydney's character is fundamentally striving for. Her paramount sense of obligation to friends and family and her own sense of loyalty is restated over and over again in *Alias*, just as Sydney's 'patriotism' and her loyalty to the CIA is also constantly invoked. Rather than cancel each other out in a schizoid blur, they clearly aim for some kind of more individualistic, transcendent reconciliation between the two.

What is fascinating about *Alias*' deployment of brainwashing, doubling technology etc., is how these techniques deepen and humanise our understanding of even such apparently inflexible and granite-like characters as Sloane and Jack. During Season Four they were both able to revisit fantasy versions of the past to better reconcile earlier mistakes with their lives in the present, especially with regards to the relationships with their respective daughters, Nadia and Sydney.

PROJECT: BRAINSTORM (AND ANOTHER MISTER SLOANE)

The appearance of an ersatz but not identical Sloane ('Pandora') has uniquely served to give greater insight into the varying permutations of the man. Nadia describes Sloane's passion for Rambaldi to Sydney explaining that, 'the closer we got to this artefact that he wanted, the more he began to change. I saw him slipping away from himself. His passion, his desperation to connect to Rambaldi, it completely overtook him. He became a different man' ('Another Mister Sloane', 4:16). This meeting of Sloane's personalities past and present is literally represented to us by the appearance of Sloane's doppelgänger, a version of Sloane before Nadia became his new priority. In the crucial episode (directed by Jennifer Garner) 'In Dreams' (4:19) the mind of the Sloane double is probed using technology developed as 'Project: Brainstorm', presumably named for the late Douglas Trumbull's eponymous 1983 movie about the recording, sharing and potential weaponising of memories. Sloane's apparent redemption is the focus of this episode, as he is forced to literally (and figuratively) come face to face with a specular version of himself, the Dionysian and morally unfettered Sloane, utterly dedicated to only one thing: Rambaldi. Using 'Brainstorm' Sloane is forced to go through something that Nadia and Sydney were unaware of – the death of his baby daughter at birth. Reliving this painful and largely suppressed memory is then used to shock the Sloane double into realising that he is not actually Sloane and so stop his evil plans. The vision of the past, psychologically a return to the womb that is complexly mapped as a fantasy of an alternate life with his wife and daughter, in fact both now dead, becomes a refuge from his previous persona now embodied in the simulacrum of Sloane, and proves almost too seductive for the real Sloane, who initially decides not to come back to reality. He only returns to reality when Nadia injects herself into the fantasy and convinces Sloane (calling him 'Dad' for the first time) that his future, and the possibility of redemption, is still worth fighting for with her by his side. This is tempered by our knowledge that the Sloane double, now revealed to be a soldier named Ned Bolger, has been psychologically destroyed by the procedure, left in a state of paranoid schizophrenia unable to separate one personality over another. Intriguingly, Marshall, who after all isn't really a doctor, directs the Brainstorm procedure. His role here is to project a wholly empirical and totally Cartesian conception of the universe, highly reminiscent of the work of Gottfried Wilhelm Leibniz (1646–1716) – the inventor of differential and integral calculus, who thought that it was possible to reduce all verbal communication worldwide to one system by the adoption of a binary language, what he termed the 'Laws of Thought'. Thus Marshall's explanations when it comes to trying to get Sloane back from his chemically induced delusional state as usual tend to reduce people to technological devices: 'Think of it like in computer terms. You can't just force quit, you have to reboot his brain.' Once again this tends to reinforce Sydney's central position in the polarised spy ethics of *Alias*. For Sydney, however, her world will always be couched in shades of grey, sometimes against all her intentions, no matter how black and white the alternatives present themselves to be.

MIRAGE

To save the life of his daughter, Jack exposes himself to a potentially lethal dose of radiation ('Nightingale', 4:14). He goes to see a trusted friend, Dr Lidell, to try and find a cure ('A Clean Conscience', 4:17) but in a devastating twist we learn that it is all a delusion brought on by radiation poisoning and that Jack has only been fantasising a cure. Marshall exclaims, 'Wow, Mr Bristow hallucinated the one man who can actually save his life. Even his delusions are lucid!' In 'Mirage' (4:18) Jack's mind is catapulted back a quarter of a century to the life he once led with Laura (Irina's cover name). Jack's family and friends at APO decide to exploit this to dislodge his memory and find Lidell (whom Jack placed in hiding in 1981) and reverse the effects of the radiation poisoning that is slowly killing him. This episode extends a device, highly reminiscent of *Mission: Impossible*, that *Alias* had first deployed in the previous season's 'Façade' (3:15), in which Ricky Gervais played a terrorist tricked into believing that he is in Russia while actually being closely monitored and manipulated in a CIA warehouse in Los Angeles. As the APO team decides that they must take control of Jack's delusion to find out where he actually relocated Lidell to twenty-five years earlier, Jack is drugged, a set approximating his house in 1981 is reconstructed and his every movement monitored. Sydney is 'cast' as her own mother and it is through this proxy that we are finally, most powerfully, able to penetrate Jack's emotional defences. Through this waking dream/

fantasy the cynical, supremely rational and at times even Machiavellian Jack finally lets his guard down. Disorientated by the effects of the radiation poisoning and finding himself a quarter of a century into his past, Jack admits the depth of his feelings for Irina and Sydney. He in fact had broken CIA protocol and told Irina/Laura of his work for the Agency. He reveals that he wishes to leave so as to be able to spend more time with his family. While earlier films had used this plot, most notably William Castle's science-fiction film *Project X* (1967), derived from two works by the British writer Leslie Purnell Davies who specialised in tales of spies, amnesia and brainwashing (see Joshi 1991), it is the oblique way that it helps brings Jack and Sydney's relationship to the fore that make it particularly satisfying and emotionally fulfilling.

CONCLUSION

Wesley Britton in his study of television espionage drama has concluded that *Alias* and other recent shows like it 'signalled an important shift in our collective thoughts on the need for less tarnished and more idealised heroes' (2004: 259). As Britton includes *24*'s utterly irredeemable Jack Bauer in this group this assertion seems slightly suspect. However, if we accept that Britton's analysis is at least partly true in explaining the appeal of Sydney Bristow as the series' prime mover, then it must also be noted that in *Alias* a potentially less traditionally heroic and more nakedly flawed protagonist has been successfully replaced and given a richness, density and complexity in both character and plot delineation that is surely unrivalled in the genre. The series' refusal to settle for a single infallible viewpoint and its embracing of emotional instability as an organising principle continues to prove to be a richly rewarding look behind the spy genre's façade of coherence and stability. Traditional television and movies aimed at a broad audience move towards elucidation through simplification, assuming a Cartesian view of an ordered universe in which its constituent parts always add up to a recognisable whole. The spy genre, however, allows for considerably more ambiguity, and *Alias* – by fusing a wide variety of generic elements – successfully toys with this precept of the genre, in which the narrative arc always reaches closure. John Clute has said of L.P. Davies' novels that they constitute '. . . a new generic amalgam: tales whose slippage among various genres is in itself a characteristic point of narrative interest' (1999: 303). *Alias*, with its relentless two steps forward, one step back approach to story and character, has made the process of narrative evolution and disclosure central to its appeal, most notably in the inward pull the viewer can experience by the foregrounding of dreams, delusions and role play. Frequently we first experience trauma internally, either as dreams or delusions that either act as portents as part of the prophecy arc (Nadia's dream of killing Sydney ('Echoes') and Sydney's dream of killing her own double ('Conscious')) or instead are part of the overarching themes of mind control, by both heroes and villains. In the climax to 'The Horizon', Sydney is able to take control of the dream state she has been forced into and uses the image of the apparently dead Vaughn to act like Virgil in Dante's afterlife in *La Divina Commedia* and guide herself back to rationality and self actualisation. Thus plots can be resolved in the objective realm, even through hallucinations and chemically induced mind control, best exemplified by Jack's treatment of radiation sickness and the Sloane double plot strand. Whereas the protagonists of *The Prisoner*, the novels of L.P. Davies or even James Bond remain resolutely unknowable, in *Alias* such gimmicks as mental conditioning, doppelgängers and artificial realities have been used in new and exciting ways to explore and not necessarily destroy personalities and so broaden the existential motifs of the spy genre.

ACKNOWLEDGEMENTS

I owe Dr Marco Angelini, my brother and constant companion for all things *Alias*, a tremendous debt. Much of what is contained above, especially as it pertains to the work of Nietzsche and Heidegger, follows directly from our discussions on the series.

3 Sydney Bristow's 'Full Disclosure'
Mythic Structure and the Fear of Motherhood

Paul Zinder

In its early history, the serial spy narrative of *Alias* is primarily concerned with prophecies hidden in ancient art designed by the Italian seer Milo Rambaldi. The episode 'Full Disclosure' (3:11) explains the means by which the radical disciples of Rambaldi intend on fulfilling his most telling prophecy. Page 47 of the Rambaldi journal depicts the Prophecy, which foretells of an intimate association between Rambaldi and the 'Chosen One', believed to be Sydney Bristow, a bond unconfirmed until the revelations of 'Full Disclosure'. As presented by Agent Kendall in his Homeric explanation of Sydney's missing years, her designation as the 'Chosen One' positions her as the unwilling surrogate mother to Rambaldi's child, his second coming. This theoretical reading proposes that the catalysts that drive Sydney to this disturbing historical moment lie in mythic archetypes, acknowledging the importance of both Christian and Greek texts. The mystical work of Rambaldi, revered by the pseudo-religious order of followers who deify him in 'Full Disclosure', justifies this specific analysis. 'All storytelling, conscious or not, follows the ancient patterns of myth' (Vogler 1998: 10), and 'Full Disclosure' revels in its allegorical roots.

Alias introduces Milo Rambaldi and Sydney Bristow as natural mythological adversaries. Rambaldi, both a Christian prophet and pagan figure throughout the series, is countered by Sydney, a Christian Messiah and pagan goddess. Modern narratives often contain universal heroes who undergo similar journeys, all dependent on mythological forerunners (Campbell 1973: 38), and Sydney Bristow is a model hero. The episode 'Full Disclosure' unites the classical Christian and Greek characters, composition, and symbology initiated in *Alias'* early years.

As the mythology of *Alias* develops over its first three seasons, Sydney's resentment of her mother's Rambaldi obsession and marriage to the Covenant's masterplan lead Sydney to fear her own potential motherhood. The narrative constructs that build to 'Full Disclosure', however, place Sydney in the dual role of parent and child, each relying on Christian and Greek precedents.

THE OLD TESTAMENT OF *ALIAS*

> This woman here depicted will possess unseen marks; signs that she will be the one to bring forth my works, bind them with fury, a burning anger.
> ('The Prophecy', 1:16)

The first two seasons of *Alias* serve as its Old Testament and found the mythology upon which 'Full Disclosure' rests. As chief architect to Pope Alexander II, Milo Rambaldi was excommunicated for proposing that 'someday, science would allow us to know God' ('Parity', 1:3), an initial presage of the Covenant's endeavour to conceive Rambaldi's offspring scientifically in 'Full Disclosure'. Arvin Sloane advocates the coming fanaticism by stating, 'Rambaldi was a prophet' ('Parity').

Prophets govern the Old Testament, as the ancient scriptures include 'many references to a coming king or anointed one' (Edinger 1986: 147). While modern Christianity traditionally locates the Messiah in its New Testament, Old Testament writings hold passages that 'refer to the Messiah by both Jewish and Christian commentators' (Edinger 1986: 147). Contemporary readings of the New Testament may focus on events in the life of Christ, but the God-man archetype appears first in the Old Testament (Edinger 1986: 126). The sketch on Rambaldi's page 47 infers that Sydney will 'bring forth [Rambaldi's] works' ('The Prophecy'), appointing Sydney the Messiah and Rambaldi a prophet in the Old Testament of *Alias*. As her defined role in the Prophecy remains shrouded until 'Full Disclosure', Sydney denies her messianic title throughout her own Old Testament.

An Old Testament requires an all-powerful Yahweh, and Jack Bristow befits the god-archetype during the first two seasons of

Alias. Jack's Almighty duality carries 'a terrible double aspect: a sea of grace met by a seething lake of fire' (Carl Jung, quoted in Edinger 1986: 48). Jack remains enigmatic as Sydney's connection to Rambaldi slowly reveals itself. When asked to identify her latest phone call as 'good guys or bad guys' in 'Dead Drop' (2:4), Sydney answers, 'neither, my father'. Jack, like Yahweh, is a 'desperate paradox' (Edinger 1986: 33). During *Alias'* Old Testament, his puzzling nature confounds Sydney, who shifts from anger to admiration for the Father she struggles to comprehend.

Early *Alias* centres on Sydney's lack of faith in Jack, and embraces Christ's assertion that 'a man's enemies shall be they of his own household' (*The Holy Bible* 1912: Matthew 10:36). Sydney slaps Jack for failing to warn her about Danny's impending assassination ('So it Begins', 1:2), reports him as the KGB agent who murdered Vaughn's father along with a group of CIA agents ('The Confession', 1:11), and insists 'I don't trust anything you say' ('Salvation', 2:6) after Jack frames Irina Derevko by wiring the house with explosives in Madagascar ('The Indicator', 2:5). Sydney often fears Jack in the Old Testament of *Alias*, failing to recognise that 'the fear of [Yahweh] is the beginning of wisdom' (*The Holy Bible* 1912: Proverbs 9:10).

But even before she readily acknowledges that her Father's intentions are just, Sydney idolises him. She boasts to Vaughn about Jack's physical display after the Hassan mission ('The Confession'), solicits Jack's 'divine guidance' (Edinger 1986: 52) on whether she should remain in graduate school ('The Coup', 1:14), and recalls that her Father carried her for miles after a childhood camping accident, referring to him as 'the strongest man in the world' ('Masquerade', 1:18). Jack, like Yahweh, is 'the union of opposites, evil as well as good' (Edinger 1986: 110).

The counterpoint to Sydney's omniscient Father is Sloane, her satanic nemesis. Sloane is former CIA, a fallen angel, with ties to both the Alliance and the Covenant. Early *Alias* bonds Sloane to Old Testament iconography. Sydney calls him 'a plague on my life' ('A Free Agent', 2:15) and his use of the Rambaldi pulse weapon in Mexico City is referred to as 'the first sign of the coming Armageddon, like the devil himself rose up to attack that church' ('Firebomb', 2:16). During the Old Testament of *Alias*, Sloane holds dominion over death. As the mastermind of SD-6, he orders Danny's elimination, which incites Sydney to dedicate her life to defeating him

('Truth Be Told', 1:1). Sloane assassinates his good friend Jean Bri-ault in a Montreal park to sway an Alliance vote ('The Prophecy') and sends Allison Doren to execute Diane Dixon in revenge for the murder of his own wife ('Endgame', 2:19). As the Old Testament Satan 'intervenes as a disturbance and hindrance to the natural order of living', Arvin Sloane serves as Sydney's 'metaphysical foe of a peaceful life' (Rivkah Schärf Kluger, quoted in Edinger 1973: 91) during the first two seasons of *Alias*.

Michael Vaughn functions as Sydney's disciple throughout the Old Testament of *Alias* and Marcus Dixon is a Judas figure in the sec-ond season. Vaughn's devotion to Sydney borders on religious. He disregards CIA policy by giving her a Christmas gift ('Spirit', 1:10), which prompts Dr Barnett to designate Vaughn as Sydney's fol-lower ('The Box, Part One', 1:12). Vaughn calls Sydney his Saviour after she rescues him from Khasinau's operating table ('The Enemy Walks In', 2:1), cementing his position as her own personal St Peter. Vaughn's eventual betrayal of Sydney mimics Peter's betrayal of Christ. Both men deny their redeemers, Vaughn through his mar-riage to Lauren Reed ('The Two', 3:1). His fervour for his Messiah, however, discounts this matrimonial pledge. After Sydney's resur-rection, Vaughn unlawfully orders a plane to hasten her to the eternal city of Rome, assisting in her escape from the government ('Prelude', 3:7).

Dixon's reverential treatment of Sydney belies his position as her Old Testament partner. At Mount Aconcagua, before Anna Espinosa wounds him, Dixon tells Sydney that 'you make it look easy' ('Time Will Tell', 1:8). After he remembers her use of an alter-nate call sign during his rescue, Dixon misplaces his allegiance (forgetting he would have died without her) and reports Sydney to Sloane as a double agent ('The Enemy Walks In'). Jack foils this Judas-like betrayal by accepting responsibility for changing her call name, assuaging Sloane. *Alias*' God soundly defeats its Judas.

The use of Christian symbology in the Old Testament of *Alias* infuses the mythological structure of 'Full Disclosure'. The Ram-baldi symbol itself contains a circle that sits between two partial triangles: <O>. The shapes used in the 'eye of Rambaldi' hold signif-icant meanings in Christian art. The circle denotes eternal life, one of Rambaldi's fixations, and indicates God's perfection (Ferguson 1961: 153). The Rambaldi symbol remains unique in its use of con-necting lines that form the sides of two separate triangles, which mirror each other outside the circle. This mandalic symbol replicates an ancient religious motif that utilises a circle and two triangles representative of 'male and female divinities' (Jung 1968: 267). As the triangle typifies the Holy Trinity in Christian art (Ferguson 1961: 153), the organisation of the shapes in the Rambaldi symbol points to a specific reading: if one partial triangle denotes Rambaldi and his unborn child, Sydney and her unborn child sit on the opposite side of the circle. The missing side of each triangle underlines Rambaldi's recognition that science would make the Holy Spirit obsolete and that his offspring could be produced without the consent of the 'Chosen One'. The Rambaldi symbol reads as a precursor to the Prophecy and the Covenant's endeavours to force an Immaculate Conception in 'Full Disclosure'.

Alias exploits the symbolic circle throughout the first season to draw Sydney closer to the Prophecy of 'Full Disclosure'. Sydney stands on a boardwalk with Vaughn, weeping about the sacrifices she's made, as multicoloured circular lights from a distant Ferris wheel frame her, creating the prominent outline of a halo ('A Broken Heart', 1:4). The Circumference, discussed extensively throughout Season One, is revealed to be a (large round) Rambaldi battery that Sydney destroys in Taipei, leading to her introduction to Irina Derevko, the mother she mistakenly believes is Rambaldi's 'Chosen One' ('Almost Thirty Years', 1:22).

The sun's significant circular form also portends the action of 'Full Disclosure'. Sent to a Spanish church to retrieve a 'golden sun' disc from a stained-glass window, Sydney engages in hand-to-hand combat with Anna Espinosa involving the use of a hymn stand as a weapon ('A Broken Heart'). The circular disc, when inserted into the Rambaldi clock, offers Sydney the coordinates to locate Rambaldi's journal ('Time Will Tell'). The journal contains page 47 (the Prophecy as revealed in 'Full Disclosure') and reinforces the symbolic weight of the circle and its connection to Rambaldi's unborn child ('Page 47', 1:15). In Christian art, the sun is symbolic of both Christ and the Virgin Mary (Ferguson 1961: 45). Rambaldi's 'golden sun' ensures the discovery of the Prophecy, which establishes Sydney's dual role as Messiah and Virgin Mother in 'Full Disclosure'.

The number 47 proves itself *Alias'* favoured number. The CIA decodes forty-seven 'distinct verifiable Rambaldi predictions' that have come true ('Q and A', 1:17), server forty-seven offers up the intel Sydney uses to destroy SD-6 ('Phase One', 2:13), and Sydney enters room forty-seven in the lucid dream that leads her to Lazarey and, ultimately, to the Rambaldi cube ('Conscious', 3:9). The number 47 combines two noteworthy Christian numbers, 40 and 7. The number 40 connotes an extended ordeal. Moses spends forty days on Mount Sinai, the raining of forty days and forty nights causes Noah's flood, and Satan tempts Christ for forty days in the wilderness (Ferguson 1961: 154). Biblical writers used the number 7 to denote 'completion and perfection' (Ferguson 1961: 154). Sydney's tortured search for her missing years (her 'ordeal') and her eventual realisation that Rambaldi chose her as the mother of his second coming (his 'completion') substantiate the potential reasoning behind the Prophecy's page number.

Alias' Old Testament provides early traces of the true meaning of page 47 as revealed in 'Full Disclosure'. After Sydney steals the blank page 47 from the Rambaldi journal in Sloane's safe, a stunned Vaughn shows her that the miracle page actually contains Rambaldi's sketch of Sydney ('Page 47'). While the meaning of the page is initially unknown, Sydney's parachuted flight past the open arms of a statue of Christ at the introduction of the following episode foreshadows the revelations to come ('The Prophecy'). After the DSR (Department of Special Research) concludes that the woman in the sketched Prophecy lives, Agent Haladki defends the government's intrusive examination of Sydney by insisting, 'it's like 666, guys. You see the writing on the kid's scalp you know there's problems at home' ('The Prophecy'). This reference to the number of the Beast is disquieting, and contextualises the apocalyptic language of the Prophecy. In addition, Irina admits that she 'could have prevented this' because Sydney was 'so small' upon her birth ('The Enemy Walks In'), acknowledging that 'the birth of the hero or divine child is accompanied typically by threats to its life' (Edinger 1987: 39).

THE NEW TESTAMENT OF *ALIAS*

Unless prevented, at vulgar cost, this woman will render the greatest power, unto utter desolation. ('The Prophecy', 1:16)

The New Testament of *Alias* commences with Sydney's own predicted resurrection as noted in her 'Full Disclosure' video message to Kendall when she requests a vow of silence upon her return to the living. When she awakes in Hong Kong she lies in the foetal position, her mind wiped clean in a pure rebirth ('The Telling', 2:22). The distinctive scar that marks her body fills Sydney with dread ('The Two'). 'Full Disclosure' draws together the Christian figures, narratives, and iconography that precede the episode to reveal the startling solution to the mystery of Sydney's missing years.

As Kendall and Sydney fly through the heavens in 'Full Disclosure', he suggests that Sydney's two-year 'death' was actually a Christ-like sacrifice undertaken by the 'Chosen One' to protect her family and followers. As the DSR studies the Rambaldi liquid at the opening of the episode, Sydney's exclusion from data secured by the study echoes her paralysis during the DSR examination of page 47 ('Q and A'). The government Pharisees will arrive at their own conclusions, without the blessing of Sydney, their Messiah. Ultimately, the Rambaldi cube and its liquid DNA vanish, forcing Kendall to break his vow and reveal the secrets Sydney (in her former life) so desperately wanted to hide.

Kendall opens his 'Full Disclosure' narrative by assuring Sydney that 'you died'. The blood Sydney sheds during her mortal confrontation with Allison Doren ('The Telling') corresponds to the redemptive blood shed by Christ (Edinger 1973: 246); her disappearance, kidnapping, and extended persecution infer the flagellation of Christ before the crucifixion (Edinger 1987: 91). The Covenant's attempts to brainwash her into becoming Julia Thorne (to serve its prophet's purpose) are thwarted by the patriarchal might given to her by Jack's involvement in Project: Christmas, the secret CIA programme that trained children to be spies ('The Indicator'). Her pseudo-God-given immunity to the Covenant's tortuous conditioning programme ('Full Disclosure') emulates the Christ of the Project's name by paralleling his victory over Satan's temptation in the wilderness (Edinger 1987: 53). She will not be turned.

Sydney convinces the Covenant that she has become Julia Thorne (her surname nominative of her own crown of thorns). On the group's orders she finds Andrian Lazarey, a Russian diplomat who knows the whereabouts of the Rambaldi cube. After anointing the cube 'the Holy Grail', Kendall explains that Sydney had been instructed to murder Lazarey after acquiring the coordinates of the cube. Lazarey is a narrative descendant of Lazarus in that he benefits from the power of the Saviour when Sydney spares his life and orchestrates his bogus assassination, which results in his own 'resurrection' ('Full Disclosure').

Surveying Kendall's folder of Rambaldi artefacts, Sydney turns to a photograph of page 47, which prompts Kendall to note that Sydney is a Christ-like 'celebrity' at Project Black Hole, the covert government bunker where Rambaldi artefacts are stored and analyzed ('Full Disclosure'). Sydney recalls that her mother had verified Sydney's position as the 'Chosen One' before bungee jumping to freedom ('The Telling'). The Covenant's strategy to fulfill the Prophecy expressed on page 47 will confirm Irina's assertion and reveal Rambaldi's endgame.

Kendall recounts that Sydney and Lazarey unearthed the Rambaldi cube themselves in Namibia after a mile-long excursion through an earthen cave. The unlocking of the cube's vault requires twelve keys ('Full Disclosure'), equal to the number of Christ's disciples (Ferguson 1961: 154). Although the CIA expects her to deliver the cube, Sydney dispatches a videotape instead. Sydney and Kendall watch her confession on a large screen above them, staring at her image, mesmerised by her words. From her electronic pulpit, Sydney preaches that 'everything gets stolen.' She has lost faith in everyone, even the CIA, so instead of bestowing the cube upon Kendall, she hides it away to protect the world from the Covenant's fundamentalism. She chooses to erase her memory, to martyr herself and rise again ('Full Disclosure').

Sydney's amnesia, however, leads her to search for her missing time and, eventually, for the cube. After Kendall questions why she 'went straight for the cube' after suffering great pain to conceal it, Sydney recalls that Sloane had given her an envelope forged with her handwriting containing a key that led her to Rome (the seat of the Vatican as well as her visions of falling angels in 'Prelude', 3:7) and eventually, to the cube. The meaning of the 'Chosen One' confirms Sydney's alarm. As Kendall reveals that the Covenant ambushed the DSR caravan to snatch the cube earlier that day (fulfilling Sydney's videotaped prediction), Sydney stares at the scar on her body, fully comprehending the horror of the Prophecy. Kendall exclaims that 'they have it all now'. The Covenant possesses both Rambaldi's DNA and Sydney's eggs, inching page 47's Prophecy closer to realization. Sydney's designation as the 'Chosen One', the Virgin Mother, may stand without her consent ('Full Disclosure'). Science does allow the Covenant to know its God.

Agent Kendall, Sydney's Angel Gabriel, performs the Annunciation. Christian scripture details that 'the power of the most High shall overshadow' the Virgin, inducing her Immaculate Conception (*The Holy Bible* 1912: Luke 1:35). 'Full Disclosure' encourages the dark reading of the Annunciation (Edinger 1987: 23) by likening Sydney's Immaculate Conception to rape. She will not conform to the Virgin Mother's 'obedience' (Edinger 1987: 26) during her own Annunciation. Sydney's Messianic obligation prevents such deference.

Sydney beseeches a follower to track the Rambaldi cube. Marshall Flinkman offers Sydney, Kendall and her other disciples (Vaughn and Dixon) the location of the fertilisation. The Covenant's attempt to immaculately conceive Sydney's child is depicted in a church setting. Sydney destroys the altar (and the remnants of the Covenant's mortal sin) with fire. In early Christian texts, 'fire appears to be an allusion to the destructive fire of judgment' (Jean Daniélou, quoted in Edinger 1987: 49). When Sydney faces a choice of vocation, she obliterates her prophesied role as Virgin Mother by embracing her place as the Saviour of mankind. This decision transfers the prophet's patriarchal authority to Sydney, making her the supreme force. Rambaldi's (demon) seed remains unborn. The Christian manifestation that permeates 'Full Disclosure' acknowledges the complex construction that precedes the episode and fulfills the expectations introduced in the Old Testament of *Alias*.

THE TWO GODDESSES

> You might want to sit down for this.
>
> Kendall ('Full Disclosure', 3:11)

'Full Disclosure' also draws upon Greek tradition in its characterisation and classical narrative drive. Just as the Sydney Bristow character appropriates archetypal patterns of both the Virgin Mother and Christ, she borrows from the paradigms of Demeter, the Greek goddess of Grain, and her child, Persephone. Sloane symbolically anoints Sydney a descendant of Demeter by bequeathing her Emily's seed box in 'Cipher' (2:3). In ancient rituals, Demeter and Persephone were referred to as 'the two goddesses' as the characters were transposable (Harris and Platzner 2001: 119). The construction of 'Full Disclosure' and Sydney's quest for her missing years suggest a kinship between Sydney and 'the two goddesses' and incorporate the mythological composition of the Demeter and Persephone tale.

The mother/daughter relationship in *Alias* originates, however, in its first season. Irina Derevko is Sydney's birth mother, and their biological bond anchors Irina to the Demeter role even before she is reunited with her daughter in the series. Several early episodes include moments that establish the Irina/Demeter affiliation. In 'A Broken Heart', Jack dreams of Irina while undergoing a psychological evaluation, only to watch her become Sydney when she turns around to face him, suggesting that mother and daughter, like Demeter and Persephone, are 'interchangeable' (Harris and Platzner 2001: 119). During one of Sydney's visits to Irina's cell, her mother tucks her own hair behind her ear, mimicking her daughter's action from moments before ('Trust Me', 2:2). As Sydney stands at the glass wall separating her from her mother, a reflection of Irina creates a dual image ('Cipher'), which anticipates an eventual passing of the Demeter archetype from mother to daughter. When Irina assures Sydney that 'it's you . . . not me' before she disappears off the side of the office building in 'The Telling', she cedes the Demeter role to her daughter, whose Season Three narrative includes many references to the ancient myth.

In the traditional telling of the story, Demeter and her daughter, Kore, wander through a field where Kore sees a beautiful narcissus (Edinger 1994: 174). After she bends and plucks the flower, the earth opens and Hades, the god of the Underworld, surfaces riding a horse drawn chariot. He snatches Kore, forces her into the earth, and rapes her (Burkert 1985: 160). After Hades claims Kore for his bride, he dubs her Persephone, which indicates her 'altered state' (Agha-Jaffar 2002: 7, 41). Persephone's father Zeus ignores the violation, leaving Demeter to hunt for her missing daughter (Agha-Jaffar 2002: 7).

The physical scar left on Sydney's cut body ('The Two') and the Covenant's theft of her eggs ('Full Disclosure') constitute bodily rape. These brutal transgressions echo the kidnapping and rape of Persephone by Hades. 'To be carried off by Hades and to celebrate marriage with Hades become common metaphors for death' (Burkert 1985: 161). Sydney's missing years signify the 'death' imposed by her own abduction. As her torturer states in 'Full Disclosure', 'the sooner you accept that you are no longer who you were, the easier this will be. Sydney Bristow is gone.'

Jack relates to the Zeus figure in this scenario; his decision to enrol Sydney in Project: Christmas removed her 'choices in life' ('The Indicator'). Sydney's childlike insistence 'I want my dad!' ('Full Disclosure') emulates Persephone's call for her unresponsive father in *The Homeric Hymn to Demeter* (quoted in Agha-Jaffar 2002: 174). Although Jack strives to assist Sydney in the recovery of her lost time throughout the third season of *Alias*, he cannot deny that her unsanctioned childhood training ultimately led to the iniquity of 'Full Disclosure'. As Persephone 'learns that her father is not nurturing and loving since he sanctioned her abduction and rape' (Agha-Jaffar 2002: 54), so Sydney holds Jack responsible for the rearing that delivers her to Arvin Sloane, her Hades ('The Indicator').

Demeter hears Persephone's cry. *The Homeric Hymn to Demeter* describes her agonised response: 'Sharp grief seized her heart' and she 'sped like a bird over dry land and sea, searching' (quoted in Agha-Jaffar 2002: 174). The third season of *Alias* initially directs Sydney into Demeter's unfortunate position. Sydney has lost – essentially – herself, and the search for her missing time becomes the chief focus of the narrative constructs leading to 'Full Disclosure'.

Demeter, livid about Zeus and Hades' patriarchal control over Persephone, utilizes her authority as Goddess of Grain to force the earth into sterility (Harris and Platzner 2001: 39). Nothing grows and starvation spreads. Irina exerts similar hegemony in early *Alias*. Irina uses a plant to sooth Sydney's bloodied skin ('The Passage, Part Two', 2:9) but threatens to withhold her support if Sydney remains with her father in the male-centric CIA ('A Free Agent'). 'By insisting on the primacy of her relationship to her daughter, Demeter challenges Zeus' self-proclaimed position as the center of her universe' (Agha-Jaffar 2002: 25). Irina opposes Jack's authority throughout the second season of *Alias*, stirring discord between father and daughter.

Demeter's aggressive behaviour ignores societal mores that traditionally label anger as a male trait (Agha-Jaffar 2002: 25). Sydney's stubborn insistence on continuing the pursuit of her missing time supersedes directives from her own patriarchal government, personified by Robert Lindsey during *Alias*' third season ('Breaking Point', 3:8).

During her search for Persephone, Demeter enters the city of Eleusis after assuming the alias of a woman (Hard 1997: 33), and, in disguise, offers to perform household tasks. Choosing to adopt a similar strategy, Sydney returns to the CIA, partners with Simon Walker as Julia Thorne, and seeks her former self ('A Missing Link',

3:4). Ancient writings depict Demeter as 'blonde . . . the color of the ripened corn' (Burkert 1985: 159) while the Julia Thorne of 'Full Disclosure' is also fair-haired, an alias Kendall has never seen before.

Mankind suffers on the brink of extinction due to the drought instituted by Demeter, forcing Zeus to act. He orders Hades to release Persephone to her mother, but his belated demand ties his daughter to Hades forever. Persephone had eaten pomegranate seeds given her by Hades (Edinger 1994: 174), which condemned her to revisit the Underworld for four months every year, before again returning above ground (Burkert 1985: 160). During those four months, the earth would grow barren to remind the world of Persephone's tribulation, but spring would return again, in gratitude to Demeter for saving her daughter's life (Harris and Platzner 2001: 116).

Although, as a member of the KGB, Irina Derevko betrayed Jack and her daughter ('The Confession'), she proves herself as caring as Demeter when she nurtures Sydney during the second season of *Alias*. Irina kills Khasinau as he prepares to gun down her daughter ('The Enemy Walks In'), she leads Sydney to a secure door in Moscow that allows her to escape from oncoming guards ('Dead Drop'), and declares her love for Sydney as mother (Demeter) and daughter (Persephone) touch the glass that separates them ('A Dark Turn', 2:17). After Irina escapes captivity in 'The Telling', however, Sydney assumes the Demeter archetype herself.

The traditional nature myth places Persephone in the role of the seed planted in the Underworld, watered by Zeus when he demands Hades to release her. She flourishes into stalks of grain to acknowledge Demeter, the Goddess of Grain (Harris and Platzner 2001: 115). Kendall's chronicle in 'Full Disclosure' grants the main players fitting mythological equivalents. Sydney (Demeter), in erasing her own memory, loses herself (Persephone). Jack (Zeus) aids the pursuit of her missing time ('Conscious'). Sloane (Hades) offers Sydney his own form of pomegranate seeds by handing her the coordinates of Lazarey's buried severed hand, directing her journey to a terrifying past ('Prelude'). Sydney's continued relationship with Sloane imposes a frequent return to the shadows of the Underworld. Eventually, she defeats the patriarchal institution by reinstating the bond between her 'new' self and her former life, just as Persephone and her mother reunite after Demeter forces Zeus to act. 'Both Demeter and Persephone undergo a fundamentally similar experience:

the death of an old self and the birth of a new one' (Agha-Jaffar 2002: 34), like Sydney after she defeats the Prophecy in 'Full Disclosure'.

During her time in Eleusis, Demeter teaches the people the Eleusinian mysteries, rituals that commemorate the stories of Demeter and Persephone (Edinger 1994: 175). Participants in the rituals were forbidden to discuss the specifics of the events (Harris and Platzner 2001: 117), so the detailed history of the mysteries correlates to Sydney's missing time. The Greater Mysteries lasted nine days to commemorate Persephone's abduction and plunge into the Underworld (Edinger 1994: 177), their length connoting the nine months of pregnancy (Agha-Jaffar 2002: 9). Sydney contacts Kendall after she's been missing for nine months, having experienced a symbolic rape by the Covenant, which they later attempt to convert into a scientific 'pregnancy' in 'Full Disclosure'. In the Greater Mysteries 'initiates were put through the process of grieving for and then reconnecting with their abducted selves' (Agha-Jaffar 2002: 11), just as Sydney mourns her lost time before Kendall offers her the revelations of 'Full Disclosure'.

Persephone loses her naivety during her experience in Hades and departs the Underworld a grown, powerful woman (Harris and Platzner 2001: 121). That is, her loss of virginity is psychological as well as physical. She recognizes that trust must be earned and that blind devotion stands unfounded. Sydney initially learns the same lesson upon discovering the true nature of SD-6 ('Truth Be Told'), but she cannot prevent her own physical violation by the Covenant. Persephone renews herself a mature woman while Sydney's fiery destruction of the Covenant's master plan in 'Full Disclosure' allows her to embark on a new life.

This mother–daughter dynamic pervades *Alias'* entire mythology and climaxes in 'Full Disclosure'. Sydney's fear of her own mother, originally established after her discovery of Irina's betrayal of Jack and murder of Vaughn's father ('The Confession'), reaches its apex when she recalls Irina's final confirmation of Sydney's role as the 'Chosen One' in 'Full Disclosure'. Her mother's words, originally spoken in 'The Telling', had been dismissed by Sydney as subterfuge. In 'Full Disclosure', for the first time, the 'Chosen One' listens. Sydney Bristow is the true Christian and Greek archetype.

The Covenant's violation of her reproductive organs impels Sydney to dread her own potential motherhood. To terminate this fear,

Sydney aborts the Prophecy and her unborn child, taking control of her own fertility, defeating the Covenant, Rambaldi, and her mother in the process. Sydney's position as Christian Saviour and Greek Goddess is thereby assured.

Part Two

IDENTITIES/ ALIASES

Family, Gender and Race in *Alias*

The New Hero
Women, Humanism and Violence in *Alias* and *Buffy the Vampire Slayer*

Elizabeth Barnes

Twenty-seven-year-old Sydney Bristow – slender, muscular, attractively 'All-American' – looks on as her partner-in-spying, Marcus Dixon, blows up a building with a remote detonator. Her face, first aghast and disbelieving, crumbles into a look of agonised suffering. Her expression betrays to viewers what Dixon himself cannot see: the physical and emotional cost of duplicity. Dixon, who believes he is working for an arm of US intelligence called SD-6, is in fact unwittingly in league with a terrorist organisation known as the Alliance. The Alliance secretly controls all SD units. Dixon doesn't know that the woman beside whom he has been working for six years is a double agent, pretending to work for SD-6 but in reality working for the CIA. Neither does he know that Sydney has just left her fellow CIA operatives in the building to gather the information she left there for them. Dixon's detonator was programmed by Sydney to malfunction. What she hadn't planned for was Dixon bringing another one along, just in case. Now the men Sydney left in the building are dead. Her brown eyes reflect the loss, the tragedy, and her own failure to protect. Her face – registering guilt, sickness and almost unbearable sorrow – is the raison d'être of the show: this is a woman who takes on the pain of the world ('Doppelgänger', 1:5).

Although ostensibly an action show premised on the conflict between world powers – one legitimate (the United States government), the others illegitimate (various global terrorist organisations) – *Alias* presents conflicts that are largely internal. In this, *Alias* represents a growing number of popular dramas featuring both male and female protagonists whose success with audiences is tied to their capacity for empathy and emotional suffering. Such suffering for the sake of others, evinced in characters like Allison Dubois in *Medium*, Jack Bauer in *24*, or Jack Malone in *Without a Trace*, is, as this list indicates, not specific to women; but female action heroes dramatise in specific and somewhat counterintuitive ways both the potentially dehumanising, because desensitising, effects of violence and the redemptive potential of emotional vulnerability. In two of the most popular contemporary examples of female heroism, *Alias* and *Buffy the Vampire Slayer*, we can see the ways in which feminine sensibility, and the empathy associated with it, becomes a test case for the future of humanism in a globally violent world. Can women, of all people, these shows implicitly ask, be violent and remain 'women': i.e., caring, nurturing, empathetic? The answer is 'yes'. Yet ultimately the foregrounding of young women not only underscores the risks to 'innocence' that violence poses, it facilitates the redemption of violence itself: violence is legitimised through its alignment with characters who understand and appreciate the nature and cost of the methods they employ, and who suffer because of it.

The suffering is key. *Alias* and *Buffy* work through questions of moral and ontological relativism by locating humanity in an image of the embattled self – a sensitive and suffering hero whose use of violence often *pains* her. The new hero's heroism resides less in her ability to defeat physically imposing opponents than in her willingness to engage in emotional battles against insensitivity and despair. Unlike their empathetic but more stoical male counterparts, Buffy and Sydney openly perform these emotional battles for their viewers, exhibiting through such performances proof of their own authenticity. White middle-class women, historically viewed as the cultural bearers of compassion and the producers of human feeling and family, are thus not so much reimagined in these shows as recontextualised; Sydney's and Buffy's implicit function as female action heroes is to redeem the world from unfeeling brutality, and to give pain, and the violence that precipitates it, meaning. More often than not the meaning of such pain eludes even them, and this in part forms the tragic quality of their battles. Although premised on an archetypal plotline of good versus evil, both *Alias* and *Buffy* reveal the difficulty of maintaining boundaries that hold, and each show undermines at points the meaningful division of good and evil, the self and what one defines the self against, to suggest the difficulty in our postmodern world of establishing an identity that is stable and reliable, 'real'.

Such epistemological uncertainty frames the action of these action shows, where external violence both produces interior conflicts and mirrors them. It also explains in part the larger-than-life settings within which the protagonists operate. Both shows feature young, beautiful, white, upper middle-class protagonists (Sydney Bristow is played by Jennifer Garner and Buffy Summers by Sarah Michelle Gellar), one of whom is a double agent for the CIA and the other who is a, well, vampire slayer. That which would normally shield them from harm – their privileged social positions – affirms the sacrificial nature of their jobs: rather than being at school associating with their friends, they are engaged in epic battles to protect the 'normal' life of others. They thus simultaneously stand apart from, and for, the viewers who watch them week after week. In *Buffy*, the battle for a loving, meaningful life takes place in the mythological world of demons who seek to return the earth to its chaotic state; in *Alias*, chaos is produced by the monstrous intellectual and financial 'elite' who seek to destroy the idealised normality of democratic life through a hierarchical power structure (terrorist 'cells') that atomises it. For both protagonists, the battle against world domination is waged for the sake of the ordinary: an unremarkable, middle-class existence. In other words, both shows move us outside the realm of the pedestrian in order, implicitly, to preserve it. Such an impulse operates on the thematic level as well: although both *Alias* and *Buffy* employ postmodern narratives of indeterminacy, unreliability and fragmentation, they do so as a means of mourning and, ideally, *recuperating* those humanist values that our decadent and cynical culture has, presumably, already moved beyond. What is perhaps the most significant weapon in both shows' arsenal of human understanding is the recurrent assertion of a core self that persists despite the atomised, violent and incoherent world that is at every moment disputing its existence. But that core self is defined by empathy: a struggling, embattled feeling for others that gives the hero her only hope for authenticity.

SLAYING THE D(R)EAD: *BUFFY*'S ONTOLOGICAL ANGST

Beginning as a witty if blackly comedic commentary on the hell that is high school, *Buffy the Vampire Slayer* developed during its seven seasons (1997–2003) into something more philosophical and – despite its puns – more deadly earnest. Its basic contention is that existence on earth is a living hell, characterised by pain, despair, loneliness, confusion and most importantly, struggle. If Heaven is peace, stasis, the end of the fight, Hell is at least productive, energetic, experiential. But it is also relentless: there is no day in the life of a slayer – that Everywoman of heroic humanity – that is not a battle. Hailed as an example of postmodernism in its self-conscious play with the conventions of gender and genre, *Buffy* ultimately relies on an understanding and acceptance of humanist values – the inherent worth of the individual and the individual's capacity for self-realisation – while locating those values in a prehistory of gods and goddesses that humanism was, historically speaking, meant to supersede. Moreover, the show, while dealing in the business of souls (and lack thereof), betrays a certain scepticism about essence: souls can be gained and lost (more than once) due to forces outside the mortal person. What we are left with is only our immediate experience, a perceptual 'reality' that changes from moment to moment. The show can thus be read as a provocative blend of existentialism, humanism and superstition; its politics, likewise, vacillate between the traditional and progressive. The show's preoccupation with issues of flesh and blood in our technological age of cloning and artificial intelligence refers us back to fundamental questions about the nature and limits of personhood, while its parodic display of monstrous power in the figure of a blonde 'Valley girl' unsettles traditional equations of heroism and entitlement with masculinity. Ultimately the attempt to differentiate precisely the human from the monstrous fails, but in the terms of the show, it is the *struggle* that matters.

Buffy's creator, Joss Whedon, has said that he intended Buffy to be not just a character, but an *icon* (Rosen 2003: 1).[1] Whedon's inspiration for the character came from years of watching horror movies in which 'bubbleheaded blondes wandered into dark alleys and got murdered by some creature.' He wanted to make a film (the original *Buffy the Vampire Slayer*) in which the blonde wanders into a dark alley and takes care of herself: deploying her powers to kill the monster (Fudge). The slayer – aka 'the Chosen One' – is always a girl chosen at birth (by whom, we don't know), who assumes her supernatural powers upon reaching puberty; from then on she exists to fight the demons who walk the earth and threaten humans with extinction. The creation of a female vampire slayer was to transform the horror genre by converting helpless femininity into a female empowerment. Since the advent of the television show, however, there has been considerable critical debate over just what kind of icon Buffy represents. Is the show feminist? What is it teaching young women today about how to govern themselves in the 'real' world? As Buffy's belatedly acquired little sister, Dawn, once complained, 'I could save the world too, if I had superpowers'. But alas, she doesn't, and neither do Buffy's viewers. Does this mean that, as Kathleen Karlyn has claimed, female heroism today resides only in the realm of fantasy? (quoted in Labi 1998: 28) And if it does, what is the fantasy the show is tapping into?

Perhaps we can address this question by considering one of the cultural anxieties the fantasy of Buffy's superpowers is presumably meant to dispel: the indeterminate status of 'humanity' and the difficulty of distinguishing the humane from the human. *Buffy* explores this anxiety through a mythology that blurs the boundaries between life and death, earthly existence and Hell. In the folklore of the show, the world as we know it, aka, Sunnydale, California (built, ironically, over a subterranean entrance to Hell that simultaneously attracts and disgorges such demons), is always on the verge of collapsing into the demon world that once was this earth. In the second episode of the show, Giles, Buffy's watcher (mentor/guide), explains to Buffy and her sidekicks, Willow and Xander, the prehistory of their reality:

Contrary to popular mythology, [this world] did not begin as a paradise. For untold aeons, demons walked the earth. They made it their home, their Hell. And in time they lost their purchase on this reality. And the way was made for mortal animals, for Man. . . . The books tell that the last demon to leave this reality fed off a human, mixed their blood. He was a human form possessed, infected by the demon's soul. He bit another and another, and so they walk the earth, feeding, killing some, mixing their blood with others to make more of their kind. Waiting for the animals to die out and the Old Ones to return. ('The Harvest', 1:2)

While invested in drawing the lines between what is human and inhuman, *Buffy* at the same time suggests that those lines are always already obscured. Humanity's potential descent into the 'other', the incipient collapse of boundaries between earth and hell, signifies the ultimate fight, and constitutes, in some fundamental way, the business of living. An awareness of this business – to battle against despair, to fight the demons within as well as without – begins in adolescence.

But it doesn't end there. Although Gellar herself once stated in an interview that *Buffy* 'basically just take[s] high school and use[s] horror as a metaphor for it' (quoted in Wilcox 2002: 3), the horror the show enacts goes beyond the challenges of maturation and socialisation. While there are a myriad of ways in which *Buffy*'s 'demons' can be said to stand in for real world problems, taken as a whole, the *Buffy* oeuvre suggests a more all-encompassing ontological angst inaugurated in, but not limited to, the teenage years. Viewers and critics alike decried the darkening vision of the show during its sixth season (after Buffy's well-intentioned friends have resurrected her from the grave, only to be informed later that they have taken her from a place of 'peace' and brought her back to this life, this 'hell'),[2] but these episodes simply make explicit what has been the show's subtext all along: the founding myth that posits humans and demons battling it out for their own 'purchase' on reality suggests realities that are serial as well as simultaneous, and contested. It is not just worlds or 'dimensions' that are split and on the verge of collapse – it is people as well. In episode after episode, humans are metamorphosed into creatures ('The Pack', 1:6; 'Go Fish', 2:20; 'Phases', 2:15; 'Beauty and the Beasts', 3:4; 'A New Man,' 4:12 etc.), doppelgängers abound ('Nightmares', 1:10; 'Doppelgangland', 3:16; 'Bad Girls', 3:14; 'Who are You?', 4:16), robots simulate people ('Ted', 2:11; 'I Was Made to Love You', 5:15; 'Intervention', 5:18; 'Bargaining Parts One and Two'. 6:1–2) and the dead come back to life . . . again and again. Fear of imminent death is secondary to the more fundamental anxiety the show rehearses about the instability of identity: if the body is not stable, what is it that tells us who we are? What separates the human from the inhuman, the living from the undead?

It is just such questions, of course, that Buffy's superhuman body means on one level to forestall. That is, one of the fantasies that *Buffy* enacts is a vision of the body as capable of exerting power and of withstanding it; a body that is strong, resilient and, most importantly, coherent. Since female bodies have historically been constructed as incoherent – as vulnerable, excitable, manipulable, excessive – a view of the female body as in control and self-possessed is particularly novel, and attractive. While vampires and other demons dematerialise on the show (they are staked, or beheaded, or chopped into bits, then turned to dust), Buffy remains firm: she is punched, cracked on the head, thrown against walls, but she is finally still standing, intact (see Karras 2002). Violence allows *Buffy* to sustain such fictions by literally performing the materiality of the body, thus apparently giving the body integrity: coherence and meaning, and coherent meaning, through physical force and stamina. The fantasy of the coherent body, however, is undercut in a number of ways. In 'Normal Again' (6:17), for instance, Buffy is poisoned and, presumably due to hallucination, finds herself in another reality. In this reality Buffy has been institutionalised for schizophrenia. Her life in Sunnydale, her friends, her superpowers are all found to be what viewers always knew them to be: fantasies of empowerment. Buffy's doctor and parents urge her to give up her fantasy world for the real one, to battle her 'internal demons' and resume her existence as a normal girl. She is on the verge of doing so (by murdering the 'fantasy' friends in her mind) when she is given an antidote to the poison and returns to Sunnydale and sanity. Although Buffy returns to 'normal', it is never made clear which illness she is really suffering from – poison or schizophrenia – or how one differentiates between reality and hallucination. The episode's final scene takes place in the hospital, thus giving that reality the last word: 'I'm afraid we've lost her', says the doctor, as Buffy, catatonic, faces the wall.

In 'Normal Again', the body fails as an index to who or *what* one is; one's physical existence may be an illusion played out in the only world that truly exists: the mind. The fantasy of the coherent (super)human body would seem, in postmodern fashion, to be nothing but play. But where material bodies fail as an index to identity, I would argue, feeling comes to take its place. Though itself no definitive marker of *biological* humanity, feeling in *Buffy* does become the basis of humanity in spirit, a spirit that even vampires may (re)acquire. Thus Angel, a vampire, is a hero on the show not simply because he has a soul, but because he loves Buffy and Buffy loves him; Spike, also a vampire, is likewise redeemed by the show through his love for Buffy – his ability to feel as a human feels. Perhaps the most dramatic example of the show's sentimental ontology comes at the end of Season Five, when Buffy leaps to her death to save her 'sister' Dawn, and all of humanity, from destruction. Dawn, it turns out, is not in fact human at all but is a mystical 'key': the shedding of her blood will unlock the gate between realities. The boundaries of Earth will disintegrate and Chaos will reign. Dawn is given human form by an ancient sect of monks, who, at the time of her incarnation, also give Buffy memories of Dawn as her little sister. The goal is to motivate the slayer to protect Dawn with her life, and although Buffy eventually discovers Dawn's true nature, the monks' plan works. In spite of being admittedly a simple 'blob of energy', Dawn *experiences* herself as a human being, just as Buffy's artificially-generated memories of Dawn evoke emotions as real to Buffy as any tangible history. It thus makes no difference what Dawn, or presumably anyone, *is*; what makes her real are Buffy's feelings about her.

Buffy's sentimental ontology points to a model for authenticity that biology alone cannot account for. In fact, one of the central tenets of the show is that the effort to be and *remain* human is a constant battle, an idea to which the existence of vampires materially attests. The willingness to engage in such a battle, and to suffer for it, is the essence of humanity. Thus in the episode 'Amends' (3:10), Angel – a vampire cursed with a soul – is saved from his past sins, and his attempt to atone for them through suicide, by his remorse. It is his unflagging suffering, the show constantly reminds us, that keeps him human. One moment of true happiness (as he had when he made love with Buffy) and he will again lose his soul, his ability to love, and his humanity. Likewise, Willow's transformation into the all-knowing, all-feeling Wicca – the ultimate empath – connects her to 'everything', but what she senses from the world is nothing but pain. Following her announcement that she can 'feel . . . everyone', she exclaims, 'Oh my God, oh, the emotion, the pain. . . . it's too much. It's just too much. I have to stop this. I'll make it go away. Oh you poor bastards. Your suffering has to end' ('The Grave', 6:22). In yet another perversion of a Christian trope, the episode concludes with Willow's attempt to end humanity's suffering by annihilating the world. Love, longing, and the capacity to suffer define the (super)human experience, a truth made most evident by our long-suffering heroine, whose love for particular individuals and for humanity in general is inextricably linked with the giving and receiving of pain.

As the medium in which Buffy and her friends live and breathe, violence is given meaning by its depiction as a potential vehicle to preserving what is most unique about being human: the ability to care for others. And caring often equals pain. In Buffy's world, then, even love relationships – the manifestation of earthly human connection – are coded as violent. When Angel loses his soul (again), Buffy must kill him in order to save the world ('Becoming, Part Two' 2:22). When he returns several episodes later, Buffy stabs Faith – a former friend and slayer turned bad – in order to save Angel's life ('Graduation Day, Part One', 3:21). In the finale to the sixth season, longtime friends Buffy and Willow try to beat each other to death after Willow has turned evil ('The Grave', 6:22). Willow's transformation is in fact prompted by love: she is grief-stricken by the murder of her lover. In *Buffy*, love initiates pain, and pain is the cause, as well as the effect, of violence. The cycles of death and rebirth on the show are paralleled by the cycles of creative and destructive impulses, by the forms of attachment that are simultaneously loving and violent. Perhaps not surprisingly then, just as Buffy is told by the First Slayer in 'Intervention' that she is 'full of Love', she is also told, 'Love will lead you to your gift', and 'Death is your gift'. Death is a gift that Buffy gives to others (soon after she will sacrifice herself for Dawn and save the world – again). But it is also the gift given *to* her: in a world where violence is a way of (preserving) life, death – even violent death – is the only path to peace.

These contradictions, paradoxes and ironies all suggest that *Buffy*'s fantasies try but fail to compensate for the dreadful anxieties they simultaneously mask. More than this, however, I would suggest that in the world of *Buffy*, the anxiety and the fantasy overlap. Jane Espenson, one of the show's head writers, has said that demons represent the pull towards inertia and breakdown: 'Disorder becomes demonized . . . as if it were an actual entity against which we struggle. Entropy as demon.' (Tonkin 2003) The fantasy of resilient bodies that cannot die obscures the fear that no one is truly alive, while anxieties about disorder/disordered bodies deflects a deathwish that all the characters (especially our hero) on some level carry. Violence is key in this scenario: a manifestation of the power that allows characters to feel more truly alive, violence also brings them closer to their oblivion – the end of struggle, the end of pain –

that they seek. Thus Buffy, when confronted with her own mortality, asks Spike how he has killed slayers in the past; he answers that all slayers have a deathwish: 'Part of you wants [death]. Not only to stop the fear and uncertainty, but because you're just a little bit in love with it. Death is your art. You make it with your hands day after day. . . . Every slayer has a deathwish. Even you' ('Fool for Love', 5:7). The fantasy of omnipotence bears the traces of what we fear: that we don't exist. Conversely, what we fear may be what we long for most: oblivion.

Viewers are redeemed from the Freudian drive to death implicit in this supernatural-humanist drama by the self-conscious irony with which the show offers up its cycles of empowerment and despair. *Buffy* capitalises on its venue as a long-running television series through narratives that loop back around and keep themselves going, much like the characters who die and are reborn, only to repeat the same cycle again.[3] At the end of the fifth season, after Buffy has died again, her tombstone reads, 'She saved the world. A lot', a humorous acknowledgement of the show's recycled plotlines, and a testament to the narrative repetitiveness endemic to successful popular genres.[4] Such humour is part of the perspective distance on reality that postmodernism offers, a distance that keeps this show from taking itself, or its serious subject matter, too seriously. At the end of every season, Buffy pulls viewers back from the edge of the abyss it has brought them to week after week – the coming Apocalypse – to discriminate between good and evil, life and death, the human and the monstrous. But it does so not on the grounds that there is a coherent, verifiable difference, but on the grounds that it is the work of the living to *make* the difference, to defend the boundaries, to slay the dread. Buffy, in defending those boundaries, proves herself an exemplar of the new hero whose love is purified in the crucible of violence, and who redeems violence itself from meaninglessness, and us, in consequence, from despair.

SYDNEY BRISTOW'S MASQUERADE

Overlapping with *Buffy the Vampire Slayer*'s penultimate season, *Alias* evinces some of the same postmodern play that both highlights and humorously disarms anxieties about apocalyptic endings at the dawn of a new century. During its five seasons (2001–6), *Alias* boasts an ever-changing list of terrorist groups (SD-6, KGB, the Alliance, the Covenant, K-Directorate, Prophet Five), seemingly remaking itself and its villains as often as its protagonist changes costume. One thing that remains constant, however, is the emotional angst with which that protagonist, Sydney Bristow, meets every new threat, every newly revealed deception. If, as I have argued, *Buffy*'s display of the coherent female body taps into cultural fantasies of empowerment – fantasies that mask, but cannot dispel, the divided feelings within – the pain engendered by such emotional ambivalence is nowhere more ably and demonstrably performed than in *Alias*'s strong but suffering heroine. Like Buffy, Sydney's spectacular body serves as both signifier of and displacement for internal conflicts; her primary battles are psychological and emotional, revealing the hero's inner world as the true site of vulnerability and struggle. Sydney's foremost 'mission', one could say, is to arm herself against the potential consequences of grief, betrayal and alienation. In its first season alone, *Alias* presents Sydney reluctantly lying to her closest friends day after day, telling them she works in a bank; after she becomes a double agent, she lies to her fellow agents in SD-6, going on missions for that organisation and then giving whatever information she finds to the CIA. When she tells her fiancé the truth about herself – that she is a spy – he is assassinated by SD-6. She then discovers that her father, Jack, from whom she has been estranged for years, is also a double agent, pretending to work for SD-6 but in reality working for the US government. Her beloved mother, whom Sydney believes died when she was six, turns out to be a Soviet spy in league with the terrorists, a fact that becomes painfully clear when Sydney confronts her mother on a mission and is shot by her in the shoulder ('The Enemy Walks In', 2:1). As if to underscore Sydney's emotional strength, her uncorrupted values, and the life she longs, but is forbidden, to lead, the show depicts Sydney doggedly taking classes at the local college in between missions; she eventually graduates with a Masters in English Literature.

Sydney's painful struggle to maintain her humanity in the midst of unrelenting violence and duplicity constitutes the central tension of *Alias*, a show that concerns itself, both literally and figuratively, with *doubling*:[5] The show implicitly asks, how can a woman who plays a part in virtually every area of her life find an authentic, feeling self? The problem is both posed and ostensibly answered by the show's suggestion that espionage is simply a performance. One of *Alias*' signature moments is Sydney dressed-up for a mission: with pink hair, with blonde hair, with punk hair; in feathers, or minks, or skin-tight leather; with high heels, with thigh-boots, in swim suits, in ball gowns and once, unforgettably, in a dominatrix outfit complete with whip. Sydney's dress is invariably outrageous – sexy, glamorous, provocative. By contrast, her appearances at home or at the spy offices are shot with little or no make-up. Sydney the spy, these masquerades imply, is exactly who Sydney is *not*. That is part of what makes them titillating. The Sydney viewers 'know' – viewers who are in on the secret that many of the other characters are ignorant of – is the fresh-faced girl who smiles at her friends when she wants to cry, and who wants to be a teacher. But if Sydney's performances are meant in effect to establish her wholesome character through startling contrast, it is a difference often lost on the character herself who claims, consistently and insistently, that she no longer knows herself because no one else really can.

In this aptly titled show, then, the greatest threat comes from within: in constantly playing a part, Sydney may finally lose her self. In the same episode where she witnesses the death of her CIA colleagues, Sydney recalls finding her fiancé, Danny, dead in their apartment, assassinated by the rogue organisation SD-6. 'I had his blood on my hands', she tells her CIA handler, Michael Vaughn: 'I feel like I'm losing my mind; like I don't know who I am anymore, or what I'm doing, or why I'm doing it.' 'I've seen who you are', Vaughn reassures her, 'missions change, the enemies have a thousand names. The one crucial thing, the one real responsibility you have is to not let your rage and your resentment and your disgust darken *you*' ('Parity', 1:3). The potential to become what one battles against is central to *Alias*, as it is in *Buffy*, and reveals the struggle involved in maintaining a coherent sense of self. In insisting that the 'enemies have a thousand names', but 'I've seen who *you* are', Vaughn frames the contest as one between anonymous evil and the self-knowing, and known, individual. Yet the show does not posit the victor as a foregone conclusion; after all, Sydney's ability to love and be loved does not keep her from having 'blood on [her] hands'. In fact, Sydney's love for Danny is indirectly responsible for his death. Danny is killed because Sydney stops lying to him: she finally tells him that she is not an agent for an international bank, but a spy. When she confronts the leader of SD-6, Arvin Sloane, with Danny's murder she accuses, 'You killed the man I love'. 'No, Agent Bristow,' Sloane replies, 'you did' ('Truth Be Told', 1:1). Sloane's reply, though self-serving, nevertheless reveals what will become a significant and recurring theme on *Alias*: we always hurt the ones we love. Though the consequences of Sydney's actions are unintended, its effect remains the same; it thus serves as a tragic initiation into a world where husbands murder their wives, mothers wound and fathers kill their children, and loved ones betray one another, over and over again.[6]

Alias' representation of love and violence as virtually inseparable modes of interaction highlights the moral ambiguity at the centre of the show, an ambiguity, as I have suggested, made manifest in the trope of doubling. Like *Buffy*, *Alias* locates its moral quandaries in plots of ontological instability – 'good' and 'evil' characters who are forced to inhabit each other's reality, both physically and psychologically. Jack Bristow's betrayal by his wife, Irina, for example, is mirrored in Michael Vaughn's similar discovery that his wife Lauren is a double agent ('Unveiled', 3.18); Sydney has a dream about a confrontation with Lauren in which Lauren then turns into Sydney herself ('Conscious', 3:9). In a particularly unsettling episode, Sydney plays the role of her own mother to a delusional Jack, hoping to gain access to Jack's past and thus save his life ('Mirage', 4:18). And in its final season, *Alias* returns to a plot about genetic cloning first introduced in Season Two, transforming Sydney's arch-nemesis, Anna Espinosa, into Sydney's 'double' – an evil version of herself whom Sydney is then forced (and glad, presumably) to kill ('I See Dead People', 5:14). The persistence of storylines about literal and psychological substitutions render legible anxieties about the shifting boundaries of identity, as well as reveal the limits of transparency. The question of whether or not one can truly know another, or even oneself, is played out against a background of bodies and relations constantly in flux; lovers, spouses, parents and parent-figures who may or may not be who, or feel what, they claim. But more than this, the doubling of persons and experience suggests that the concepts of good and evil themselves may double for each other, rendering love and the authenticity it signifies and should engender, another casualty of war.

Perhaps nowhere is the doubling of identity and its psychological costs rendered more explicit than in *Alias'* third season, when we learn that Sydney has been transformed into that which she most fears becoming: a cold-blooded killer. At the end of Season Two, Sydney discovers that her friend Francie has been 'doubled', and in a battle between the two Sydney is shot and left for dead. When we next see her, she is in a safe house in Hong Kong and two years have passed. Though Sydney herself has no recollection of the missing time, we eventually discover that she was abducted by a new terrorist organisation, the Covenant, and made to take on a new identity: Julia Thorne. As the result of an apparent brainwashing, Sydney, alias Thorne, is made to murder for the Covenant. We learn this through a videotape that Sydney herself has made. She confesses on the tape not only to the murder of an innocent man, but to her *pretence* at being brainwashed ('Full Disclosure', 3:11). Despite a six-month ordeal of torture and coercion, Sydney resists the captors' tactics to change her; her strength and essential integrity are thus reaffirmed. However, this also means that when she kills, Sydney does it as herself, rather than as her alter ego, Julia Thorne. And this is a torture too painful for her. In an effort to protect the whereabouts of a weapon she obtained while with the Covenant, and as an escape from the memories that now plague her, Sydney goes to a neurosurgeon and has the memories of her last two years removed. She records this information on a videotape for the benefit of the CIA, but she asks never to be told what is on it. She couldn't live with the knowledge, she tells them, of who she had pretended to be. Although through medical intervention Sydney is returned, for a time, to her identity as the ingénue, such an act lays bare the aggressive and artificial means of recovered 'innocence'. Her return is achieved only through a physical removal of experience, a surgical sleight of hand, one that reveals the extent to which the preservation of self (as well as the preservation of the free world) involves a struggle painful, violent and at best, temporary.

If *Alias* appears, simultaneously, to authenticate Sydney for viewers even as it continually undermines such confirmations, this is no accident. The battle for a sincere and empathetic self is ongoing, the show implies, just as the suffering that demonstrates such empathy must be every day endured. Thus Sydney's struggle to remain genuine in the face of corruption and violence is constantly reestablished: with every new costume, Sydney must reconfirm her essential identity. Her success is attested to in the series' final episodes. In the ironically titled 'There's Only One Sydney Bristow' (5:12) (the episode in which Sydney is 'doubled' by Anna), longtime friend Will counters Sydney's now familiar (and somewhat accurate) lament that 'the people I love, sooner or later, something terrible happens to them' with the assurance that her fight against evil has not gone unappreciated: 'Sydney, you save the world every-day and you never ask for anything in return. I think I speak for everyone who loves you when I say, Thank you for watching over us.' Likewise, Arvin Sloane, when face to face with Sydney's double, tells her that despite Anna's appearance, 'You're nothing like her. . . . You crave power. . . . Sydney, on the other hand, is driven by a sense of duty, of loyalty to those she loves. That's where she gets her strength.' 'It's also what makes her weak,' Anna/Sydney replies 'Attachments are a vulnerability which are easily exploited' ('I See Dead People'). To a certain extent, of course, Anna is right. Sydney has been told before that her 'major weakness' as a spy is her empa-thy ('Breaking Point', 3:8). But, like Sloane, what viewers have come to recognise is the power of Sydney's 'weakness'. Her strength lies in her feelings, just as her heroism is defined by her willingness to endure the sufferings of a divided and embattled self. In this world where aliases prove the rule rather than the exception, *Alias'* saving grace is Sydney herself – a woman vulnerable to the forces both of love and love's dark double, but whose very struggle to remain whole and true despite these assaults constitutes her 'true' identity. It is because of this struggle that viewers and characters alike can say (with only a hint of irony), 'There is only one Sydney Bristow.'

Taken together, *Buffy* and its sister-drama *Alias* lay the foundation for a re-humanising of the postmodern, post-9/11 television drama, a foundation based on the hero's capacity to *experience* as well as to inflict pain, and thus prove herself human. Far from becoming mir-ror images of their more traditional masculine counterparts, Buffy Summers and Sydney Bristow are not only 'all American' (read: young, pretty and white), but 'all woman'. They are saved from the potentially corrupting influence of power and violence through their empathetic sensitivity to pain and their tendency to internalise the pain that they wittingly and unwittingly inflict.[7] In the mythol-ogy of both shows, it is womanhood itself, and the feelings associated with it, that proves redemptive. *Buffy* converts despair into hope in the end by rearticulating power as collaborative rather than isolating; the paradigm of the 'lone hero' (historically a male model) is superseded by the vision of an army of female slayers who all work together ('Chosen', 7:22). Likewise in *Alias*, love for others ultimately defines the hero's representative humanity. In the series' final episode, Sloane and Irina's perverse attempt to gain both eternal life and eternal power through Rambaldi's invention of the 'Horizon' is contrasted with Sydney's 'natural' means of gaining immortality: i.e. having children. Sydney's daughter, Isabelle, while clearly another double for Sydney, testifies to the *difference* between Sydney and her own mother-double, Irina. Unlike her 'evil' mother, Sydney chooses to give life and then protect that life with her own. She thus chooses love over power and individual gain, with all the potential suffering that such a choice implies ('All the Time in the World', 5:17). Yet, as we have seen, it is just this capacity to suffer, to stay emotionally connected when such connections hurt more than blows or bullets, that proves the hero's source of strength, and her redemption. It is also, as I have tried to argue, the key to redeeming violence itself. By conceiving of aggression as not only a staple of the world in which women must do battle but as a necessary means of achieving and/or preserving emotional connection, these shows reimagine violence as constitutive of the emotional pain that proves one's humanity, a humanity that is inextricably linked with female sensibility. The use of violence is thus ultimately legitimised through its connection to, and connecting of, emotional subjects – specifically, through its performance in the hands of women who love as well as kill, and who kill, we are constantly reminded, because they love.

Aliases, Alienation and Agency:

The Physical Integrity of Sydney Bristow

Deborah Finding and Alice MacLachlan

> It's this damn body. I have the uncontrollable urge to act like a girl scout.
>
> Sydney, posing as her own double ('No Hard Feelings', 5:15)

On one level, the very conceit of *Alias* is radical. The show is structured around a sympathetic female protagonist who can become anyone and who is strong and independent, even in situations of extreme danger or degradation. She must regularly rely on her own capacity for deception and violence, and as viewers we cheer for her the more successfully she lies and fights. We are led to understand that Sydney survives in a very male world of international espionage by relying primarily on her own physical strength, her ingenuity, and even her female sexuality, and that moreover, she retains a certain moral integrity at the same time. This situates *Alias* in relation to other recent television shows like *Xena: Warrior Princess* and *Buffy the Vampire Slayer*, which portray women whose strength resides in their physical power. All three shows begin from the premise of female near-invulnerability, and yet in all three, the concept of total female power actually serves to expose the contradictions inherent in representations of female physicality: as enticing and reassuring, fearsome and vulnerable, manipulative and manipulated. In the case of *Alias*, this is particularly evident in the social and institutional configurations of Sydney's capabilities; she is strong partly in virtue of her relationship to other individuals (e.g. her father, her mission partners) and to powerful institutions

(SD-6, the CIA, APO). The construction of her physical strength and her vulnerability is thus in part social; 'Loss and vulnerability seem to follow from our being socially constituted bodies, attached to others, at risk of losing those attachments, exposed to others, at risk of violence by virtue of that exposure' (Butler 2004: 20).

Thus the show should be credited with both representing female physical power, and with recognising it as far from unproblematic. At the same time, *Alias* remains unwilling to truly push boundaries. Instead, it relies on a dualism inherent in the disguise-conceit; the further Sydney's aliases depart from the feminine and the 'good', the more heavily her own purity is reinforced. She must appear ambivalent about her own physical potential for both violence and sexuality. Exploring the relationship between Sydney's physical integrity and her personal agency – demonstrated in her capacity to assume physical difference in her aliases, her sexual identity and her physical power – not only illuminates a particularly compelling case of embodied identity, it also demonstrates how the concept of *Alias* both challenges female identity on television and ultimately opts to 'play it safe'. We take up this question in several stages, examining Sydney's relationship to her aliases (those of individual missions and the extended alias of Julia Thorne), the character's sexual identity and her relationship to her own physical prowess.

Sydney's physicality is certainly presented as powerful. She can punch, kick and disarm men twice her size; she is fast, agile and resourceful. We understand her to be enticing – and thus disarming – even in her vulnerability, and this is reinforced in each spy escapade when she inevitably turns initial situational disadvantages into opportunities to strike, disarm and escape. But does this power *belong* to Sydney? Can she claim it?

The material nature of Sydney's body suggests that this is the case. Jennifer Garner's physique, while conforming to the slender ideal demanded by Hollywood, is still strikingly tall, strong and athletic, so much so that media descriptions of *Alias* inevitably mention her shoulder and leg muscles. In other words, Garner's portrayal of Sydney stands out as a *physically* plausible superwoman even among other female-led action dramas. Indeed, this may be why the writers of *Alias* have emphasised the 'softer', more feminine aspects of her personality in Sydney's life with Francie (e.g. their desire for massages, shopping trips and cocktail nights). This is not merely a static visual presentation; we see Sydney actively inhabiting her body in her personal, non-spy life, when she jogs with Will, plays hockey with Vaughn, does Pilates, or plays mini-golf with her friends. Moreover, Sydney's body has a strong presence in the show's narrative. Not only does it (possibly) hold the key to the mysterious figure of Rambaldi but many of the dramatic events that mark the story arc of *Alias* are literally written on Garner/Bristow's body, from Sydney's mysterious scar in Season Three to the effects of Garner's pregnancy in Season Five.

A viewer's first impression of Sydney's physical identity is as something she can change, adapt and *use*, that is, as the site of her ability to assume an alias. Sydney Bristow's life is composed of a number of aliases: those she assumes for individual missions and the roles she must enact as part of her fragmented identity (spy at SD-6, double agent for the CIA and grad student/banker). For each individual mission she is assigned, Sydney must adopt not only a costume and accent but also an entire *persona* – complete with backstory, relationships and usually a seductive set of manners – to manage the tasks she undertakes. It is not simply that Sydney must disguise her own identity (a negative task); she must create and assume a wholly new one (a positive manifestation) in order to succeed. Moreover, her ability to do this is, quite literally, a matter of life and death. Sydney must consciously, and thus conscientiously, perform herself as Other to maintain her own security. She risks her self each time she does so.

Yet despite this risk to Sydney's physical wellbeing, her physicality is, in one sense, the only thing she retains across these multiple narratives. Sydney's aliases are her body, and the role she enacts is always an enticing combination of vulnerable and strong, from the slightly drunken secretary in trouble with her boss at the Chinese embassy ('Truth Be Told', 1:1) to the bookish graduate student eager to see the Smithsonian's special collections ('Blood Ties', 3:20). Indeed, part of the ingenuity of *Alias* is its Clark Kent/Superman approach to Sydney's disguises: to viewers' amusement they are rarely more than a wig or an outfit. And while her fellow spies Dixon and Vaughn will dress up as *characters*, the essence of Sydney's aliases is often no more than a particular sexual type or fantasy (the drunken flirt, the bookish virgin). Indeed, Sydney's aliases fit so neatly into the hetero-normative categories of (feminine) young, sexual and desirable that their exceptions are memorable. In 'Firebomb' (2:16), Sydney dresses not as virgin or whore but crone, as an old woman visiting a Catholic cathedral. In this case, it is a woman she must convince, not a man she must overpower.

In Season Five, the character of Sydney's aliases changes again, but this time one set of feminine tropes is substituted for another – equally gendered – physical stereotype: the brash and hormonal pregnant woman. Sydney warns Vaughn's murderer that her interrogation will be especially violent because of her hormones ('. . . 1 . . .', 5:2), and a few episodes later, she blusters past an embarrassed security guard by threatening that if she does not speak with the Chinese general she will have to speak to his fiancée instead, presumably to inform her of the child's paternity ('Solo', 5:6). The mysterious and fearful potential of the female body remains her primary weapon. Moreover, it is telling that the writers felt compelled to introduce a new character, Rachel, who must take on a prostitute alias after Jack tells Sydney there are 'certain' things she can no longer do. If Sydney is to become the Madonna figure, someone else must assume the whore.

Reliance on stereotypical and often highly sexualised personas helps prop up the conceit of *Alias*; in assuming them, Sydney is both wholly Other than herself and clearly identifiable as Sydney – to the television viewer, if not to the villains she hoodwinks. Indeed, the reliance on stereotype reinforces the continuity of her physical self at the same time as it emphasises the contrast between the 'bad', sexual type she becomes, and the morally/sexually pure individual she is. As viewers, we easily identify the stereotype, but reject it as descriptive of Sydney. The contrast does not challenge our sense of her as 'pure'; it reinforces it. Moreover, it distances Sydney from her own physicality, since her physicality can go places – and take on roles – that she, Sydney, cannot follow.

Of course, continuity of the physical does not guarantee that Sydney's aliases will not threaten her physical integrity. Like fellow superheroes Xena and Buffy, Sydney regularly experiences violence against her body and severe physical pain in combat situations. The body in pain can seem alien and obstructive; it no longer appears to belong to the individual who inhabits it (Scarry 1985). Yet Sydney's missions alienate her from her physicality in another way. Unlike Buffy or Xena, Sydney must use her sexuality as much as, or more than, her physical strength. She seduces as frequently as she assaults. Even when Sydney plays a supposedly 'asexual' character this is also a sexual ploy, since the alias' lack of sexuality is itself an enticement; for example, the shy and bookish virgin. Sydney reacts visibly to this challenge in one of the series' most famous episodes, 'Phase One' (2:13), which opens with her striding into a garish bedroom, dressed as a call girl in red lingerie, apparently awaiting approval from a large man sprawled out in bed. A few minutes later, the power has shifted and Sydney demands, 'What was wrong with the black one? Do you think it is comfortable wearing clothes like this?' to the same man – whom she now has in a chokehold – while held aboard his personal plane. In this case, it is not the alias but Sydney herself who has been degraded. While on one level this reads as an allusion to post-feminist fantasy, since Sydney can both 'pull off' the ultimately sexual call girl outfit and be self-aware enough to reject it, it also articulates an increasingly desperate struggle to claim her own body. It is she, Sydney, who must wear the red lingerie, after all. Sydney has no choice but to change from the black underwear into the red underwear in order to maintain her cover. She is still performing sexually for a man who believes he is coercing and paying her to do exactly this. That it is the CIA, rather than the man, who will ultimately reward her financially for her performance does not alter the sex-for-work dynamic, and Sydney still risks being alienated from her body-as-asset.

The assaults on Sydney's physical self culminate in her 'lost years', and her shadow existence as Julia Thorne. Both Sydney and the viewer have only a vague sense of her life as Julia. We learn that she suffered six months of torture and 'conditioning' but did not break (due in part to her conditioning at her father's hands as part of Project: Christmas), that following her brainwashing she had to undergo a test of loyalty which she passed by killing a man, that she apparently killed another man, and that she spent many months working for the Covenant while secretly reporting back to Director Kendall. Through flashbacks the viewers are informed – as is Sydney – that, 'the sooner you accept that you are no longer who you were, the easier this will be. Sydney Bristow is gone' ('Full Disclosure', 3:11). The irony of this statement is that while Sydney survives as Sydney, she must eventually expel her alias, Julia, from her memory, since she *cannot* accept that she (Julia) is whom she (Sydney) was. It is Julia Thorne who has to go. This alias is unique in that she does not *choose* to be Julia, yet she must sustain it continuously over a period of time, and in doing so take on a level of sexual and moral 'otherness' so extreme that she cannot assimilate Julia and retain her basic integrity. Sydney must literally wipe Julia from herself (her memory) in order to go on.

What is it about Julia that Sydney cannot assimilate as she can her other aliases? Partly, perhaps, it is her complicity in violence, as she must kill a helpless man in order to survive her loyalty test. Yet it is apparent that her choices in this situation were limited at best. The other 'murder' she apparently commits is literally undone; in fact she saved the man's life and worked against the 'bad guys' as she had always done. We are told little else about her life as Julia, with one exception: Sydney discovers that, as Julia, she had a passionate and dark sexual relationship with Simon Walker, a charismatic, unpredictable killer and thief.

The relationship between Sydney and Simon is partly so intriguing because we are never told exactly why it came about. While *Alias* tends to reinforce the stereotype that certain sexual proclivities go hand in hand with villainy, it is hard to understand why Sydney would need to prove something to the Covenant in a sexual relationship as she might with an act of violence. Sydney-as-Julia worked for Simon on a number of heists, so the sexual consummation of their partnership could have been a contingent need born out of the situation, or equally, it could have been a genuine sexual attraction. If it were the former, then Sydney's sleeping with Simon represents the terminus of the sexually manipulative aspects of her aliases. That sex for the job was even once a possibility means it could have always been a possibility. The fear of alienation and self-loss that has been hinted at in quips and rejoinders to her targets (such as the lingerie comment on the plane in 'Phase One') is suddenly manifested. This possibility also represents a morally grey area for Sydney – that is, the limits to what she will use as a means to her end – that remains unexplored, in part because of her memory loss. Sydney literally cuts off access to Julia, for both herself and the viewers. In doing so she performs a very deliberate act that mimics the psychological process of 'mental splitting'. Many psychologists and psychiatrists (e.g. Herman 1994; Terr 1994) claim that traumatic events that threaten to overwhelm the personality may actually cause the mind to divide. This process protects the individual from intense distress because it results in one part holding the memory of which the other is not conscious. Like the spy's need to compartmentalise in order to survive, some even 'develop multiple personalities that enable one or more "selves" to emerge unscathed from the abuse' (Brison 2002: 47).

Yet fans of *Alias* appear far more distressed by the second reason for Sydney to sleep with Simon: that she felt genuine attraction. Unlike Buffy or Xena, Sydney demonstrates little interest in darker characters. Danny, her fiancé, Vaughn and even Will are represented as solid, upright and kind; only her ex Noah Hicks ('Snowman', 1:19) displays a hint of darkness, and Sydney is clearly repelled by this. Even if Sydney-as-Julia was interested in Simon, the show insists, she had to become a wholly different person first. The implication is that Sydney-as-Sydney is not even responsible for Julia's actions. The reactions of fans indicates that nothing short of a complete division of self will protect their image of Sydney, as the following fan-board postings indicate:

tazzer416: I thought it was very weird that of all the things he could say about Sydulia [Sydney/Julia] it was that she was freaky in bed. I mean, I'm sure Syd's not a prude, but come on. Then I thought, that really sounds like Lauren.

toria55: In the world that I live in, Simon and Sydney never had sex. Our sweet little Sydney would never prostitute herself for her job. She has too many mother issues [to] deal with. Sydney hypnotized Simon into believing that they were having sex.

(http://sd-1.net/index.php?showtopic=30859&st=0)

This displacement of the sexually 'bad' from Sydney onto Lauren (Reed) – even when it requires inventing plot devices – indicates how much the show's characterisation of Sydney depends on her constant reinforcement as sexually pure. She may play out her aliases, but she must be different from them. Nor is it only fans that insist on denying the possibility that Sydney-as-Julia reveals anything about Sydney herself. Vaughn learns of her sexual relationship but ignores it, and Jack goes even further: he murders Simon (and loses valuable information) to stop him from sharing the details of their affair.

Simon: I wasn't kidding, about screwing your daughter. She's the wildest girl I ever had.

Jack: Tell me about Julia, if you want to live.

Simon: You wanna know how she likes it? She . . . (Jack shoots him)

('Repercussions', 3:5)

Despite Sydney's erasure of Julia and the almost dogged insistence by character and fan alike that she cannot resemble what Julia appeared to be, there is textual evidence that Sydney's own sexuality may resemble Julia's. Consider, for example, this exchange between Sydney and Vaughn before a mission ('Search and Rescue', 4:21):

> Vaughn: How do you want to play this?
> Sydney: You want to be rough, or you want me to be rough?
> Vaughn: You're always rough.
> Sydney: No, I'm not!
> Vaughn: Yes, you are!
> Sydney: That's not true!
> Vaughn: Yes, it is!
> Sydney: Do you mean at home or on ops?
> Vaughn: Both! (pause) Hey, I'm not complaining.
> Sydney: If I'm rough, it's because you like it when I'm rough.

While this scene is played for comic effect (Jack and Marshall are monitoring the conversation), it does suggest that the distance between Sydney and Vaughn as they are, and the supposedly 'deviant' couple they are about to portray, is smaller than one might suppose. Nor is the image of the female action hero who secretly (or not so secretly) likes rough or unconventional sex uncommon. In *Buffy*, it is represented as a dominant feature of Faith's personality, and a more subdued and conflicted aspect of Buffy's. The implication is either that violent work leads to a craving for release through equally violent sex or that the hero can only combat darkness because she possesses it, and that this darkness must manifest itself through 'dark' sexual play.

Nevertheless, *Alias* resists this connection between power and sexuality more than *Buffy* or other comparable series do. In 'Second Double' (2:21), Sydney's relationship to sexuality is played ambivalently. Earlier in the episode, the issue of voyeurism is introduced when tapes of Vaughn and Sydney are found. Both are called for a briefing and left to witness what, it is clear, Jack and Kendall have already seen. Later, at a Berlin BDSM club, they engage in some sexual banter:

> Vaughn: I'm glad I'm not the one in leather.
> Sydney: You'd look cute in a teddy.

Soon Sydney is both overpowering and dominating her target, except this is the illusion, rather than the reveal; he wants her to be his dominatrix. When Vaughn enters, however, they immediately 'snap out' of the sexual role-playing, almost exaggerating their supposed 'normality' for the benefit of a bewildered target.

Sydney: (smiling) Hello, honey.
Vaughn: (sing-song) Hello, dear.

Once again, the relationship between sex, power and violence is played for comic effect. This is a relatively safe move, after two potentially unorthodox sexual moments between Sydney and Vaughn (the tapes of their sex, their pleasure in BDSM costumes) earlier in the episode. *Alias* hints at, but quickly demurs from, any genuine exploration of sexual role-playing in a world based on the interplay of deceit, power relations, violence and sexuality. It remains provocatively suggestive, rather than genuinely subversive. The latter would be a show that provided a female character so in command of both her physical power and her sexuality that she could both own and enjoy them. The comedy of unorthodox sex provides a safer 'third way'.

Of course, while *Alias* refrains from allowing Sydney to be genuinely sexually powerful, neither does the show's premise consider the possibility of her sexual vulnerability. Sydney is shown facing brutal torture at a number of points, and enduring severe physical hardship at others, but the question of sexual violence is almost never raised. Yet, presumably, Sydney's life places her at significant risk of sexual violence, especially given the peculiarly seductive nature of her missions. She is often alone with a large and violent man who has every reason to think she is there purely for his sexual pleasure. Sydney never expresses concern that she is vulnerable in this way, and the writers work to ensure that the viewers remain equally blithe. That Sydney will never fail in a fight or a mission nor experience her body as a site of sexual vulnerability leaves us free to appreciate scenes in terms of genre satisfaction or comic relief. Despite being ostensibly more 'realist', in this way *Alias* fails a test of realism passed by more obviously fantastic shows like *Buffy*.

There is one other significant difference between Sydney's physical power and that of other female super-figures. Unlike Wonder Woman, Xena or Buffy, Sydney is not a 'lone wolf' figure. The former are depicted as standing wholly outside and even against institutional power establishments; Sydney is powerful in part because of her access to institutional resources and her partnerships with others. But not all institutional access is empowering. When

Devlin argues against her incarceration in 'The Prophecy' (1:16) he calls her 'an asset' – some*thing* of material value to the agency – and notes that she is extremely 'well-placed' in her current mission at SD-6. Describing her value in material and spatial terms emphasises her physical power at the expense of her individual agency, even her personhood. The euphemistic language of combat and strategy reminds the viewer that in subjecting her physical power to the demands of the CIA, Sydney has surrendered something of her identity.

The conflict between Sydney's physical identity and her institutional affiliation becomes overtly threatening to her wellbeing at several points. She is forcibly incarcerated, not for anything for which she can claim responsibility, but for events she cannot remember and knowledge she does not have ('Breaking Point', 3:8) or for genetic facts beyond her control: the size of her heart, the shape of her face and the message presumably encoded in her mysterious DNA ('Q and A', 1:17). Held in turn by the DSR, the FBI and even the CIA, Sydney is shown a fairly insidious side of the agencies she serves. Given the threatening and duplicitous nature of almost every institution that co-opts her professional prowess, Sydney's dogged faith in what she does can sometimes appear surprisingly naive. Yet this naivety can be read as a strategy for reconciling herself to her own power and her capacity for violence, and thus as evidence of Sydney's own ambivalence. The doubts and fears that come from the exertion of power are not unfamiliar to the action genre, yet in Sydney's case they are particularly amplified. Partly, it seems, the viewer is encouraged to sympathise with her *because* she doesn't really want to be a spy (as shown in her commitment to graduate school, her thoughts of 'getting out' after SD-6 goes down, etc.). While Sydney wields tremendous power, she does so reluctantly. Viewers are encouraged to understand the morality of her work, not the method, as central to her identity.

Sydney may appear ambivalent towards her spy identity throughout the series, but the real challenge only emerges with her pregnancy in Season Five. If female superheroes remain uncommon, a pregnant female superhero is genuinely groundbreaking; only Xena had previously entered this territory (Suro 2001). And a lack of pregnant action heroes is understandable; the potential conflict between Sydney's spy-identity and her motherhood is clear, as Irina's prediction to Sydney during her labour reveals:

Irina: I looked at you, so fragile, all I could think was, 'How could I have made such a terrible mistake?' And at that moment, I was sure of one thing: I couldn't be an agent and a mother. I'd either fail at one or both. And I chose to fail at being a mother. In time you'll learn. You can't do both.

Sydney: Watch me.   ('Maternal Instinct', 5:11)

This is a genuine challenge posed to Sydney; can she sustain both identities, and at what cost? Sydney's pregnancy – which is, after all, a physical capacity – represents a new physical vulnerability, alluded to when Dixon jokes that she must refrain from active duty because she 'waddles' ('SOS', 5:10). It may be a moral vulnerability as well. For the first time, the 'rightness' of what Sydney does is seriously questioned. In 'Mockingbird' (5:4), Sydney poses as a rich pregnant woman gambling at a casino, rubbing her belly for extra luck. After a few wins, Dixon (disguised as another gambler) tells her, 'This is disgusting . . . You're pregnant. You shouldn't be in a casino. You should be at home.' Once again, the line between Sydney's alias and her own identity blurs. Of course, the belief that pregnancy makes women too 'pure', too morally elevated for vices like gambling seems (and is meant to seem) very reactionary. Nonetheless, Dixon's words remind the viewer of Sydney's own decision to continue in a dangerous job, risking her safety and that of her foetus. This decision jars with her usual determination to protect the weak and vulnerable at all cost. Nor does *Alias* shy away from this moral ambiguity; viewers are led to see Sydney's decision as both questionable and triumphant, as the following exchange demonstrates:

Casino Manager: I have seen some despicable acts of cheating in my time, but a pregnant woman using her own baby to escape suspicion? I don't know how you live with yourself.

Sydney: What can I say sir? (drops Southern accent) I'm not like other moms (shoots him).   ('Mockingbird', 5:4)

Sydney may not actually be a pregnant gambling cheat, but the parallel to her own actions is unmistakable; both she and her character rely on the social respect pregnancy garners to escape suspicion (and in both cases, suspicion is justified). Yet just as she previously relied on her sexual prowess and romantic allure without qualm, here Sydney appears to experience no internal conflict; she even reverts away from her type to speak in her own voice.

Sydney's motherhood is the final development in a show that has consistently returned to themes of biological determinism. Her family is composed almost entirely of ruthless intelligence agents: her parents are both agents, her half-sister is recruited in a manner similar to Sydney herself, even her two aunts (Katya and Elena) and Sloane, the father of her half-sister, are all implicated in a web of international espionage. The message that biology is destiny repeats itself through several seasons. For instance, when Sloane suggests that he may be Sydney's real father, viewers are led to believe that more than her relationship with Jack is at stake: Sydney's self-identity is also implicated. When she sets off to discover her half-sister, Jack warns her that whomever she finds will be the product of 'Irina Derevko and Arvin Sloane' and is therefore untrustworthy, insinuating that the sins of the parents may be written into the self-hood of the child. Indeed, this hint of biological destiny re-emerges at the end of Season Four, when Irina hints that Nadia is remarkable, in part because her parentage is not what it seems ('Before the Flood', 4:22). For Sydney, this genetic implication is a double-edged sword. Her father remains an enigmatic figure: a source of support and sporadic affection, but someone whom she ultimately does not know and cannot always understand. Her mother is first an illusion, then revealed a villain, then emerges as a complicated sometime ally. She turns herself in, which is a double play, but the audience is led to understand that even this double-dealing is a smoke screen for a deeper concern from a message in her earrings ('Truth Takes Time', 2:18).

Perhaps most threatening, however, is Sydney's possible genetic connection to Rambaldi, since it implies she is claimed by a male individual (Rambaldi) and by a set of male institutions (the agencies who perceive her as a security threat). Milo Rambaldi is the mystical backdrop to *Alias* – the quintessential male genius, clearly modelled on Leonardo da Vinci. He is referred to in turn as an inventor, a prophet, and a genius, with connections to the papacy and to secret underground movements. Rambaldi's ultimate 'end game' is the goal pursued by almost every villain on *Alias*, and is never satisfactorily resolved, despite the final climactic showdown between Sloane and the Bristows. But it is unquestionably bound up with Sydney's genetic inheritance and her ultimate fate. At one point Sydney comments, 'Rambaldi made a habit of hiding his real work in ordinary things' ('The Prophecy'). The irony is that she herself may be an 'ordinary thing' disguising the genius' design. Her body and all its power and capability is merely a vehicle for the projects of another.

Rambaldi's connection to Sydney represents the ultimate twist on a show that centres on a presumably independent powerful female figure. The origin of her power is wholly externally located and she is thus somehow diminished. This appropriation of physical self is a familiar theme in female superhero narratives, and is reminiscent of the moment in *Buffy* when Buffy discovers that her [female] Slayer power originates in the violent manipulation of women by men ('Get it Done', 7:15). Of course, the 'strings' attached to Sydney's power were already more evident, given her closer links to institutions, but it remains an equally threatening possibility; we first see Sydney register the Prophecy's implications (that she is the subject of Rambaldi's words) in a flash of fear. Moreover, this moment is prompted by another character's narration of when, and how, she first knew her cancer was fatal ('Reckoning', 1:6).

Like Buffy, Sydney must reclaim her physicality in an act of strength: torching the lab where her eggs were apparently stolen and harvested by the Covenant. This moment is powerful on any number of levels: she simultaneously learns the secret of her lost years, destroys the consequences of her violation (the removal of her eggs), and undoes what Rambaldi may have wanted done: his DNA mixed with that of the supposed 'Chosen One.' If both Sydney and Buffy have their power claimed by another in being 'chosen', they are also capable of using that very power to choose and so re-claim their selves.

The twists and turns of *Alias'* fairly ambitious narrative arcs may toy with Sydney's power, her integrity and her sense of self, but all of these seem to remain relatively intact. She suffers but does not succumb to the threats imposed by institutional appropriation of her physicality, by the socially and biologically determining aspects of her life course, and by the physical and moral strain of her peculiarly fragmented professional life. Yet, because Sydney is never faced with a risk that could plausibly destroy her, or a burden beyond what she can bear, there is a sense in which *Alias* deprives her, and the viewer, of the potential to be truly subversive. In Sydney Bristow, television is offered a heroine who is strong and resourceful, and who successfully owns her physical and sexual power with both determination and integrity. Yet much is sacrificed in the effort to keep Sydney sympathetic; she remains unable to incorporate moral ambiguity into her self-identity, unwilling to transgress the boundaries of sexual and social purity, and ultimately ambivalent in her relationship to her own capacity for power, violence and sexuality. *Alias* is thus an exercise in temptation; it hints at but cannot reveal what the physicality of a female superhero could be.

6 Can't Live With 'Em, Can Shoot 'Em

Alias and the (Thermo) Nuclear Family

Simon Brown and Stacey Abbott

> What got me excited was the idea of telling the story of the world's most dysfunctional family, and telling it through the spy/intelligence/action-adventure genre.
>
> J.J. Abrams (quoted in Gross 2002: 35)

> TV tends to orient its programming towards its presumed audience, to try to include the audience's own conception of themselves into the texture of the programmes. Hence broadcast TV gives central place to the series of cultural preoccupations that accompany the nuclear family: to heterosexual romance, to the stability of marriage, to the notions of masculine careers and feminine domesticity, to the conception of innocence of childhood, to the division of the world in public and private spheres.
>
> (Ellis 1992: 115)

As Abrams states, *Alias* has at its heart the idea of family, and as such is part of a long established television tradition. Not surprisingly given the medium's location within the domestic space, television has focused upon the family and the domestic as the subject for its narratives, both comedic and (melo)dramatic. The situation comedy and the soap opera both take the family as its centrepiece. In writing about the absent patriarch in *Six Feet Under* Joanna di Mattia asserts that the 'conventions of American television [are] repeatedly constructed around a version of the nuclear family in which patriarchal authority is reinforced' (2005: 153). *Six Feet Under*, she argues, contests these conventions, and it is not alone in doing so, as *Alias* equally challenges the 'cultural preoccupations' that surround the nuclear family, as outlined by Ellis, as well as the nuclear family itself. In this chapter we will examine how *Alias* renegotiates the representation of the domestic and the notion of family within the wider context of the changing landscape of masculinity and patriarchy in contemporary television.

Di Mattia's description owes a debt to the legacy of family-oriented television that has developed since the medium's early days, in which an ideal conception/representation of the family was created. In the 1950s, popular comedian comedies such as *The Honeymooners* and *I Love Lucy*, which focused upon the often zany or ridiculous antics of their star comedians, Jackie Gleason and Lucille Ball respectively, were gradually replaced by family situation comedies based upon 'real' family experiences. As Mary Beth Harolovich (1989) argues, this emphasis upon realism was based upon representing not necessarily everyone's family experiences, but rather the experiences of television's target middle-class audiences. Series such as *Father Knows Best*, *Leave it to Beaver*, *Ozzie and Harriet*, *My Three Sons* and *The Donna Reed Show* constructed an image of the domestic space, the family, and the 'homemaker' that sold a particular lifestyle, and with it a conception of the ideal father, mother and child. Nina A. Leibman has pointed out that these series position men as the all-knowing patriarchal force within the family, while the wife is there to reaffirm women's place within the home. These series, even *The Donna Reed Show* helmed by a strong lead actress, present the 'good' wife as being anti-careerist and self-effacing, fully understanding that her place is in the home to support the will of the father. As Leibman argues, according to television of the 1950s, 'familial success' is predicated on 'an uncontested structural valuation of paternal fatherhood and masculine dominance' (1995: 216).

While this vision of the all-American family has undergone changes over the years, particularly based around the role of the wife and mother within the household and the employment sector, many contemporary family comedies *Growing Pains, Family Ties, The Cosby Show, That Seventies Show* and *Malcolm in the Middle* have continued to reinforce this classic vision of the nuclear family. There has, however, been a trend within recent television series towards valorising alternative over biological families as a means of critiquing or challenging patriarchal norms. As Jes Battis explains, the aim of these series is to 'introduce the image of the "chosen" family – the surrogate sphere of friends who sometimes succeed, and sometimes fail, to recuperate ideals that the characters' biological families cannot properly transmit' (2005: 18). Depending upon the sphere in which the series operates, the chosen family can be drawn from friends and/or neighbours (*Friends, Sex and the City, Desperate Housewives*), from work (*The West Wing, Without a Trace*) or from a mixture of the two (*The X-Files, Buffy the Vampire Slayer, Angel*). The difference in origins means that in general the alternative work family tends to be more distant and formal than that drawn from non-work environments, but even so work colleagues become surrogate families. In doing so the work family tends to reorganise itself within the patriarchal structure of an efficient and relatively harmonious pseudo-nuclear family which is contrasted with a representation of a chaotic and dysfunctional real family. For example, President Bartlett is a strong yet tender patriarchal figure watching over his West Wing family who in turn experience trauma in their relations with their own fathers (Toby's is a hitman, Sam's has a twenty-year affair, CJ's has Alzheimer's and Josh's dies).

Alias is unique in that it seeks to reinstate the biological family at the heart of the narrative and as a source of support for its main character Sydney Bristow by reconfiguring the separation between chosen family and biological family. At the same time it contests the biological family by offering a distorted representation of conventional family roles and gender dynamics. While the series begins by offering Will and Francie, and likewise Dixon and Marshall, as the chosen family, by the end of Season Two this has been stripped away so that the only person Sydney can truly rely on at the beginning of Season Three is her father, Jack, who unlike everyone else was convinced Sydney was still alive and waited for her. This, however, does not mean that the series offers a conservative restoration of 'traditional' family values in the form of *Father Knows Best*, for while Jack always *wants* the best for Sydney, he does not always *know* what is best for her. Instead the series attempts to offer a site for the constant negotiation of family and its many meanings. At the beginning of Season Four Sydney's family dynamics are renegotiated again when Sydney finds herself once more estranged from her biological father and dealing with her mother's death, yet surrounded by a comforting and closeted extended family in APO. This family too is broken down and renegotiated in Season Five, with Vaughn's apparent death, Weiss' promotion and Nadia's coma taking them out of the family unit, while Sloane is in jail (again), and

Sydney's pregnancy pushes father and daughter closer once more. Throughout its five seasons, the concept of family in *Alias* is fluid, fluctuating between friends-as-family (Will and Francie), family-as-family (the Bristows, the Derevkos, the Sloanes, the Reeds), lover-as-family-to-be (Vaughn, baby Bristow) and colleagues-as-family (at SD-6, CIA or APO).

Not only does *Alias* renegotiate the family unit but also the idea of the domestic and domestic sphere as the space where this renegotiation takes place. This sets *Alias* apart from many American quality television shows, where the domestic sphere is almost entirely absent; the action is confined to the workplace, and home is usually either a functional place of food and sleep or a metaphoric space of isolation. Jack Malone's apartment in *Without a Trace* is glimpsed as a sphere of dysfunction or, after his wife's departure, an empty space representing an empty life filled only with work. Once Jack Bauer's wife leaves the house in search of their daughter Kim on the first day of *24*, we never return to Jack's domestic space. In *The West Wing*, Leo McGarry's house is only seen once, notably at the moment his marriage breaks down. These series encompass a world in which work is more important than family, so that the work family becomes the surrogate as characters sacrifice their family life for a life in which they serve a global imperative, be it political or matters of international security. This is actually done in *24*, where family characters are not part of the action but are often brought into the action and sacrificed to it.[1] *Alias*, however, contains no such distinction; matters of family (be it friends, family, colleagues, lover) and matters of global significance are intertwined. So, for example in the finale of 'Countdown' (2:20), while the CIA hunts for a bioweapon that they believe is about to set off a cataclysmic global event prophesied by Rambaldi, the actual event is in fact the very personal matter of Sloane's discovery that he has a daughter. As a result of this entangling of family and work matters, *Alias* pays more attention to the domestic space but does so not because this is the location of family, but because the domestic space becomes part of the action.

In 'So it Begins' (1:2) a contrast is established between SD-6 and Sydney's apartment, which she will eventually share with Francie and Will. Her friends, who are separate from work, represent comfort and security. They drink wine, eat ice cream and talk supportively in a home that is open plan, decorated in warm earthy

colours and lit by golden slanting sunshine. This stands in opposition to SD-6 where the space is lit with harsh blues, filled with
metallic surfaces and broken down into small meeting rooms, corri-
dors and cubby-holes where hidden and secret actions take place.
Yet there the contrast ends. Both spaces are equated with lying. Sydney must lie to her friends about her job, and she must lie to her
colleagues at SD-6 about her 'other' job as a double agent and the
real nature of the organisation. Thus there is no distinction between
the domestic and the workplace in terms of what it represents to
Sydney. Apart from Sloane (and initially Jack), both spaces are filled
with respected and loved people to whom she must lie on a daily
basis; this for a woman whose first major act of the series was to tell
her fiancé the truth because she could not go on lying to him, and
this leads to his death. This establishes the home space as Eden,
made safe by lies and dangerous by the introduction of knowledge
and the truth. Once the truth enters the home space it becomes a
place of death, much more so than the three work locations of SD-6,
the CIA and APO and the numerous highly dangerous locations visited on missions. Danny is killed in his home ('Truth be Told', 1:1).
Sloane's wife Emily is killed twice in or around her home, once by
Sloane ('Almost Thirty Years', 1:22) and once by Dixon ('Truth Takes
Time', 2:18), while Sydney is abducted by the Covenant from her
home ('The Telling', 2:22). Both Will and Sydney are captured in so-
called safe houses, Will from a CIA safe house ('Rendezvous', 1:21),
Syd from a safe house she herself set up as Julia Thorne ('Prelude',
3:7). Vaughn vents his anger at Lauren's betrayal by burning down
his house because 'it wasn't a happy home' ('Authorized Personnel
Only, Part 1', 4:1).

Furthermore, over the course of the first two seasons, the workplace becomes less fraught with lies and duplicity when SD-6 is
disbanded and Sydney's need to lie at work is diminished, but the
domestic space becomes more so. When, for example, Will begins to
investigate Danny's death against Sydney's wishes, she cannot tell
him that this is for his own safety. Meanwhile, Francie and Sydney
are trying to uncover the infidelity of Francie's fiancé, which initially
appears benign until the truth is uncovered. Finally Will, having discovered too much about Danny's death, is brought into the CIA, and
must keep the truth, like Syd, from Francie. Thus by the end of Season One, Sydney is still lying to Francie, but has an ally in Will, yet
Francie, by the middle of Season Two is revealed to have been

doubled by Allison and is now lying to both of them. By the finale of Season Two, Will is stabbed and lying in a bath (a deliberate echo of Danny), the false Francie is supposedly dead, Sydney is unconscious, and the home space is destroyed by fire ('The Telling'). This marks a shift within the series as the domestic space has become so much a part of the action that the distinction is no longer required. When Sydney is seen in her home in Season Three it is in the company of her friend and colleague Weiss, and then finally in Season Four she invites her sister and spy partner, Nadia, to move in, joined later by the duplicitous Sophia (aka Elena Derevko).[2] The other domestic space glimpsed in the third series is the home of Lauren and Vaughn, which is likewise represented as a place in which work is discussed. Also, for Lauren the home is literally a place of work as her marriage is simply a part of her job as double agent for the terrorist organisation the Covenant. Lauren often refers to her relationship with Vaughn as 'doing her job', a situation reversed when Vaughn uncovers the truth, and then is forced to make love to Lauren while Sydney and Marshall listen in. When Vaughn later apologises to Sydney, she shrugs it off, telling him, 'you were just doing your job' ('Hourglass', 3:19).

By the end of Season Two, Sydney has been reunited with her biological family but this has not taken place in the domestic sphere – rendering the domestic sphere redundant – and all future family conflicts, both biological and otherwise, will be played out in the workplace, except for the brief time that Elena lives with Sydney and Nadia. The initial conversations between Sydney and her estranged father, thrust together in their shared roles as double agents for the CIA, tend to take place in parking garages and venues outside SD-6 (though never, of course, at home). Gradually, however, this relationship, complicated further by the struggle for Sydney between Jack and Vaughn, penetrates the workspace, firstly in the cage (the location for Sydney's meetings with her CIA handler), then SD-6, then the rotunda at CIA headquarters and finally APO. The ability of Sydney and Jack to discuss their relationship at work is facilitated in part by the demise of SD-6, but more importantly by the arrival of Sydney's mother Irina Derevko at CIA HQ, reconfiguring the workspace as the location where domestic issues are addressed and resolved. Sydney, Jack and Irina work out their relationship issues almost entirely within the space of the rotunda and Irina's cell. Thus this space ceases to be the main alternative site for the exploration of the non-biological family, but rather the main site for the negotiation of the biological family.

The increasing domestication of CIA HQ is a result of the series' hybridised nature as a spy/melodrama, which facilitates the constant negotiation of the meaning of family that preoccupies the narrative. This hybridity enables the show's creators to bombard the audience with images that undermine traditional expectations of family. In 'The Enemy Walks In' (2:1) Sydney's reunion with her mother culminates in Irina shooting her; in 'Remnants' (3:10) the villainous Sark tortures his father with a blowtorch; in 'The Frame' (3:17) Lauren's mother shoots Lauren's father in cold blood; and in 'Legacy' (3:21) Sloane abducts his recently discovered daughter Nadia in order to inject her with Rambaldi fluid, which will draw from her the key to Rambaldi's elusive (and somewhat flexible) endgame. Yet these moments of family horror are mirrored by moments of tenderness: Lauren's father offers to forgive her and cover up her treasonous acts ('The Frame'); Sloane takes care of his terminally-ill wife Emily ('Rendezvous'); Irina and Jack fight over who will tend to Sydney's gun-shot wound ('The Passage, Part Two', 2:9); and Sydney thanks her father after learning that he tried to save Danny's life ('So it Begins').

Of course the primary focus for the series' exploration of family is the Bristows. While the series is replete with dysfunctional, or questionable, families, it is the Bristows' transgressive journey from the ultimate in estranged relations to a form of functional dysfunctionality that preoccupies the series' narrative arc. For instance, in 'Truth Be Told' when Danny calls Sydney's father to ask for her hand in marriage according to tradition, Jack responds with a coldly cynical and humorous response:

> I may become your father-in-law . . . that is just fine. But I will not be used as part of a charming little anecdote you tell your friends at cocktail parties so that they can see what a quaint, old fashioned guy Danny really is. Are we clear? . . . Good . . . then welcome to the family.

This speech establishes Jack as cold, unsentimental and resentful of any attempt to define his position as a father through traditional conventions. His last words to Danny, 'welcome to the family', echo with irony and disdain.[3] In the final episode of the same season, however, Jack demonstrates his absolute devotion to Sydney and his definition of fatherhood by brutally torturing and murdering Steven Haladki, a CIA operative who put Sydney at risk by exposing her position as a double agent ('Almost Thirty Years'). In this he demonstrates that while he is unwilling to be civil to her boyfriend, he will, quite literally, kill for her, not because Haladki is a direct threat to her but because his actions dared to put her in danger. Here conventions of the spy genre, torture and murder, become the means through which Jack expresses his fatherly love for Sydney.

Another knowingly transgressive representation of family occurs in the Season Two episode 'The Passage, Part One' (2:8) when Irina is temporarily released from CIA custody so that the Bristows can go on their first mission together to disarm nuclear weapons held by terrorists in Kashmir. Not convinced that Irina is trustworthy, Jack forces her to wear an ornate necklace filled with C-4, which he gently places around her neck like a string of pearls. Should she try to escape or betray them in any way, Jack informs her, he will detonate the C-4 and blow her head off. The accessories of a loving marriage are utilised to literally bind Irina to Jack. Later, while undercover as a 'normal' family on holiday, an immigration officer comments on how beautiful Irina's necklace is, to which she ironically responds, 'an anniversary gift from my husband' as she lovingly caresses the chain and kisses Jack on the lips. Here the performance of the ideal, loving couple thinly veils the threat of violence and death. In fact, it is through the act of violence that the Bristows demonstrate that they can function as a family. When captured by the terrorists, Irina, in league with Jack, uses the necklace as a grenade to distract their captors and to gain the upper hand in battle. The sequence ends with the family, each armed with an automatic weapon, firing in unison at the terrorists as they work together to defeat their enemy. As Sydney later tells Vaughn, 'some people go miniature golfing with their parents. We go to India and look for nukes' ('The Passage, Part Two'). In the world of *Alias*, family bonds are expressed through action rather than words.

While the series consistently offers contradictory images of family through the hybridity of spy and melodrama conventions, it is through the past relationship of Jack and his wife Irina (aka Laura Bristow) that *Alias* deconstructs the classic image of the 'all-knowing father' and the 'passive', 'self-effacing' mother. Here the series directly engages with the legacy of the televisual family, revealing it to be a construct, and it demonstrates that the image of the 'passive' wife can simply be subterfuge for hidden activity. In two episodes the audience is given a brief glimpse into Jack and Laura's marriage, albeit glimpses channelled through Jack's memory and ones that seem to both evoke and question the image of the ideal TV family. Firstly, in 'A Broken Heart' (1:4), Jack undergoes his regular psyche evaluation at SD-6, which involves questioning under hypnosis. As he is gradually led into a hypnotic state by the promise that he is safe and relaxed, he envisions a brightly lit, white-walled nursery in which a woman is holding a baby. As the camera tilts up, the image of Jack's wife Laura is revealed, staring lovingly into the camera as she rocks her baby to sleep. This image dissolves to a close-up of Jack still under hypnosis being told that he is safe and comfortable. As the scene dissolves back to Jack's vision of his wife and child, however, the camera again tilts up, but this time to reveal that Sydney has taken the place of her mother as she turns to warn Jack that 'it is only a matter of time before I find out the truth'. Jack wakes up abruptly from this vision, no longer safe and comfortable, and must leave the interrogation room, demonstrably shaken. The lyrical quality of the initial dream sequence, with its crisp and clean imagery and Laura's dress and performance evoking the perfect nurturing mother, is disrupted by the suggestion that it is based upon lies. It is only later in Season One that the truth that 'Sydney' talks about in the dream is revealed to be the fact that Sydney's mother Laura Bristow was actually Irina Derevko, a Russian spy posing as a perfect wife and mother to gain state secrets. The image of the self-effacing wife and mother serves as a useful shield for her own duplicity. Both Jack and Sydney's perception of their family is therefore shattered by this revelation and Jack's status as the all-knowing husband and father is called into question as he has clearly been manipulated by Irina, never seeing through her lies.

This image of the Bristow family is once again used to undermine traditional gender roles and to suggest the inherent duplicity within family relations in the episode 'Mirage' (4:18) in which Jack, suffering from delusions caused by a form of radiation sickness, mistakes Sydney for his wife Laura. To acquire the necessary information from Jack that will help find his cure, Sydney takes on her mother's alias as Laura Bristow in a carefully constructed recreation of the Bristow home of her childhood. In this alias, Sydney wears a flow-ered dress and pink cardigan, and enters into 'their house' carrying the groceries. This is a far cry from her usual, highly eroticised weekly disguises (such as the blue rubber dress in 'So it Begins' or the geisha in 'The Counteragent', 2:7), for she is the image of the all-American homemaker. In this performance, Sydney must 'play' the loving and supportive wife, making plans to have dinner with her husband's colleagues, listening to him talk about the demands of his job and being understanding when he informs her that he will have to miss their daughter's birthday because of work. The fact that he works as a CIA agent is only the first of a series of disruptions to this ideal image of the family. As Sydney proceeds with the charade of being the perfect wife, the audience is reminded that the real Laura was herself performing the role. Jack asks Sydney/Laura, 'how can you be so perfect? Loving mother . . . beautiful wife . . . just by standing there?' The answer is she can't, isn't and wasn't. This sequence reminds us that Sydney, like Laura/Irina before her, is playing at being the 'perfect wife' in order to acquire information and that Jack is a victim of their performances. Here it is the wife and daughter who are shown to be in control while the father is blindly following their lead. Furthermore, the duplicity portrayed in this sequence is underscored by a threat of danger as Jack not only reveals that he had informed Laura that he was a spy (an act that reveals his own complicity in her acts of treason) but his declaration to Sydney that he plans to quit the CIA (a declaration we can only assume he is re-enacting from memory) suggests that he was about to outlive his usefulness to her mission. This is reiterated at the scene's end when, having provided the information that was needed, the blissful image of Jack sitting by the child-Sydney playing the piano is violently disrupted by the entrance of two med-techs who sedate him. The act is no longer necessary.

These glimpses into Jack and Laura/Irina's past, therefore, serve to uncover the inherent duplicity in this representation of the ideal family and yet also reveal the honesty of the emotion between Jack and his daughter. He conceals the truth about her mother so that Sydney will not needlessly suffer the pain that he did, and Sydney poses as her own mother so that she can save Jack's life. Furthermore, this performance enables Sydney to reconcile her own feelings about her father's absences in her childhood as she tells him that 'the work you do is important' only to be finally told what has been implicit throughout the series, 'not as important as her [Sydney] . . . or you [Laura]'. Through these layers of performance and deceit, the series deliberately presents the Bristows as a dysfunctional family that is desperately striving toward functionality.

At the centre of this transition within the Bristow family is Jack. As discussed, many contemporary American television series possess alternative patriarchal figures or remove the father figure (*The West Wing, Buffy, Six Feet Under*) to challenge the traditional patriarchal family structure. *Alias*, however, attempts to place the 'father' under the microscope by situating Jack Bristow at the heart of its fractured family. While Sydney's character arc revolves around personal growth with regards to trauma and issues of identity, and Irina remains a moral and emotional enigma, it is Jack who is shown to undergo the most overt process of social and emotional development. Throughout the five years of the series, the audience has witnessed Jack's gradual transformation from the estranged and emotionally detached father first presented in 'Truth be Told' to the proud grandfather-to-be helping Sydney build a crib in 'Fait Accompli' (5:7). But Jack's apparent move from taciturn CIA agent to accessible new family man is not a linear progression nor is it designed to reinstate him as the head of the family. Instead it introduces fundamental questions about the nature of fatherhood and masculinity into the matrix of a post-feminist action series.[4]

As Joanna di Mattia argues, 'the ideal American man is one in total control of his emotions: stoic, silent, disengaged and not prone to moments of self-disclosure' (2005: 151). At first glance this seems an apt description of Jack but as the narrative of *Alias* progresses, Jack is revealed to be an emotionally injured man. The betrayal by Irina, we find out, caused him to have a breakdown and when she turns herself in to the CIA he must take compassionate leave, begins to drink and then must go and see the CIA therapist. As such, it becomes increasingly clear that Jack is defined by his emotions and that they determine his often-duplicitous actions. His distrust of Irina causes him to blow up the house in Madasgascar in order to prove her treachery ('Dead Drop', 2:4); it is his love for Sydney that fuels his efforts to conceal her apparent murder of Lazarey; because of his sense of betrayal at the revelation that Sloane had an affair with Irina, Jack withholds evidence that will exonerate Sloane of treason ('Unveiled', 3:18); and it his need to protect Sydney that instigates his assassination of Irina when it appears that she has put a contract out on Sydney's life. This linking of emotion and action ostensibly separates Jack from the traditional image of the action man, who, as Stella Bruzzi suggests 'has seldom proved a successful father, for "action" signals a representational dependence on the body, physicality and strength, all attributes that the father . . . most notably lacks' (2005: 132). That Jack *is* an action man is in no doubt, yet Jack's actions are defined by cold intellect, cunning, planning and contacts, rather than kung fu and karate, and fuelled by emotion. In her analysis of the contemporary action genre, Susan Jeffords has argued that the dominant image of masculinity from the 1980s to the 1990s has shifted from 'hard-bodied' action heroes who crash through doors and kill whoever they want, towards sensitive new men who 'get doors slammed in their faces, or they are forced to stand patiently outside them while women inside decide whether to see them or not' (1993: 198). Jack, however, seems to represent something new, for he doesn't kick down doors, nor does he wait for them to be opened, rather he knows someone who can get a key so he can break in and torture the occupant quietly – all for the sake of protecting his daughter. In this respect Jack directly addresses and undermines the traditional idea that father *knows* best. It is precisely his experience and calculating intellectualism that places Jack in a position of authority, while it is his emotions that cause him to doubt himself and make wrong or questionable decisions, as in 'The Descent' (4:20) when he tells Sydney:

> I have gone over the details a thousand times in my mind. Each one added up to the same conclusion . . . that your life was in danger and your mother was the lethal threat . . . I've lived my life trusting in the veracity of details and in doing so I lost sight of the one thing I know to be true. . . . Your mother would never hurt you . . .

While Sydney comforts Jack by telling him that she has never questioned his motives, she knows he has her best interests at heart, she has often throughout the series challenged his methods and his decisions.

Jeffords further argues that in the early 1990s action films 'families provide both the motivation for and the resolution of changing masculine heroisms' (1993: 200). The tension between the roles of action man and father is resolved through his return to his family. Karen Schneider takes this argument further by suggesting that a new genre of 'family action thriller' has emerged in which the family is not only the salvation of the hero but more significantly, the action narrative is structured around the 'rearticulation of the traditional – white, bourgeois, patriarchal – family' (1999: 4) and its ultimate salvation. While in many ways the potential restoration of the Bristow nuclear family is a thematic focus of *Alias*, its serial structure is designed to deny this. The family is never restored because the story never ends.

Significantly, of course, the story *has* ended. Although Rambaldi and page 47 were resurrected for the finale, bringing the show full circle, fundamentally the final episodes are all about family. While the focus is upon the Bristows and the Sloanes, even Tom, Rachel and Marshall have denouements that are linked to family. Having failed to save his wife, Tom sacrifices himself to save the staff of APO (interestingly the most moving scene of the finale); with Prophet Five destroyed Rachel's family is safe so she can leave APO, but she chooses to stand with her chosen family; and after having been kidnapped Marshall works with his wife both to bring down Sloane and to prove himself in the eyes of his son.

The major catalyst for the end of the series is Sloane's killing of Nadia. This accidental event finally shatters Sloane's moral compass and leaves him free to embrace his Rambaldi obsession. Since the end of Season Two, and arguably even before, Sloane has walked the line between sin and redemption, but it is this single crime against family which is finally irredeemable. Nadia returns in the final episodes as part spirit guide, part guilt-created manifestation, but finally abandons him. Jack traps him, but it is Nadia who punishes him. She leaves Sloane an immortal, trapped for eternity in the Rambaldi tomb, her abandonment the final accusation of Sloane's failure as a father, as well as a rejection of his assertion of patriarchal authority over her life and death. Indeed *Alias* ends with a total rejection of patriarchal authority. Jack's decision to blow himself up, leaving Sloane trapped within the detritus of his magnificent obsession, is his final exertion of his televisual paternal authority – he does in this instance 'know what is best' for Sydney. At the same time he releases her from the influence of the three major patriarchal figures who have attempted to control her life since before her birth. With patriarchy effectively overthrown, Sydney's final battle is not with Sloane but with Irina. The dysfunctional Bristow family overturn their progress and seemingly reach the end of their trajectory with the over-protective but ultimately 'good' Jack putting Sydney above all things and the duplicitous Irina choosing power and glory. The Bristow family unit is irreparably fractured.

Yet the final image left to us is of Sydney and Vaughn as a happy nuclear family. We see them in their beachfront property, visited by

Dixon, and for the first time in *Alias* we see a home space in which work is comfortably situated and lies are absent. This is not a domestic space as a place of work but a home in which, it is made clear, work poses no threat. So, do the final images of the show overturn that which has gone before, the negotiation of biological family, the tension between work and home space, to present a comfortably conservative rearticulation of the nuclear family? The events within this final episode, as well as the narrative trajectory leading up to it since the first episode of Season Five, seem to be striving towards the restoration of the nuclear family shown in these final moments, but the path is strewn with significant disruptions that serve to undermine this notion; Vaughn is shot and killed, Sydney's baby is threatened (by Irina, who later delivers it), Nadia is killed by Sloane, Marshall is kidnapped, Tom's wife's murder is revealed and, finally, both Jack and Irina are killed. Although by the end the family dysfunctions in Sydney's life are ostensibly resolved and the two main characters responsible for it, Jack and Irina, are dead, these disruptions signal the continued importance in the series of questioning traditional televisual images of family in a world where this conception of the nuclear family no longer exists. Far from selling an image of an ideal American family, what *Alias* offers is an extreme example of family as battleground, where conflict may pull it apart, but also has the power to bring it together. Finally the 'happy' ending is not what matters because it is the unending nature of serial television that provides satisfaction for the audience: that Sloane will turn evil again, that Irina will turn up again, and that Jack and Sydney will reconcile and be driven apart once more.

7 Alias' Inversion of White Heroes and Brown Foes

Jennifer R. Young

No other television show approaches human relationships the way *Alias* does. Sydney Bristow qualifies as the modern-day super-woman. Few would argue at how well she saves the day in virtually every episode. Arvin Sloane wins the prize as the ultimate manipulator. Whether he is working with or against the CIA, the Covenant, the Alliance, Authorized Personnel Only (APO), Prophet Five or some other unknown, Sloane fabricates or foils many of the missions, counter-missions, and extractions. Jack Bristow prowls along as the consummate operative. Despite his dubious actions, Jack remains the ever-present watchdog. And of course, there is no denying the appeal of other characters like the tech genius Marshall Flinkman, the elusive Irina Derevko, or Julian Sark, a sly Sloane in training.

Creator J.J. Abrams and his crew make the world of *Alias* as ethnically diverse as the actual world in which its viewers live. While many of the central characters are of European descent, some are from historically underrepresented ethnic groups. Other characters and guest roles include those from parts of the world – Middle East, Asia, Africa, Central and South America – that viewers rarely see in primetime network television programming. Not only does *Alias* expose viewers to some serious, mature, and sophisticated characters who are non-American or non-white, but the show has several subplot developments that add dimension to the lives of the entire ensemble cast. It takes only one episode's viewing to recognise *Alias'* many facets of multiculturalism.

Since the 1950s, American dramas and sitcoms have had some semblance of diversity, but the principal characters and subplots were frequently directed toward either white or black audiences. For a long time, television diversity mainly referred to these two ethnic groups. Consider early dramas like *Star Trek, Mission: Impossible,*

I Spy and *Julia*, or dramas in the 1990s like *I'll Fly Away*, *Sweet Justice* and *In the Heat of the Night*. As reflected in sitcoms from *Amos 'n' Andy* and *The Jeffersons* to *The Andy Griffith Show* and *All in the Family*, television programming resembled its segregated audiences, what Herman Gray calls pluralist or separate-but-equal discourse, in which American television continues to promote parallel worlds where little interaction exists between people of different ethnicities (1995: 87–9).[1]

'Narrow casting' in the 1990s was a turning point for black audiences since networks began to employ marketing strategies to reach black audiences (this was due in large part to the popular success of *The Cosby Show*) (Gray 1995: 59–60; Bogle 2001: 430–2;).[2] At the same time, sitcoms and dramas continued to have fictitious worlds where neighbourhoods and circumstances were predominately centred on white characters (as in *Seinfeld*, *Everybody Loves Raymond*, *Sex and the City*, *Friends*), Latinos (*21 Jump Street*, *New York Undercover*, *George Lopez*, *Freddie*), or Blacks (*Homicide*, *City of Angels*, *Frank's Place*, *The Bernie Mac Show*, *Everybody Hates Chris*). Networks assumed that shows with black actors would best appeal to black audiences, while shows with white actors would appeal to everybody since most viewers are used to watching this majority group. However, Herman Gray and cultural critics like Paul Gilroy, Stuart Hall, George Lipsitz, and Kobena Merar would agree that these assumptions lead to a dominant discourse in which minorities are conservatively mobilised, demonised, or eroticised (Gray 1995: 5). Recounting Gramsci's concept of hegemony, George Lipsitz provides the minority perspective regarding a lack of cultural leadership: 'Culture exists as a form of politics, as a means of reshaping individual and collective practice for specified interests, and as long as individuals perceive their interests as unfulfilled, culture retains an oppositional potential'(quoted in Brown 1990: 212).[3] In other words, when 'blackness' is depicted as menacing and 'whiteness' is used to resemble heroic valour, not all audiences (of varying ethnic groups) find this appealing (Gray 1995: 85). Shows like *Alias* challenge long-existing visual patterns of degradation by confounding the ethnic affiliations of the good guys, bad guys, and everyone in between.

In the efforts to debunk age-old stereotypes, contemporary television shows have diverse casts. But how visible are these cultures? Herman Gray identifies the question of ethnic visibility as the 'assimilation and discourse of invisibility'. Invisibility is the term used to describe minority actors/characters integrated into predominantly white worlds, void of any hint of their cultural traditions, social struggles, racial conflicts or cultural differences (Gray 1995: 85). Due to these invisibilities, minority characters are rendered culturally white, invisible of race representations. If viewers see people of different ethnicities but there are no other cultural signifiers or storylines dedicated to diverse characters, these casts have less chance of appealing to non-white audiences. By describing feminist discourse in television, critic Mary Ellen Brown presents a formula for identifying authentic characters:

> Feminine discourse involves speaking practices among women or other non-dominant groups where they can talk directly, where their opinions are valued, and where listeners share the same or similar perceptions of the world. This validation has to do with the mutual recognitions of those restrictions by the participants in the group.
>
> (Brown 1990: 206)

By showing viewers the public and private spheres of all the principal characters (regardless of their ethnicities), *Alias* has numerous methods to counter such hegemonic forces.

Aside from the aliases that the characters assume, the show's global settings, multiple languages, and ensemble multicultural cast give viewers programming that is more realistic to their everyday desegregated lives. *Alias* is not the first contemporary show to have an ethnic mix of recurring characters that have integrity, sincerity, and purpose. Recent American programmes like *Ally McBeal, NYPD Blue, Law & Order, ER, 24, Lost* and *Grey's Anatomy* have enjoyed high viewer ratings, even with principal cast members of varying ethnic groups. Similarly, *Alias* has universal appeal for mixed ethnic audiences. Its multiple perspectives on ethnicity, nationality and culture are progressive for primetime television. To use Donald Bogle's words, *Alias* spectators have weekly access to 'tube neighbors'. Having the same people of colour in American living rooms at the same time with the same tangle of relationships every week alters perceptions and attitudes by making African Americans and other minority groups familiar. 'They become neighbors of sorts', Bogle explains (2001: 6). *Alias* offers an inversion of character motivations, actions and reactions, and a fluid way of conveying dimensionality without seeming contrite.

'OLÉ, OLÉ, OLÉ, OLÁ!' DIVERSITY OF LANGUAGE, LOCATION AND COSTUME

Virtually every episode of *Alias* has at least one foreign setting. Push-throughs that spell the name of some city in the world often introduce the foreign scenes. Audio – which could be as simple as a swooshing noise or as involved as an orchestra arrangement – accompanies the word as it moves toward the foreground of the screen. *Alias* compliments its viewers by not identifying country locations. Viewers are left to their own wits to decipher nations based on the names of villages, towns, and cities. They are given additional cultural cues through the use of music, *Alias*' effective way of communicating foreign settings.

Beyond foreign locations, the audience gets to hear multiple languages. *Alias* is one of the few American network television shows to have intelligent people speaking in their native tongues. Likewise, the American characters – no matter what their ethnicity – are shown interacting in other languages and dialects. *Alias* even dares to have episodes that feature the use of foreign languages where subtitles may or may not be provided. Furthermore Sydney is the most multidimensional character on the show. Her heritage reveals a Russian mother, an American father, an Argentinian sister, and an alleged Italian ancestor, the prophet Milo Rambaldi. She speaks dozens of languages and dialects. In earlier seasons her best friend is African American, and later her boyfriend/fiancé is revealed to be French. Sydney oozes diversity.

By casting an international net, *Alias* establishes expectations for global citizenry. When terrorists strike in one place, the CIA agents work to prevent destruction somewhere else. In 'Firebomb' (2:16), for example, a weapon resembling a neutron bomb explodes in Mexico City, causing the people in the Vatican embassy and local church to spontaneously combust. Urgent situations like 'Firebomb' occur often, and the agents repeatedly stress how they go to work to protect their country and the world. In 'The Two' (3:1) Sloane explains the motivations behind starting Omnifam, his world relief organisation based in Zurich. In this same episode, viewers learn that he helped dismantle over two dozen terrorist cells around the world. While he is as devious as the characters get, Sloane has redeeming qualities through his humanitarian efforts. Whether viewers believe his good intentions or not, part of Season Three is dedicated to the notion of Sloane as a man without country, but a son of the world.

The Derevko sisters are also examples of global citizenry. Irina, Katya and Elena slip in and out of the American borders, usually without detection. It is unclear what their allegiances are or to whom. While Katya reveals her untrustworthiness in 'Resurrection' (3:22) and Elena proves herself in 'Before the Flood' (4:22) to have ill motives, viewers are left from one season to the next with the ambiguous actions of Irina. Devoted to the Covenant, Prophet Five or another covert initiative, she gives her daughter Sydney hints that suggest her true intentions are to protect not only Sydney and Jack, but the global community. Like Sloane, Irina appears to be an unfeeling and covert independent who does damage on the side of evil, but who claims to be doing it for the greater good of the world. Her utilitarian approach does not necessarily include devotion to her daughter, former husband, or even native Russia. Still, Irina is a woman of the world and supposedly a protector of it.

Being a show about espionage, the agents are always saving the world, yet this does not make *Alias* monolithic. Terrorists do not come from one region of the world, like the Middle East. Criminals-at-large like Daniel Ryan in 'Façade' (3:15) or Toni Cummings in 'Legacy' (3:21) sometimes work with the CIA to solve dangerous situations. CIA operatives cannot always be trusted as good guys. *Alias'* people and places are interconnected, moving the programme beyond the dualism of good guy–bad guy. One of the show's strengths is how no situation is cut and dried. At times the agents go rogue, break the law, or compromise missions for desired results. Previous spy shows like *I Spy* and *Mission: Impossible* had more definitive bad guys to apprehend. *Alias'* storylines are more convoluted, forcing the characters to consider the causes and effects of their actions: strategy is essential.

Images of the cities, squares, villages and townspeople of these international locations reinforce the show's attempts to recreate these places authentically. In 'A Broken Heart' (1:4) Sydney and Anna Espinosa fight inside a church in Málaga, and its architecture reflects Spanish origin. 'The Orphan' (4:12) shows Cesar Marquez and Nadia sharing coffee at a marketplace in Buenos Aires. Narrow streets, vendors, the everyday words on the cafés and shops, the clothing of the townspeople and the music of the scene all indicate some semblance of Argentine life.

Costumes reflecting the ethnicity and nationality of the people help make the aliases more credible. In 'Reckoning' (1:6) Sydney and

Dixon disguise themselves as wealthy buyers at a London photo gallery. Dressed in full geisha costume in 'The Counteragent' (2:7), Sydney finds the antidote for Vaughn. In 'There's Only One Sydney Bristow' (5:12) Will and Sydney pretend to be part of the French elite as they bribe the train attendant to give them a first-class cabin, a secure place to track down Anna Espinosa electronically.

Arguably, many of the aliases are caricatures.[4] Dixon's are probably the most problematic in terms of ethnic representation and stereotypes. In 'The Coup' (1.14) Dixon acts as a Jamaican diplomat who has an inclination for gambling. While Dixon's alias is meant to distract the K-Directorate agent with whom he plays cards in a Vegas casino, it is Dixon's large afro, assumed mannerisms, and acquired accent that are distracting. In 'The Awful Truth' (4:3) Dixon wears a dreadlock wig when he and Sydney hack into a bank safe in the Bahamas. The intention may not be to impersonate a Rastafarian, but this alias does fulfill a stereotype of a happy-go-lucky (inebriated from the elixir of life) Caribbean man. He plays a computer hacker in 'A Clean Conscience' (4:17), yet his characteristics loosely resemble pimp stereotypes. By regressing into such stereotypes, *Alias* engages in the pluralist discourse to which Herman Gray categorises some television programming. From misguided portrayals of African-American men as angry, truculent, and arrogant in 1970s dramas like *Shaft*, *Tenafly* and *Paris* to clownish and indolent portrayals of Black men in 1990 sitcoms like *Martin* and *The Fresh Prince of Bel Air*, it seems that a twenty-first-century programme like *Alias* could abandon such ill-informed characterisations altogether.

Alias loses its aim of appealing to many different audiences when Dixon dons these aliases. Usually, Sydney is dressed in sexy dresses and wigs, but Dixon is taking on cultural signifiers relating to sacred African customs and Caribbean religions on the one hand, and characters resembling blaxploitation films of the 1970s on the other. Such aliases distract (and offend) viewers from watching the agents succeed with the actual missions. This flaw may be the result of a lack of cultural guidance on race representation issues. What is confusing is how the show can have alias stereotypes for Dixon on the one hand, but then portray him with great dimension in the private sphere of his family life or in public moments as director of the Los Angeles branch of the CIA.[5]

Costumes together with location settings and languages are supposed to add texture to these international conflicts. Although the aliases are more visual than culturally driven, *Alias* is still one of the few American television programmes to integrate this global fabric into their world. *24*, *The West Wing* and *Commander in Chief* are shows that deal more with issues of homeland security whereas *Alias* deals with global security issues. Aside from presenting some images that do not necessarily ring true within the character of the show, *Alias* takes chances with topics and global situations that no other show has taken.

DIVERSITY OF CASTING

What makes *Alias* truly unique is the multicultural and multinational cast of characters. The actors, who are international, play characters with heritages different from their own. The Derevkos are supposed to be Russian but are played by a Swede, an Italian/Swede and a Brazilian. Sydney's number one enemy Anna Espinosa has multiple ethnic traits, although the actor who portrays Anna is Cuban American. Sark is English, but the actor is an American. Vaughn is a Frenchman playing an American, but the actor who portrays him is an American who grew up in France.

The series is populated by an international array of characters on the sides of good and evil. More importantly, much like the main characters, the minor characters blur lines between good and evil. Toni Cummings is a mercenary but fights alongside Sydney and Vaughn to rescue Nadia ('Legacy'). Anna Espinosa is on the side of evil, but is colourful, attractive and fun in a way that means that the audience can root for her escapes from incarceration and her ability to repeatedly dodge death. *Alias* has many recurring characters – like Thomas Brill, Professor Choy, Kazari Bomani, Daniel Ryan, Lauren Reed, Renée Rienne, Dr Lee and Dr Jain – who add to the show's setting of global diversity.

While we cannot be certain that the *Alias* producers, writers and directors engage in colour-blind casting, it is significant to note that the characters are not generally driven by the stereotypes of their ethnicity. Aside from the characters speaking with varying accents, dialects, and in foreign languages, their bio sketches seem to be filled with competence and intelligence rather than ethnic flamboyance. Sydney's professor, Professor Choy, expects his graduate students to do their work ('Parity', 1:3). Thomas Brille listens to funk music in the park while he plays chess and plans multimillion-dollar extractions ('Breaking Point', 3:8). CIA medical doctor Dr Jain may draw little attention as the doctor who helps Sydney recover from a vampire bite ('Nocturne', 4:6) and Nadia return from a medically induced coma ('The Road Home', 4:11), but he plays his role straight, not hiding his accent, but not acknowledging it either. Even though the cultural signifiers become secondary to most of the characters of colour on *Alias*, what seems most significant is how everyone interacts with each other without hints of bias, prejudice, or racism.

FRANCIE CALFO/ALLISON DOREN

> I had nothing against [Francie]; she was just a casualty of circumstance.
> Allison Doren ('Prelude', 3:7)

Aside from the television show *Girlfriends*, a programme about the friendships, professional challenges and romantic lives of African-American women, American television has little representation of young black single women. Critics like Donald Bogle and Herman Gray have also noted the significance of *Living Single*, *Sister Sister* and *Moesha*. These same shows, however, have received criticism for female stereotypes. For instance, Bogle notes the fascination with romance and sex on *Living Single*, a flaw in the storylines considering all four women have booming professional careers and sisterly bonds that have nothing to do with romance (2001: 427). Still, Bogle and others do applaud these shows for doing three things well: presenting the look of full-figured women who seem comfortable with their bodies; not including colourism subtext (the internalised racist notion that light-coloured blacks are more beautiful than those with darker complexions); and providing overall intelligent conversations that exist between women and their families. Unlike shows that turn African-American characters into caricatures through extreme language, gestures, and mannerisms, *Girlfriends*, *Living Single*, *Sister Sister* and *Moesha* have moments in which serious issues are not trivialised or used as the punch lines (Gray 1995: 35–56; Bogle 2001: 422–32).

Returning to the textual strategies in *Alias*, notice how Francie and Allison do not solely exist for the advancement of Sydney's plot. Despite starting as peripheral characters, both contribute significantly to the show's major storylines. Season One emphasises

Francie's desire for relationships of integrity with her friends, family and significant other. Race, class and economic challenges inform her disposition as an African American. Viewers see Francie as a woman unafraid to speak her mind in 'So it Begins' (1:2), when she recounts her day at a dinner celebration for her boyfriend: 'So [the client] says to me, "hey, Honey, I asked for the butter like an hour ago." So I'm sitting there thinking, oh no . . . you asked the other black girl for butter, you rich entitled son of a bitch.' Francie is a working woman who does not lose sight of her self-worth.

Francie's boyfriend Charlie, who is also black, is portrayed as a respectable law student. We learn that he is a first-generation college graduate. Instead of becoming a lawyer, early episodes imply that Charlie may pursue a singing career. The fact that he exercises his privilege to pursue another career suggests a lack of previous bad experiences or choices. His prerogative affirms positive characteristics like decision-making, critical thinking, and commitment to his true identity. So, instead of being portrayed as a law student who was once an at-risk child from humble beginnings, the writers take a different approach by not getting into the logistics of his upbringing. Viewers are able to imagine numerous possibilities for Charlie without a prescribed backstory that usually involves poverty, lack of education and instability.

Despite his brief appearances in Season One, Charlie has dimension. His mannerisms are polished. He speaks Standard English; he does not fulfill the role of the cool black guy around for urban dialect and wise jokes. Like Francie, his outward appearance suggests that he is comfortable interacting in middle-class circles (whether he is or not). Beyond character sketch, we get to see Francie and Charlie interact with one another in good times and bad. In 'A Broken Heart' Francie confronts Charlie about his affair. Their conversation takes place in a restaurant. She does not make a scene or intentionally set out to emasculate him. Francie speaks in hushed tones, careful not to make a fool of herself or Charlie. Viewers get to see two African-American characters acting as adults instead of adolescents, the stereotype that usually prevails.

Francie is crucial to helping Sydney get over the tragedy of her fiancé's death. In many ways she is an emotional centre for Sydney but does get sidelined when Will learns the truth about Sydney's double life. As Francie moves from the peripheral character as Sydney's friend and is literally replaced by Allison the double spy, her role becomes part of the major storyline. Allison gets to have fight scenes, sex scenes and spicy interactions with Sloane, all things that Sydney does. In her few appearances, Allison is intimate with both Will and Sark. Sark is the only other character who gets as many sex scenes as Allison. Black sexuality on primetime television is uncommon. Jeanie Boulet on *ER* has intimate relationships, but she contracts the HIV virus from her husband. *ER* writers used her storyline to highlight important issues regarding AIDS and the black community, especially black women. However, some viewers could take offence at the fact that out of all the sexually active *ER* characters, Jeanie – whose private life is not a part of the show – contracts HIV. While black television characters are known to have partnerships, this is rarely shown at length on the screen. As one journalist notes, 'black actors are seldom afforded the opportunity to portray characters involved in tender, sensitive love scenes that display the depth of the attraction between a man and a woman'(Anon 1991: 162).

Allison is one of three characters to undergo genetic alteration. The doctor whose genetics are altered in Season Two does not have as large a role as Allison. In fact, the doctor is only used to unveil the genetic lab. The third person to undergo alteration is Anna Espinosa. In 'There's Only One Sydney Bristow' Anna turns into a genetic copy of Sydney. Two of these three genetic copies, therefore, are black women. While it is a compliment to the characters that they are good enough to be doubles and spies, it is also disturbing to see these two manipulated and experimented upon in ways in which the others are not subjected, and Anna is 'made white' in her transformation into Sydney.

Ethnicity does not seem to be an issue for the ways in which others interact with Francie, Allison, or Charlie. While the audience sees the visual distinction between the characters, everyone seems to share the same interests in art, music, clothing, people and food. For a while, Charlie and Francie are together, but there are few other people of ethnic diversity in their friendship circle. Most of their friends are white. In this way it seems odd that there are no cultural signifiers to indicate difference, especially on a show that is filled with visually diverse people and places. Perhaps this is why the international scenes are so vibrant. When the characters are back in Los Angeles, the tone is much more muted. For instance, the aliases are grand and extravagant but the characters dress in plain black clothes, with understated hair and makeup, reconfiguring themselves as blank canvases in between missions.[6]

MARCUS DIXON

> Sloane has no authority in this room.
>
> Marcus Dixon ('Prelude', 3:7)

Marcus Dixon is the unsung hero. With his own set of complexities, Dixon's actions are motivated by two things: his devotion to his loved ones and his allegiance to his country, in that order. Dixon handles his responsibilities with maturity, ranging from family man – both husband and father – to mentor and partner, from CIA division head to field operative. Like the other characters, Dixon is a skilled linguist, marksman, technician, mathematician, analyst, medic and martial artist.

His sense of duty is clear from the start. In the pilot episode, Sydney is secretly excited about her boyfriend Danny's marriage proposal. On a plane ride overseas Sydney asks Dixon how he balances his work and private life. He says in earnest, 'Diane is married to an investment analyst who loves his job. I'm protecting her from the truth. If there's one rule you don't break, that's the rule you don't break.' Dixon lies to his wife to protect her and their children. He stands by the lie as the seasons progress, and as Dixon's character develops, viewers get to see the maturity of his choices and decisions.

'Endgame' (2:19) shows the intimacy between Dixon and his wife Diane. After a tragic accident in the field, Dixon requests a transfer. While she had known for several episodes (since 'A Free Agent', 2:15) about Dixon's career as an agent, Diane openly expresses herself: 'When you first told me the truth, I said I didn't know who you were. I was wrong. I just didn't know what you did. I have always known who you are. You are the most decent man I know. Whatever you decide, I'll be with you.' Dixon and Diane display an unwavering commitment to each other. Somehow, their relationship withstands the lie that Dixon has been keeping for over a decade. *Alias* portrays a solid relationship through this black couple, one of the few, if not only, healthy relationships on the show.

Years after Diane's passing, we see Dixon dating Director Hayden Chase. Diane and Chase are the only two women that Dixon has relationships with. It is significant to note how both women share the same ethnicity as Dixon. Some, like Jack and Irina, Jack and Katya, Sark and Allison, Nadia and Weiss, have partnered with those from different backgrounds. What makes *Alias* unique is that the narrative does not make a big deal of people dating inside or outside their ethnicity.

When it comes to his professional life, Dixon is forthright. When he feels manipulated or disrespected he directly addresses the issue. Dixon does not cower in corners, waiting for someone else to take control. For example, in 'The Nemesis' (3:6) he uses the power of his position as CIA director to get justice. Before a mission to pursue Allison Doren, Dixon gives Sydney the following order:

> I want her dead. The order from Langley is to bring her in dead or alive. She killed my wife. She killed your best friend, so I look at this as an opportunity. The only reason I hesitated before was that I hoped that she might have more information for you, but now that we know there's no hope for that, I want that bitch dead.

Dixon is not an angry man. However, he is subjected to the most cruelty. His wife is murdered in 'Endgame'; his children are kidnapped in 'Taken' (3:16); he gets attacked or shot (several episodes), or falls victim to toxic chemicals in 'Tuesday' (4:13). Despite all of these trials, Dixon keeps his poise, a mark of a mature agent who tries to keep the balance between right and wrong. At the same time, this episode proves that Dixon is no pushover. Through these moments Dixon is given equal depth in his emotional representation as the series' main characters, Sydney, Vaughn and Sloane. In fact, next to Sydney, he appears to be the most in touch with his emotions (in a productive sense) while the others repress or compartmentalise their emotions.

Dixon's showdowns with Arvin Sloane are the most appealing moments, because the audience is exposed to a black male character asserting his power and intelligence without using physical intimidation. Dixon does not stoop to Sloane's level. Where Sloane has threatened others with violence, Dixon fights him with knowledge. When Dixon serves as CIA director in 'Prelude' he has a commanding presence. Hooded and handcuffed, Sloane is brought into the Los Angeles branch. On Dixon's cue, the guards remove Sloane's black hood. Dixon steps closer to Sloane. Sloane fixes his smug expression and speaks first, realising that Dixon is in charge: 'I always knew you were destined for great things.' Unresponsive, Dixon spins around and tells the guards to bring Sloane to the briefing room. Though Sloane tries to dominate the conversation, Dixon cuts him off, uses harsh tones, and gives commands to the others to indicate his power. He does not use the same manipulative leadership tactics as Sloane but takes the wellbeing of his team into consideration. Others have respect, appreciation and admiration for Dixon, reactions that the agents have never linked to Sloane, even when he becomes a worldwide humanitarian.

With a perverse change of events, Sloane resumes his post as director in Season Four. 'Nocturne' shows Sloane exercising his power over Dixon. Dixon advises him that sending Sydney out in the field following a recent trauma is a tactical error. Sloane responds by questioning Dixon about his eleven loyal years with SD-6. 'Do your job, and I'll do mine', Sloane says to Dixon. After Sydney is healed, Sloane tells Dixon that he was right. Sending Sydney was a tactical error. Dixon looks Sloane square in the eyes and calmly says,

> I [would have] said this earlier, but when I get done it's likely you'll have me relieved of my position and I didn't want that to happen while Sydney was in the field. I've asked myself countless times why I never saw the true nature of SD-6. For a while I punished myself over it. Finally I realised my only failure was that of imagination. Despite all the evil I'd encountered I'd never imagined a person could exist, someone as thoroughly toxic as yourself. I won't make that mistake again. You want us to believe you've reformed, that for the love of your daughter you've decided to listen to the better angels of your nature. Arvin, let's be honest. You don't have any. And on that inevitable day when your true motive reveals itself, I promise you, I'll be there. I'll be waiting.

Critical to the *Alias* cast, Dixon serves as a moral guard, in strong contrast to Sloane. While Sloane is driven by Rambaldi's prophecies, Dixon is motivated by his need to protect his loved ones and the world from catastrophic tragedy. Dixon goes against Langley orders; he steals information from systems; he goes on rogue missions, all for good reasons. The contrast between Dixon and Sloane, good and evil, is a nice twist from old stereotypes that make the dark man evil and the lighter man good.

CONCLUSION

In June 1950 an author for *Ebony* magazine suggested that children exposed to diversity through television programming would 'finally lay Jim Crow to rest' (quoted in MacDonald 1992: 14). J. Fred MacDonald notes that Ed Sullivan's variety programme, which started in 1948, sometimes included talent from underrepresented ethnic groups. Despite criticism, threats and anxious advertisers, Sullivan invited singers, dancers, sportsmen and political leaders of differing ethnicities to his show *Toast of the Town* (later called *The Ed Sullivan Show*). MacDonald explains, 'Sullivan felt that by bringing [different] personalities directly into the homes of Americans, TV would undermine racism. He believed that white adults and children, seeing and appreciating black talent, would be forced to reassess racist stereotyping and their own prejudices' (1992: 14). As host of the *Tonight* show from 1954 to 1957, Steve Allen was another entertainer who occasionally used his show to address issues of civil rights, brotherhood, and American patriotism (MacDonald 1992: 15) While television programming in the decades of segregation was hardly diverse, critics recognised the power that integrated shows would have on changing apathetic actions and attitudes regarding race.

Much in the way of progressive dramas, comedies and variety shows that came before it, *Alias* challenges the ways in which ethnicity and nationality are portrayed. The show does not make a mockery of non-White or international characters. All of the *Alias* characters have some dimension of integrity, whether their motives are good or not. With an ensemble cast of talented characters, *Alias* pushes its audience to consider their views regarding race. Television content is important, but Jane Feuer explains how television programming is affected by advertisers:

> It is a truism in the industry that the purpose of commercial television is not to deliver programming to the people but rather to 'deliver' audiences to advertisers. Of course this mechanistic interpretation does not explain why some programmes succeed with the mass audience and others don't, a factor that the industry would dearly love to be able to predict. The television series is both commodity and text. (1984: 2)

The flip side of Feuer's argument works as well: television may be for advertising, but advertisers need to market to their ideal audience. With a show as diverse as *Alias*, marketers have taken notice and have responded to audience interests. It is not unusual to see car commercials advertised with Spanish voiceovers, or to see a black middle-class mother buying Midas tyres, or a diverse group of college students using their Dell computers. Audiences may be geared toward advertisers, but it is nice to see a show like *Alias* cause advertisers to consider the audience and the context of the television programme.

The writers, directors, and producers of *Alias* succeeded in completing a series that suggests what human responsibility should look like on a global scale. Whether television viewers are uncomfortable, turned off, curious, or intrigued by these new images of human interaction, *Alias* banishes old dichotomies of looking at race and power in matters of binary opposition. Like the real world, *Alias* is not simply composed of black and white people. Though a fictitious show, *Alias* acknowledges the reality of one human race. The characters are interdependent on each other for survival to the point where humanity trumps ethnic divide. Ultimately, the show suggests that every character is some shade of brown.

Part Three

TERROR/
COUNTER TERROR

Truth and Morality Post-9/11

8 The Good, the Bad and the Justified

Moral Ambiguity in *Alias*

Sharon Sutherland and Sarah Swan

Just nineteen days after the 11 September 2001 terrorist attacks on American targets, *Alias*, with its plotlines of terrorism and government intrigues, premiered on the American Broadcasting Company network. The series has served as a window into a new era in US international relations since then, complete with espionage, national security issues and violence. Like other television shows in recent years, *Alias* exemplifies a shift towards an ever more morally ambiguous vision of this period. *Alias* presents a world in which the separation between good and evil is constantly shifting: the audience shares with the protagonist continuing uncertainty about the moral consequences of her actions because they are never sure who is or is not an enemy of the nation and potentially a terrorist. As legal scholars, we are interested in popular representations of morality, and particularly intrigued by the slipperiness of the moral landscape in *Alias*. With its coincidentally opportune launch date, its explicit interest in terrorism, and its many morally complex characters, *Alias* provides us with a vehicle for examining shifts in popular moral thinking since 9/11. In this chapter, we examine *Alias'* connections with, and unique manifestations of, the recurrent theme of moral ambiguity, and contrast *Alias'* reading with that of *24*, the other morally ambiguous thriller launched in the fall of 2001. In doing so, we consider the more specific question: what does *Alias* tell us about popular moral thinking on the topic of 'justifications' for apparently immoral or illegal acts?

For legal scholars, 'justification' has a special meaning distinguishing it from 'excuses': a justification, if proven, negates the wrongness of the criminal act, while an excuse negates only the culpability of the person committing the act. To illustrate: in special circumstances, such as where a person is provoked or suffers from a mental disorder, it is considered unfair to blame that person for their actions, so we, as a society, excuse him or her. In other situations, such as a person killing in defence of herself, or killing in defence of her child, we accept that the act itself was not wrong, but justified. Accepted legal justifications are manifestations of societal morality: we impose sanctions on acts that we consider morally wrong, while we forgive as morally acceptable those acts that fit into one of the traditional categories of justification.[1]

Popular television dramas, including *Alias*, offer us an alternative definition of justification: Sydney Bristow lives in a world where deceit, violence, theft, and even murder are justified by assumptions that normally unsavoury and even illegal actions are necessary to fight against terrorism, and that a morally righteous few – always including our protagonist – are justified in doing whatever it takes to carry out their mission. In the case of *Alias*, these new parameters operate despite the fact that our protagonist is often entirely mistaken or at least conflicted about which 'side' her own family members are on. As Simon points out in discussing other popular culture texts, enjoying *Alias* 'is not tantamount to embracing' its 'moral premises', yet the popularity of the series seems to 'depend strongly on the imaginative identification of the audience with [the heroine]. Such identification seems to imply at least openness to the moral assumptions on which [her] portrayal as [an] attractive [person] depends'(2001: 440). In other words, the very fact that *Alias* succeeded in drawing a loyal audience over five seasons suggests that at least some portion of the American population is comfortable with the moral ambiguity of Sydney's choices and is open to the moral assumptions underlying them.

MORAL AMBIGUITY: ANDY SIPOWICZ IS A HERO?

J.J. Abrams, the show's creator, recognises that 'every episode' of *Alias* 'has obviously taken on a different tenor and different sort of emotional approach because of the world we live in since [9/11]' (audio commentary for 'Façade', S3:D4). While clearly influenced over its five seasons by Western responses to that event, *Alias* was, of course, conceived before those terrorist attacks. Its earliest episodes, while seemingly prescient in light of the manner in which the programme's very premise tapped into its audience's concerns with national security, clearly built upon already growing themes of moral ambiguity in television programming. Legal shows of the late 1980s and early 1990s such as *L.A. Law* and *Law & Order* are often cited for the introduction of 'uncertainty, ambiguity and doubt' into stories that would previously have had black and white answers, heroes and villains (Sumser 1996: 155). Critics praised these programmes specifically for challenging viewers to reach their own conclusions about difficult moral issues (Gillers 1989: 1610), and it became *de rigueur* in the legal genre to raise issues that created discomfort in viewers and were not easily resolvable.

Similarly, while 'early television crime drama portrayed an ordered universe where evil was punished and good triumphed,' 'moral uncertainty' was seen to invade crime shows 'in which lawyers do not play a significant role' in the mid-1990s (Lane 2001: 138–9). *NYPD Blue* and *Homicide: Life on the Streets*, for example, both created worlds in which guilt is not always clear, and police officers do not always have a reliable moral compass. As Lane notes, '[q]uestions of right and wrong , good and evil, do not boil down to "just the facts, ma'am" . . .'(2001: 140). Andy Sipowicz (Dennis Franz) is the epitome of the conflicted law enforcement officer that evolved during these years, and in some ways a trailblazer for morally challenged counter-terrorist agents like Sydney. Beginning as an alcoholic racist with a vicious temper, Sipowicz gave us a highly complex character study of a man struggling to be good in a world that was just as complex and morally ambiguous as he was. One of the qualities that distinguished *NYPD Blue* from the majority of its precursors and led to its critical acclaim was its ability to allow for a multiplicity of views (Lavery 2001), and Sipowicz provides a challenging lens for those views.

The popularity of morally challenged characters on increasingly morally complex shows has continued with more recent series like *The Shield, Lost* and *The Sopranos*. Every one of these shows has a lead character who has killed and tortured. Justification for illegal and morally culpable actions on these shows seems to rely on character complexity: the audience is given enough information to know that the protagonist has reasons for his actions, and perhaps even to identify with some of them. Legally, some of these reasons might be considered mitigation leading to a reduced sentence, but they do not negate the wrongness of the acts. Similarly, the fact that these characters are often remorseful, or at least troubled, by their own actions, might be a factor to consider at sentencing, but only on television does it convince the jury of viewers that the act might be anything but criminal.

One obvious pattern that appears from these examples is the fact that the conflicted characters portrayed in these series are almost all male.[2] Female protagonists are not missing in this era, but they do seem to engage differently with the moral ambiguity of their worlds. Unlike the male character whose behaviour is implicitly justified by complex character development, the female heroine facing morally ambiguous choices more commonly engages in explicit moral questioning and reasoning, walking viewers through her difficult choices. Buffy, for example, questions her own choices repeatedly in *Buffy the Vampire Slayer*, developing confidence in her reasoning as she matures, but she is never permitted to be complacent in moral decision-making: any easy answers she seeks to adopt are quickly shown to be inadequate.[3]

Abrams also presents two more recent examples of female protagonists facing difficult choices: the central character of *Felicity* (Keri Russell) and *Lost*'s Kate Austen (Evangeline Lilly). Although these characters come from the same creator, their moral challenges are very different from each other's and Sydney's. Felicity's dilemmas are the small, normal challenges of a young adult: should I go to medical school to please my parents or follow my dream to go to art school? Should I date the loyal, cute, but nerdy Noel, or the confused and potentially troublesome Ben? The questions do not have the global importance of Sydney's life-or-death counter-terrorist decisions or Buffy's apocalypse-ending choices, but Felicity's approach to them nonetheless shares characteristics with these two heroes. Felicity revisits and rethinks every decision she makes, seeking some confirmation that she is making the 'right' choice. Decisions are not easy for the female protagonist, who, like Buffy and Sydney to varying degrees, relies on friends to validate choices made.

Kate Austen falls into a separate category of female protagonist: sharing the supernatural terrain with Buffy and, to a lesser degree with Sydney, Kate has many secrets that the audience is slowly learning about. She killed her stepfather; she was morally culpable in the death of her childhood sweetheart, Tom; and she led an armed bank robbery to retrieve a keepsake Tom gave her before his death.

Yet Kate seems to be one of the 'good guys': on the island, she is one of the strong providers and protectors of the survivors. More like the men of *Lost* and less like the pattern of earlier female protagonists, Kate internalises her evident moral conflicts. As a post-*Alias* character, Kate may best be seen as a further shift in the portrayal of women in morally challenging circumstances, whereas Buffy and Felicity are Sydney's prototypes.

SYDNEY'S MORAL STRUGGLES

For a tough, super-agent action hero, Sydney, like Buffy, is remarkably sensitive to the moral consequences of her actions, often attempting to tease out the moral basis and ramifications of her decisions. She asks herself: is my action justified? Is this choice 'right'? For example, early in the series Sydney holds herself responsible for the death of an agent, stating, in a phrase fraught with literal and figurative meaning, that she had his blood on her hands ('A Broken Heart', 1:4). Two episodes later, in the aptly titled 'Reckoning' (1:6), she is horrified when her body count increases fourfold: four CIA agents are killed in an explosion when Dixon activates a second detonator that Sydney was not aware of. She berates herself, insisting that the men died because of her secret double-agent status, and lamenting her choice to keep hidden the true nature of SD-6 and her affiliation with the CIA. Although her CIA handler, Michael Vaughn, reassures her that their deaths were not in vain, that they died for their country, and that the revelation of her true loyalties would only lead to more deaths, Sydney looks unconvinced, and still uneasy about her blameworthiness in the scenario. The audience, too, wonders where to place Sydney's actions on the spectrum of moral responsibility: we empathise with her, but are also not completely soothed by Vaughn's rationalisations.

When Sydney kills Noah Hicks, aka the assassin 'The Snowman', she is again conflicted about her homicidal role ('Snowman', 1:19). His death was arguably self-defence (and perhaps even somewhat accidental): in an intense fight scene, during which Noah is disguised as the Snowman and Sydney is unaware of his true identity, Noah overpowers her. Although he can stab her at that moment, he pauses. Sydney seizes the opportunity his hesitation presents to kick him off of her, and he rolls onto the knife and dies. Sydney chastises herself for causing his death, and expresses her remorse and confusion to Vaughn. He offers her the same type of moral massage as in the previous situation, pointing out the parameters constricting Sydney's operational decision, and the cold facts: 'Noah Hicks was an assassin. If you hadn't killed him, he would have killed you.' In this instance, the audience feels less agony over the death than Sydney feels. The situation is not black and white: we have seen Noah's own hesitation and cannot be certain that he really would have killed Sydney, but we are still able to categorise this killing as 'self-defence', a category of defence that is generally agreed to be morally innocent. Most common-law-based legal systems recognise self-defence as a justification for homicide, holding that when one is faced with the option of kill or be killed, it is not morally repugnant to choose survival. Although Noah's hesitation complicates Sydney's justification, the somewhat accidental nature of his death assures us that she responded to a clear threat with only the force necessary to ensure her own safety. Additionally, Vaughn puts the argument into the simplest terms possible, saying 'Hicks was a bad guy.' In a sense unique to television, Vaughn's characterisation of Hicks allows us to dismiss Sydney's actions on the grounds that these are the rules of engagement: on television, the good guys live, and the bad guys die.

While the death of Hicks is arguably justified by self-defence, the perceived death of Andrian Lazarey is more complex. Sydney's horror at what she believes to be her murder of Lazarey is perhaps the best example of her moral questioning. As she watches the video of herself slitting the man's throat, her feelings of shock and dismay are obvious. She assesses her moral responsibility immediately, deciding that her killing an unarmed man is inexcusable. She assumes, in keeping with the standard notions of criminal law, that unless there is an immediate threat to her life, the killing is not justified. Her father, Jack, cautions her against her assumption: 'Your remorse is premature. Without knowing the circumstances, you can't be sure you didn't have just cause' ('Succession', 3:2). Sydney, though, will not exonerate herself so readily. She ruminates on what she has done: 'I killed a man . . . I killed a defenceless man in cold blood. What was I thinking? Did I know it was Sark's father? What would compel me to do something like this? Did someone condition me? . . .' ('A Missing Link', 3:4). The killing was apparently not self-defence, and Sydney cannot comprehend another moral justification for what she has done.

Interestingly, at this point in the series, the audience trusts Sydney more than she trusts herself. As our hero, we believe that Sydney will act in morally acceptable ways. We trust the hero to do what needs to be done, while still maintaining integrity and adherence to a high moral standard. Although the show tests how far our blind faith will go, we do not fully believe that Sydney would have killed 'in cold blood', and we are rewarded when we, and Sydney, discover that the 'murder' is an elaborate fake. Her moral disquiet and questioning of self-identity is halted, and the audience is proven right in their faith in her. Unlike with Andy Sipowicz and Tony Soprano, we do not have to believe that Sydney is good despite doing bad things: Sydney's own moral despair at the thought that she could commit such an act convinced us she was innocent.

More morally disturbing than these previous acts, however, is an action Sydney takes when supposedly brainwashed as Julia Thorne. In order to convince the Covenant that her loyalty lies with them, Sydney, aka Julia, must kill a man ('Full Disclosure', 3:11). Since the Covenant would kill her if she did not kill the man, Sydney is faced with a complex moral dilemma: she must kill an innocent person, or someone else will kill her. While killing an attacker to save one's own life is legally justified as self-defence, killing an innocent person is not. Most common law jurisdictions do recognise an excuse of duress where threats made 'actually overwhelmed the defendant's will and would have overwhelmed the will of a person of ordinary courage, . . . so that his or her entire behavior was involuntary' ('Duress', *Wikipedia*). As an excuse, a finding of duress indicates society's condemnation for the act committed, but excuse of the actor under the circumstances. A defence of duress, however, is frequently excluded by statute in cases of murder on the basis that murder is so morally reprehensible that it cannot be excused even under the most extreme coercion. Legally, then, Sydney's choice to kill could not be excused: she would be culpable for this action at law.

Unsurprisingly, Sydney questions intensely the morality of her choice to kill in these circumstances. In these scenes, Assistant Director Kendall plays the role of comforter, reassuring her that she had no choice – that the man was dead no matter what she did. Sydney does not accept this as justification, stating 'That doesn't lessen what I did.' Kendall disagrees, arguing that if she had not killed the man, the Covenant would have killed them both ('Full Disclosure').

Sydney will not accept forgiveness, again assigning herself moral culpability, while those around her rationalise her actions. Kendall excuses her execution of the man on the grounds that her actions had no real consequence – the man was as good as dead either way. Sydney does not accept this reasoning, deciding instead that killing is killing, and the man is dead because of her. To her, whether he would have died anyway is irrelevant. As an audience, we may have sympathy for Sydney's dilemma, but again we are not asked to accept her as a morally ambiguous actor. Much like Buffy before her, Sydney is harder on herself than her friends are. While her friends rationalise and excuse murder in these circumstances, Sydney's moral compass is aligned with that of many of our lawmakers: she does not believe that her actions were excusable.

Sydney's moral questioning sharply contrasts with the decisiveness of another television action hero on a similar show launched the same fall as *Alias*: Jack Bauer of *24*. Whereas Sydney needs constant reassurance from those around her that her killings are justified, Bauer asks approval from no one. Bauer kills when he believes it is necessary, and he makes no apologies for it. He rarely questions the morality of his own actions, even when others do. For example, when Jack kills Nina Myers (Sarah Chalke) out of what looks like pure vengeance for her killing his wife, he refuses to apologise. His daughter asks him what he told his boss about Nina's death, and he responds: 'I said I wasn't sorry that Nina was dead. I wasn't sorry that I shot her . . . she posed an immediate threat to you, to me and to thousands of innocent people' (3:15).

Sydney's killing of the Covenant prisoner is something that Bauer would do. Like Sydney, Bauer sacrifices the lives of others in order to pledge allegiance to the bad guys, and deceive them into thinking he is one of them. Bauer allows the bad guys to kill an innocent phone company worker. The worker's friend is shocked when Bauer identifies himself as a 'good guy', disbelieving that anyone 'good' could allow such a thing, for any reason (2:1). Bauer's actions differ slightly from Sydney's, in that the phone worker might have lived had Bauer made a different choice, yet even though his actions are more morally suspect, Bauer never questions whether he was justified in his actions. He simply accepts that in the battle for good, there will be some casualties.

JACK V. JACK

Although Jack Bauer shares few moral struggles with Sydney, he does have a remarkable similarity to Sydney's father, Jack Bristow. Both men are unwavering in their belief that moral compromises are necessary and justified when the protection of family is at issue. Both men make whatever sacrifices are necessary for the ultimate good, adhering to the utilitarian view that the ends justify the means, particularly when the ends are saving family members.

Sydney struggles with the decisions and actions of her father. In 'Spirit' (1:10), Sydney judges her father's decision to sacrifice Russek's life for hers. She believes Russek's death to be unjustified, claiming that he had done nothing wrong, but was killed because of what her father did. Vaughn defends her father, and offers little sympathy for one of the bad guys:

> Russek wasn't such an innocent. You want to know about Russek? He was an early member of SD-6. He knew he was working for the bad guys. He was the leader of at least a dozen operations that stole weapons and chemicals and intel and sold them to the enemies of the United States for cash to fund more SD-6 operations. Just like the one that killed your fiancé. He got what he deserved!

Vaughn, at least, finds Jack Bristow's motivation for his actions persuasive, challenging Sydney to consider what she would have done if it had been her daughter.

Sydney, though, does not blame her father for long. When the bad guys take her father prisoner in Cuba she instantly switches into protection mode, telling Vaughn that since he understands what her father did for her, he'll understand what she has to do for her father now. Reflecting back on her rescue mission in 'The Confession' (1:11) she explains to Vaughn that she now accepts that when a loved one is in trouble, there is nothing that she would not do: 'Last week when I learned what my father did for me, sacrificing Russek, it made me sick. But now, I know I would have done the exact same thing.' In this way, Sydney resembles her father; however, while Sydney states that she would do anything to protect her father, she is not required to follow through on this vow. If she were, we can be certain her moral conscience would engage and cause her to criticise her decision intensely, in a way that her father never questions his own. Whereas Jack insists that his actions do not affect his fundamentally good character, since every 'morally questionable thing' he has done was 'to protect Sydney' ('Succession', 3:2), Sydney constantly worries about the impact of her actions.

One of the several occasions on which Jack Bristow protects Sydney by participating in a murder is the death of Javier Perez, the man with information about Sydney's work as Julia Thorne. If Javier were to reveal the information he has about Sydney, the government would subject her to dangerous invasive procedures that could permanently harm or perhaps kill her. That said, the threat to Sydney that Javier represents is not imminent. Nevertheless, Jack eliminates the risk he poses by eliminating him. In order to have the opportunity to do so, Jack orchestrates the kidnapping of Lauren and Vaughn as they are on the way to the prison housing Javier. After their release, and after Javier is found hanging dead in his cell, Vaughn realizes what Jack has done. He denounces Jack's actions, threatening that if Jack ever endangers Lauren again, he will kill him. Jack recognises Vaughn's sentiments as familiar, and points out the hypocrisy in Vaughn's position with his retort: 'Then perhaps you finally understand the moral compromises you'll make when someone you love is in danger' ('Prelude', 3:7).

Like Jack Bristow, Bauer fully understands the moral compromises a man will make when his family is in danger. Although impenetrable and invincible in many respects, Bauer has one weakness: his family. Bauer is willing to do whatever the terrorists tell him when they have the leverage of his kidnapped wife and daughter in Season One. He repeatedly deceives the Counter-Terrorist Unit (CTU), and his colleagues, in order to get his family back safely, taking risks in the process that many later blame him for. In the utilitarian view of these men, nothing done in the protection of family can be wrong.

Of course, Jack Bristow and Bauer share characteristics with a long line of revenge tragedy protagonists and action film heroes whose vendettas against villains, criminals and terrorists are launched by actual or threatened harm to their families and a need for justice and vengeance.[4] Historically, audiences have been forgiving of illegal actions against criminals who threaten or harm one's family. Legally, defence of others in imminent peril has long served to justify otherwise criminal acts. Yet Jack Bristow's actions to protect Sydney through covert murders go further than we have been accustomed to accept, and Bauer's choices to save his family members verge on treason and threaten the lives of countless civilians.

For the most part, Bauer's actions when his family is threatened generally fall short of murder, except where there is a direct and proportionate threat of death, and therefore test the boundaries of the excuse of duress. The obvious exception is his killing of Nina Myers, the woman who killed his wife and would have killed his daughter. In that case, however, Jack is exonerated by a television audience comfortable with a tradition of retributive justice for villains like Nina. Jack Bristow's actions, on the other hand, fail the test of duress and even retribution, and are not saved by any existing legal excuse. Instead, the audience sees Sydney struggling with her own ability to excuse her father's actions. The audience is more inclined to forgive Jack than Sydney is, simply because of the strength of our support for Sydney, but support for Jack demands acceptance of actions that push beyond our previously accepted categories of justification and excuse, and move into the purely utilitarian.

THE GOVERNMENT'S MORALITY

In addition to the concern about the moral choices of individuals, another central concern of *Alias* is the morality of the government and governmental agencies. The theme resonates with post-9/11 critiques of the US government and its war on terrorism, but just as *Alias* tapped into a pre-existing development of moral ambiguity, so too did it draw on a growing paranoia about the secret and illicit operations of government. The most obvious example of this development was *The X-Files*, a programme based on the premise that a conspiracy exists to keep the 'truth' (about paranormal events and alien colonisation of earth amongst other truths) hidden from the American people. Many other examples also exist. For example, *The West Wing*'s President Jed Bartlet, a president who is shown weekly to be highly morally reflective, orders the murder of a Qumari diplomat known to be a terrorist and participates in a cover-up of the murder. The audience is willing to believe that this righteous man could order a murder at least in part because it fits well within a tradition of immoral and deceitful popular culture government officials.

In *24*, Bauer's CTU is almost always victim to a spy within; and Season Five takes the corruption in government much further than in the past, showing first the president's aide, Walt Cummings, and then implicating the president himself in supplying terrorists with military-grade nerve gas. Both attempt to justify their actions as being for the good of the country, but in the world of 24 actions can only be justified in two ways: through demonstration that the ends justifiy the means, or through the support of Jack Bauer, who provides the accepted moral perspective for the show.

Alias also explores the question of whether the government itself behaves morally, or even legally. In 'A Higher Echelon' (2:11), we learn about an incredibly invasive communication monitoring system created by the government. As the television screen shows a satellite hovering over the earth, Sydney's voice explains the situation:

> Some people think there's a conspiracy. That the government eavesdrops on everyone. It's no conspiracy. Right now, satellites and ground stations are listening in. Faxes, e-mail communication, phone calls, are all routed to high-speed voice and optical recognition computers. They can analyse words spoken and written in any common language on Earth. The system's called Echelon.

When Will asks the obvious question about the legality of Echelon, concluding that it is a shameless violation of the Constitution, Sydney responds that the National Security Agency claims it is one of its most important weapons against terrorism, and is not an abuse of the system. Given the constant, pervasive presence of terrorism that we see on the series, and the increase in governmental surveillance powers since 9/11, we accept this analysis, believing that the efficacy of Echelon justifies the infringement of privacy rights.

We see the government's use of morally questionable tactics again when it needs the information stored somewhere in Sydney's brain. Lauren's expressed naivety that the government would not force dangerous invasive procedures on its own agents is quickly dismissed by Vaughn, who explains that the government will simply ship Sydney to Moscow and have the procedures performed there ('Prelude'). Indeed, the government extends brutal treatment to Sydney at Camp Williams, torturing her both mentally and physically. When the doctor inflicting this pain tells Sydney that her cellmate is a journalist in the Middle East who would not reveal his source, on the belief that the First Amendment of the Constitution would protect him, we believe him, and believe the government would unlawfully detain such a person.

The foundation for this belief may well be a piece of real-world law often highlighted on the show: the legislative response to 9/11, the USA Patriot Act.[5] With the stated purpose of deterring and punishing terrorism in America and around the world, and 'enhancing law enforcement investigative tools', the Patriot Act allows the government to respond much more forcefully to perceived threats, and to people perceived to be threats. The Patriot Act is both feared and revered in the series, depending on the situation and who it is being used against. Similarly, techniques like the Inferno protocol are also presented as dualities: necessary tools when used by the government, horrific violations when used by terrorists. The Inferno protocol is an interrogation procedure that, we are told, causes cardiac arrest in fifty per cent of its subjects. We are asked to accept its use on Sark as justified, while at the same time provoked into horror when Vaughn is threatened with the same treatment.

As the American government in *Alias* moves towards employing tactics similar to those used by the terrorists, and works with former terrorists when their interests are aligned, the morality of the government's actions are increasingly called into question.[6] However, given the constant reality of terrorism, the means resorted to seem necessary. The series asks us to accept that a war of this nature cannot be fought on the usual terms of engagement; moral lines must soften and bend in order to accommodate the necessary weapons such a battle requires. With the Patriot Act, the law has shifted, and the audience is asked to shift its moral judgement and appreciate the task of the government. While we are at times uncomfortable with the massive power of the governmental agencies and the new slippery morality portrayed in the series, and clearly distressed when the government threatens our heroine, we understand that the complexity of the situation demands a nuanced response, one which may not fit clearly into our established moral justifications.

CONCLUSION

Although the fictional world of *Alias* is unnaturally rife with violence and death, it promotes reflection on a real world of uncertainty and fear. Our sense of right and wrong, in particular, is challenged by the actions and responses of the characters and the government. Sydney offers us the opportunity to question the moral lines we draw: when she queries her own moral choices we not only sympathise, but learn which justifications for illegal and seemingly immoral actions we accept ourselves, and in what contexts. Self-defence is almost glibly presented and accepted, but other situations – such as Sydney's killing of the 'unimportant man' – ask the audience to accept justifications that are not reflected in our historical criminal law. In other words, accepting Sydney as the moral lens on this world means condoning much more utilitarian moral assumptions than our courts (and by extension our society) have accepted in the past.

Sydney's choice in that situation resonates with the image of morality her father offers: a utilitarian view that the ends will justify the means. According to her father's moral code, that rule is never more true than when the end is the protection of family. *24*'s Jack Bauer would stoically agree: both men come from the male heroic tradition in which moral questioning is not an option. Instead, they do what they believe is right, and since their methods are successful, we are led to accept that this brand of morality is acceptable as well. The American government, also, uses this type of reasoning to justify surveillance, intense interrogation techniques and torture.

The complexity and ambiguity surrounding moral decision-making that we see in *Alias* is part of a trend in television. There is no more black and white: all is grey. Heroes are still heroes, but they make choices differently and operate within realities different to those of the heroes of a decade ago. As *Alias* winds down its final season, we are sure to see our heroes presented with more morally complex issues, and they will undoubtedly be forced to make difficult decisions. As we watch their choices, we are presented with an opportunity to pose our own questions about the manner in which their moral world influences and is influenced by ours. Our criminal law tells us that we have historically abhorred some of the choices we now cheer in *Alias*. We have already seen the law change with the introduction of the Patriot Act. As viewers, we are confronted with moral questions that resonate within the many choices that Sydney faces: to what degree does *Alias* show us the future of our societal morality, and to what degree is it simply a reflection of our fears?

9 Reflections of Deleuze
An *Alias*-ed Critique of Truth

Dyrk Ashton

Alias is one of the most fascinating works of visual media, film or television, to come along in quite some time. The series' creators have produced a show that is not only intelligent and entertaining, but on a deeply philosophical level slyly critiques the form of truth itself. *Alias* presents us with a world where we never really know who people are, let alone who's a good guy and who's a bad guy. In *Alias*, who is good and who is bad, or what is true and what is false about any character, event, or organisation, is difficult, if not impossible, to determine, and affiliations, allegiances, motives, names and identities constantly change in a consistently frenetic upheaval of franchise.

The events of 9/11 have shaken our foundations of comfort and security. This can be seen as a wake-up call, forcing us to perceive a different reality of the world where anything can happen at any time. *Alias*, airing in the aftermath of the destruction of the Twin Towers, reflects this new reality. But a world where anything can happen at any time means not just that every moment has potential for bad things to happen, but also the potential for good, for growth, for change, for creativity. The world of *Alias* may be an uncomfortable one of uncertainty and insecurity, but it is not all doom and gloom. It is a world of ever-present possibility where truth can be created and re-created in every successive present moment.

The pre-9/11 television series *The X-Files* presented a world where truth is something that exists, or pre-exists, to be un-earthed or discovered. Hence, the theme appearing in the opening title sequence and in various episodes, 'The Truth is out there'. This kind of truth, Truth with a big 'T', is the traditional form of truth. It is Platonic in nature, assuming ideals, the possibility of Truth and the legitimacy of judgement. Truth of this sort can be thought of as being universal, unequivocal, and for all intents and purposes, fact. Truth with a small 't', on the other hand, can be considered to be local, arguable, a shifting concept where what may be true for one person is not true for another, and what is true in one moment may not be the next. There are certainly deceptions and doubles in *The X-Files*, with the shape-shifting aliens, clones of Mulder's sister, and double identities of certain characters being conspicuous examples, but *The X-Files* gives little pieces of what is assumed to be some transcendental Truth. It is implicit that these pieces will eventually fit together in some overarching whole or greater Truth of what is going to happen; of what the greater plan is. Regardless of the many lies, deceits, wrong turns and cover-ups, *The X-Files* presents a world where there is Truth, and in knowing the Truth about things we can then judge anything contrary to this Truth to be false. We are led to believe that Truth can be found, that we can be certain about things, that we can know who the good guys and who the bad guys are, as well as exactly what they are up to, and in knowing the Truth we will be better off – because we can then do something about it.

Uncertainty leads to feelings of insecurity and makes us uncomfortable, and this is exactly what the world of *Alias* is all about. *Alias* is not preoccupied with a search for truth itself and never assumes that one truth is the Truth. It questions every truth – because it could simply be another falsehood. Unlike *The X-Files*, *Alias* performs a fundamental critique of the idea of Truth, presenting a world where truth is never fixed, reliable, or something pre-existent to be found, but instead is created, questioned and re-created all the time. What is true changes constantly. And if truth changes – if there is no Truth with a big 'T' – then judgement, or the very ability to judge, is also called into question. How many times in the series has Sydney judged the shifty and ever-shifting Sloane, only consistently to be both wrong and right about him at the same time? If she had killed him any of the many times she wanted to, Elena Derevko may have indeed destroyed the world with the Rambaldi device ('Search and Rescue', 'Before the Flood', 4:21 and 22). Each character in the series may at any moment be forced to trust any other with their life, for the moment, with every possibility that they could be wrong, or right, in their instantaneous judgement to trust or not to trust. Good characters do bad things, and bad characters do good things. How are we to judge in such a world, where the very ability to judge may not be possible, and perhaps not even valuable?

What is most interesting regarding *Alias'* critique of Truth is that it is accomplished not only through narrative structures or storyline, and rarely if ever through philosophical statements spouted by a character in dialogue, but on a deeper, metaphorical level through the thematic, recurrent use of doubled images: aliases, doppelgängers, double identities and duplicitous characters, even duplicitous organisations, settings, objects and events.

French philosopher Gilles Deleuze writes in his *Cinema 2: The Time-Image*, that the Second World War brought about a changed perception of the world, particularly as a result of the Holocaust and use of atomic bombs in Japan (Deleuze 1989: xi). The world was suddenly a place where the impossible was possible; the horrific an immediate and very real prospect. The comfortable, secure, commonsense Truth of the world had been called into question. According to Deleuze, there were films that emerged in the late 1940s that conveyed this changed perception, in part, through the presentation of what Deleuze speaks of as 'reflections', which are essentially doubled images (1989: 70). The appearance of doubles in *Alias* can be seen as a sign of similar changes in our perception in the wake of the bombing of the Twin Towers. The world of *Alias* can be read through the cinematic philosophy of Deleuze as a 'proliferation of reflections' – a world of doubled, duplicitous, even multiplicitous, reflected images (Bogue 2003: 122).

Deleuze begins his discussion of reflections with the idea of a character and their reflection in a mirror (1989: 70). Think of this in terms of a shot or a series of shots in a film or on a television screen, where we are presented with two images, one the character, and the other a reflection of the character. These images may also be presented in the same shot, as a doubled image. We are faced with the difficult situation of determining which image is the real character, and which is the reflection. Unless we are given a context where the camera pulls back or there is a cut to a wider shot so we can see the outline of the mirror, we simply cannot tell which is which. Consider that the camera does pull back, or there is a series of cuts to wider shots, but we find ourselves in a hall of mirrors, with reflections upon reflections, extending into infinity. The hall of mirrors itself appears in films such as *Enter the Dragon* (1973) starring Bruce Lee, and Orson Welles' *The Lady from Shanghai* (1948). In these scenes there is no context by which to judge which images are the real characters among all the reflections.

Now, we can extend the idea of mirrored or doubled images and think of one being true and one being false (Deleuze 1989: 274), or any number of what could be called opposites, such as good and bad, friend and enemy, right and wrong.[1] In addition, we can think of the context we would need to be able to judge which images are real and which are reflections as Truth. What if there is no context? What if there is context, but it constantly changes? What if the world is in reality a kind of hall of mirrors, a proliferation of reflections, where we simply cannot definitively discern once and for all between what is real image and what is reflection, what is true and what is false, good and bad, friend and enemy, right and wrong? This is indeed a reality of the world; a nature of the Real, according to Deleuze. And this is the world of *Alias*.

Deleuze scholar Ronald Bogue writes that Deleuze treats the appearance of reflections in films

> in the broadest sense of the term. At times he speaks of actual mirror images in such films, at others of mechanical reproductions of images in photos, films, or video clips. But he also treats paintings and theatrical performances as reflections of objects, extending the notion as well to include simulations, mimings, and the enactment of roles as so many mirror images. Finally, he treats resemblances and correspondences between objects, settings, characters, and actions as reflections – perhaps prismatically distorted, tinted, bleached or clouded, but reflections nonetheless.   (Bogue 2003: 121)

Alias thematically presents us with a multitude of levels of what can be seen as doubles or reflections, from simple double identities and doppelgängers to more complex forms such as duplicitous affiliations and allegiances: Sydney and her father Jack Bristow have been double agents for the CIA and SD-6; SD-6 has a double identity as the already doubled Credit Dauphine/CIA; Jack had a double identity as an aircraft parts exporter and a secret agent; Sydney's mother had a double identity as devoted wife Laura Bristow and Soviet agent Irina Derevko; Sydney was also Julia Thorne; Vaughn's wife Lauren Reed was a double agent for the Covenant; Lauren literally doubled Sydney to steal information from the CIA; agent Jim Lennox (played by Ethan Hawke) and Francie were doubled via Project Helix; Sydney is doubled by her arch-enemy Anna Espinosa in a similar process; Sloane is doubled by 'Another Mister Sloane' (4:16), which is yet another kind of doubling – not of body, likeness or name – but of the mind.

The episode 'Conscious' (3:9), when Sydney actually doubles her-self, provides a particularly interesting example of not only doubling but also the indiscernibility of true and false that can be seen in reflected images. Season Three began with Sydney having lost her memory of the previous two years. In 'Conscious', she sub-mits herself to an experimental procedure in the hopes of retrieving these lost memories. She lies on a medical table and is put into a lucid dream state. In these scenes, Sydney is doubled on multiple levels. First, we see Sydney lying on the table, but we also see her walking around in her dream, dressed in white. There is an image of her on the table, and there is an image of her in the dream. But which is the real or true Sydney? Common sense dictates that she cannot be in both places, so we might say that one image is her body on the table and the other her mind; that her body is the true image of Syd-ney, and the image in the dream her false image, or a reflection of her mind. But can we really separate them so easily? Isn't each image just as much Sydney, just as true, as the other?

In the dream, Sydney comes face to face with an image of Lauren Reed. Even in the real world of *Alias*, outside the dream, Lauren can be seen as a double or reflection of Sydney, a darker version of Syd-ney, on a number of levels (for example, Lauren works with the CIA while being a secret agent for the Covenant, just as Sydney was an agent for SD-6 while being a secret agent for the CIA). The doctor who has induced Sydney's dream state comments that the image of Lauren is not necessarily a memory of Lauren, but stands in for another image that Sydney has not yet faced – which turns out to be another image of Sydney herself. The image of Lauren here is then a reflection or double of Sydney on two levels – she is both a double of the Sydney we see, and of the Sydney that we will see, at the same time. The various reflections of Sydney proliferate further when Lauren becomes another Sydney, dressed in black.

Faced with these two Sydneys in the dream, we might immedi-ately assume that the first one introduced, Sydney-in-white, is the real, original or true Sydney (though there is still the Sydney lying on the table), and the second, Sydney-in-black, is a copy, or false Sydney – much like we might assume that first there is a person and then there is a reflection of that person in a mirror. In addition, putting one Sydney in white and the other in black represents the traditional signs for good and evil, so we may be led immediately to believe that the true Sydney-in-white is good, and the false

Sydney-in-black is bad. This belief is further supported when Sydney-in-black opposes Sydney-in-white, fights her, even tries to kill her. Now, we may also assume that Sydney-in-white is right, doing the right thing, in trying to find her lost memories, and that conversely Sydney-in-black is wrong, and perhaps even think of Sydney-in-white as friend and Sydney-in-black as enemy. We come to find out, however, that Sydney-in-black is indeed a true Sydney, and is trying to protect Sydney-in-white from the events that Sydney herself purposely had erased from memory. This does not turn the tables, however, making Sydney-in-white false, wrong, bad, or enemy, and Sydney-in-black the opposite, but presents us with a situation where each image of Sydney is both true and false, right and wrong, good and bad, friend and enemy. This doubled image stands in as a strong metaphor for the indiscernibility of the true and the false in a Deleuzian sense.

The implications of seeing the world as a proliferation of reflections to the traditional form of Truth can be quite profound. For Deleuze, the appearance of doubled images, or 'reflections', can stand in for the appearance of the actual and the virtual, the past and the present, the true and the false, as well as the good and the bad. In our normal, everyday world, we must have either one or the other of any of these dualities – something cannot be both actual and virtual, past and present, true and false, good and bad – that just doesn't make sense. But in doubled images in film, Deleuze says that we have the opportunity to see both at the same time. According to Deleuze, in the world of the Real, in reality, we never have just one or the other of any of these, but both at the same time, in every image, in every present moment. But how can that be?

To explore this concept more fully, we must look into the relationship between the form of truth and the form of time. According to Deleuze (and many other philosophers throughout history, including St Augustine, Kant, Hegel, Liebniz and Nietzsche), the conception of any kind of truth is intrinsically tied to a conception of the form of time. The traditional idea of Truth requires that there be a consistency, an ideal, a whole, to the world. The Truth pre-exists to be discovered and revealed through a linear progression of time. The form of time, then, must be a consistent, unbroken line that runs through and connects everything. The present is current, now, and is merely a point that moves at a constant and consistent pace along the line of time. This movement of the present is measured chronologically, by calculated ticks of a clock, or the movement of the Earth as it rotates in space. This is a traditional, commonsense, everyday conception of time, and it provides us with a context for our everyday lives much as Truth does. It is also the nice curvilinear, chronolinear form of time understood and espoused by Friedrich Hegel and Karl Marx, both being terrifically influential on Western thought and society to this day, where the line of time is a picture of eternity, static, and we simply move along it in a dialectical unfolding of the Ideal.[2]

Now, in this form of time, as time moves on, the present becomes the past as we head into the future. But there is another important aspect to this that must be considered. For Deleuze, the present is 'actual', and the past is entirely 'virtual' (and the past exists only as memory, so memory is also virtual) (Bogue 2003: 116–19). The actual is what we can recognise, name, make use of in the present moment, and the virtual here must be understood as not a fake, copy, or simulation (such as in 'virtual reality'), but as potential and possibility. If time is linear, then our existence proceeds from virtual past to actual present to virtual future, with each moving present moment actualising the virtual past through memory (calling up the past, our memories, so we know where and who we are right now and can recognise things around us) and proceeding to the future. The virtual and actual follow each other in a logical progression, just like the present and past. Consider the discovery of electricity. In a linear progression of time, electrical energy existed first as a virtuality for humankind. It had potential to be actualised, or discovered, named and put to use. Once this happened, it became no longer virtual, but actual. The same can be said of the inventions of Milo Rambaldi in *Alias*. They existed as virtual, as potential, until discovered, deciphered, constructed and used, becoming then actualised.

Now, the revealing of the true and the false, and the good and the bad, can be thought of as proceeding along the line of time in the same way. At any one time, or present moment, something is either true or false, good or bad, and through time we can know whether something, or someone, is one or the other. This is the fundamental structure of the world presented by *The X-Files*.

Deleuze, however, challenges us to consider the question – what if time is not linear and chronological? What then happens to Truth? Drawing upon French philosopher Henri Bergson, Deleuze claims that time is indeed not chrono-linear at all. For Deleuze, time itself is simply change, and exists as coinciding (doubled) past and present in every moment. This is Bergson's 'originary' form of time (Deleuze 1989: 81–2, 98, 271).[3]

At its fundamental level, Bergson's (and Deleuze's) logic is that we cannot measure the present moment – not because it is so infinitesimally small, but because it is simply immeasurable. There is no point we can look at or calculate and say 'that's it, that's the present'. Once we try to fix it, capture it, it is not gone, but has become wrapped up and carried along as past in another present moment in a constant process of change. There cannot be a point where the present ends and past begins, or where the present ends and the future begins. Therefore, the past must co-exist with the present or be simultaneous with the present. The distinction between the two is indiscernible, we cannot tell which is which. What we have, then, is really a continual past-present. The past is not behind us or fixed, as we normally think it to be, but exists only in every present moment, as memory.[4]

What, you may ask, does the originary form of time have to do with truth, doubles or reflections? If past and present co-exist, then everything, including ourselves, is doubled at every moment. There is, in every present moment, both a past me and a present me, doubled, co-existing or mutual. Everything we see, everything we are, has two sides, past and present, and each one reflects the other. This is presented most clearly in *Alias* in 'Conscious', where Sydney is shown to co-exist as both actual/present self and virtual/past memory of self. Second, if Bergson's originary form of time is the Real form of time, then chrono-linear time is entirely imaginary, merely an idea that we cling to in order to make sense of the world and of our lives; to provide ourselves with a grounding for where, when, and who we are in time, and with commonsense relationships between past, present and future moments or events. Third, if the past is virtual and the present actual, and past and present co-exist in every present moment, then everything must be both actual and virtual in every present moment as well. And if everything has a virtual quality, contains virtuality, then everything, in every present moment, has potential and possibility. Anything and everything contains in every moment the potential to be either true or false, good or bad – and this describes entirely the world of *Alias*. There is no consistent, buried Truth waiting to be un-earthed. The traditional form of Truth, like the chrono-linear form of time, is imaginary, because the only universal Truth (and the universal Truth of *Alias*) is that everything changes.

With the form of originary time, truth can only be re-created in every present moment through memory and present thought (including thoughts of the future). We cannot rely or count on Truth, or on the past. This is not terrible, however. For Deleuze, it is an opportunity to change the world at any time, in any moment, for the better. We simply do not have to be slaves to the past – it can be undone at any moment (Deleuze 1989: 274). This way of seeing the world is not as comfortable, not as secure, but it opens life and thought to multiple possibilities from which linear time, habit, common sense and a belief in Truth close us off. Truth in the traditional sense is static, fixed, resisting change, whereas truth as it emerges through originary time promotes, causes and allows for change – change for the bad, perhaps, but also for the good.

The appearance of reflections in films or television shows can be seen to have the ability to give us, if not a conscious comprehension of the Real forms of time and truth, at least an intuition of it, a sense or feeling of it, if we are receptive to it. This experience can be disturbing, different, strange, although we may not know why. To be presented with two images of the same person (such as two Sydneys) can be uncomfortable as we commonsensically, habitually, try to determine which is the real one and which is not – because they both cannot exist at the same time – not in our everyday, common-sense world, anyway. Yet, through Deleuze, this can be thought of as how everything exists all the time. Sydney Bristow lives in a world that is not comfortable, not secure, a different reality – but this can be seen, from a Deleuzian point of view, to be closer to the Real world than the one we construct for ourselves to live in every day.

Even in the traditional conception of Truth, where it can be revealed in the linear progression of time, we know that things can change in the future. Once things become past, however, we think of them as being fixed, and past events as having revealed truth. But the past is only memory. Memory can be faulty, or even erased as in Sydney's case, and we have all seen that what we may have thought of past events as being true can indeed be proven false. This is a consistent theme in *Alias*. The past is virtual, has potential for being both true and false. Therefore we cannot (and probably should not) count on the past to determine even present events, let alone the future – in part because this virtual past co-exists in every present moment, as a virtual side to every actual present instant. But only in seeing or being aware of this virtuality in everything in every moment can we deal effectively with the reality of the world. This is exactly what most of the characters in *Alias* do. Sydney in particular has come to realise this reality of the world, and does the best she can to deal with it, as difficult or painful as it may be.

On a basic level, the term 'alias' itself embodies the idea of a doubling as well as the indiscernibility between true and false. An alias is commonly thought of as something, usually a name, that is false or fake. It is also, however, synonymous with 'other name'. The Latin *alias dictus* translates to 'otherwise called'. When Sidney Bristow assumes an alias she doubles herself. She is both a true Sydney and a false Sydney, both a true image and a false image at the same time. When we as viewers see Sydney using an alias, we see a doubled image. The truth is not that she is Sydney posing as someone else, with a false identity, but that she is both. An important element to this is that an alias, a false name, can be by definition equally as legitimate, as useful, as true, even as good, as any other name. When Sydney assumes an alias, she does so because it is useful and with good intentions. In Nietzschean terms, the use of an alias in this manner can be seen as having the 'power of the false' (Deleuze 1989: 132), releasing the false as a creative mode of living life and surviving in the world that is equally, if not more, legitimate than living the true.

When faced with aliases, the characters in the story most often do not know that the person is posing as someone else. We as the viewers know when Sidney or Vaughn are using aliases, but does it really matter? In the case of Vaughn, for four seasons we thought we knew the real Vaughn from the alias Vaughn, but we did not (as revealed in 'Before the Flood'). And neither did Sydney. We only knew one name from an 'other' name. There was yet another identity for Vaughn – but is the alias Vaughn any less legitimate, true, or real than his birth name, especially to Sydney? What is real and what is not, true and false, right and wrong, is in this case not only indiscernible, but ambiguous. In finding out Vaughn's birth name, have we discovered Truth, or have we simply been given an 'other' name by which to know Vaughn? We may get a fuller picture of Vaughn as the series progresses, but does any one truth outweigh any other? We may get the feeling that we discover the final Truth about Sloane, or Irina Derevko, but do we ever really know the full, whole, complete, final and fixed Truth about them, other than that they have all along been simply paradoxical figures? Is there any such thing as final Truth? And does it really matter? Why search for pre-existing Truth, when creative falsehood can be more valuable to survival for the good guys as well as the bad guys in their ongoing everyday existence and anything we may think is true, even believe to be true, can be proven false at any time? These are some of the questions that the philosophy of *Alias* poses. *Alias*, however, does not espouse a nihilistic existentialism, but posits the possibility of a creative outpouring of life.

The search for the Rambaldi artefact in *Alias* and the emphasis on prophecy and fate do not disclose a belief in a fundamental teleological metaphysics of the world (as *The X-Files* does), but appear in *Alias* in purposeful juxtaposition to a philosophical foundation of the celebration of free will and creative falsehood. Though each episode and season are ultimately subsumed by commonsense coordinates of time and space, the series constantly and on many levels critiques this view of the world. In *Alias* we get a sense that to defeat evil or 'make the world safe . . . for the people you love', as Sydney puts it ('Solo', 5:6) is perhaps not even possible, but is something that we must strive for at all costs, regardless of our own comfort. Sydney claims that to do this we must understand that we have no choice in the matter ('Solo'). But we always have a choice, and Sydney knows it, no matter what she may say at the moment to help herself or others to cope with a difficult situation.

Alias may present a world of constant, even chaotic change, where the earth shifts beneath our feet and our moorings are loosed – much like what we experienced with the attack on the Twin Towers – but in *Alias* this condition brings about a world where the characters survive through constant creativity, a creation of truth in every present moment, and the willingness to see the world as it is, as uncomfortable and even dangerous as that may be. They see the virtual potential for the true and false and good and bad in every moment, in every person, situation or event. And they are willing to do something about it, through a Nietzschean creative invention and generosity – in their self-sacrifice, their taking-on of the burden of the Real, protecting the world, and trying to make it a better place. They know that they may not succeed, but they accept that this is what they must do, this is how they must live, in a world where there is no Truth, but multiple truths, constantly re-created, each as legitimate as the other, in every moment of their lives. *Alias* is a testament to the belief that nothing is determined, that we have choices to make, that free will exists, that our lives can be re-made in every moment, and we do not have to be weighed down by the past or by what has happened before us or to us. The series not only poses questions and critiques Truth, but also presents a possible manner in which to live life in an unstable, insecure, post-9/11 world.

Part Four

AUTHORIZED PERSONNEL/ UNAUTHORIZED PERSONNEL

Alias and Beyond

10 Accusatory Glances
The Evolution and Dissolution of the *Alias* Fandom in Narrative History

Hillary Robson

> *Alias* has brought me some of the best friends I've ever had, so I will always love it for that. And part of me will always love Sydney Bristow, fierce and damaged and brilliant with her dyed red hair and yearning for normal. (Thorne 2006)

As series creator J.J. Abrams stated in a March 2006 article in *Entertainment Weekly*, 'despite a premise that seemed to have mass appeal, *Alias* was probably not a mainstream show' (quoted in Jensen 2006: 18) Abrams' comments are not unwarranted: *Alias* never did reach a wider audience than an average of 10 million regular viewers in the USA and Canada, even after DVD releases and syndication on the TNT network. But it did manage to gather a group of dedicated, appointment-viewing fans who spent time discussing the series on message boards, building fansites, and purchasing official merchandise, including DVD box sets, t-shirts, video games and trading cards. These fans formed an interconnected network of *Alias* devotees, freely giving their time and money in support of a series that would eventually provide five seasons of exhilarating storytelling. Beyond this, *Alias* fans, while sharing similarity in the scope of typical fandom behaviours, are unique in the rapidity with which they developed, aided by the internet, into a fan community based on intense discourse and creative endeavours.

Today, the internet plays an indispensable role for fans, allowing them to discuss, research, interpret, and promote their fandoms around the globe. In 2001, the initial development of the *Alias* fandom relied heavily on the power of the internet. From the first season, ABC, Touchstone and Bad Robot Productions used the web to help ensure its success, introducing a host of 'pseudo' websites, such as Creditdauphine.com and an interactive chat applet 'game' that fabricated a secretive dead drop environment for fans. Such official online components integrated seamlessly with the highly technological elements of the show: Sydney's spy gadgets, for example, relied on fantastic cutting-edge (or even non-existent) technology. The online visibility inspired fans to create their own reverential websites, which, in turn, aided the producers in furthering (and securing) a strong fanbase. The internet remained the primary source of engagement and expression of fandom experiences for *Alias* throughout the series' run, providing a location for active discussion within the fan community, primarily through websites, blogs and discussion boards.

ALIAS FANSITES AND DISCUSSION BOARDS

Discussion fansites and boards launched soon after the pilot episode for fans to discuss Sydney Bristow's adventures as a double agent beyond the ABC-sanctioned official forums. While ABC's official site offered plot and character synopses, fansites provided more comprehensive indices for the more discerning *Alias* fans, with unofficial episode transcripts, music references, notes on geographic locations, recurring themes, and screenshots from previously aired episodes. The SD-6.com fansite was one of the first content-comprehensive sites, providing series information, airdates, character guides and the SD-1.net message boards. The latter has been a localised source for fan engagement since the fall of 2001, a cyberspace where fans gathered to discuss previously aired and upcoming episodes, spoilers and casting news, as well as to post fan fiction and art. Though not the only *Alias* fansite to publish fan works, SD-1.net was the first to allow fans to post their stories without the approval of site owners in an open forum, allowing for 'feedback' from other fans; it consistently received the largest number of postings and became the preferred site for 'newbies' publishing their first stories, finding beta readers (editors for their writing), and forming friendships.

When the series' popularity exploded in the middle of Season One, a proliferation of *Alias*-themed websites hit the net. A great number of these sites were free, courtesy of Geocities or other free hosting providers, yet as web traffic exceeded free bandwidth limits, site owners were forced to either purchase domains or to close down their sites. The longevity of fansites was also affected by a natural process of attrition; individual enthusiasms for the series that drove the creation of websites waned, diminished by the time and effort required to maintain a quality site. Popular fansites SD-6.com, Alias-TV.com, and Have-Dog-Alias.com juggled these demands by providing specialised content such as episode synopses, character dossiers, fan fiction and art.

It was not until the second season that the pre-eminent fansite, Alias-Media.com, launched, providing fans with a fully *Alias*-based venue that offered comprehensive news, screen captures and links about the series maintained by site visitors and owner Gertie Beth. As a testimony to visitor popularity, by April 2006 the site had logged over 78 million page views since its launch in the fall of 2002 (Alias-Media.com). Based upon the level of professionalism reflected in site design and constant maintenance, Alias-Media.com was different from the fansites of Season One, providing visitors with a one-stop-shop for all the *Alias* content that they could ever hope for.

Many fans indicate that their first foray into the *Alias* fandom was facilitated by the website TelevisionWithoutPity.com (TWOP), where there were both episode reviews and discussion boards. One fan, Lauren, recalls stumbling on to the *Alias* forums at TWOP and how it helped her to form lasting friendships with other *Alias* fans:

> I remember thinking how smart and careful everyone seemed to be in their analysis of the show. I managed to find a group of girls that were around my age that decided to talk on instant messenger about the show. We started having almost nightly chats and while we did talk about *Alias* or television a lot, we also talked about other things that were going on in our real lives.   (Lauren 2004)

Lauren's experience is similar to that of many *Alias* fans: compelled by interest generated by the show itself, they turned to the internet to obtain additional information about the series. Many of those fans visited the popular websites and their message boards when the official news channels dried up due to the lack of regular maintenance of the ABC official sites during the summer hiatus. Judging by the fan experiences collected for this chapter, the interaction with and between *Alias* enthusiasts and the friendships between those fans are the primary reason they have remained so invested in the fandom. The role of community is a common trend for fan scholar researchers and communication theorists, where these interactions are considered important elements of participatory culture.

A fan community, as Matt Hills explains in *Fan Cultures*, 'rather than merely imagining itself as coexistent in empty clocked time, constitutes itself precisely through a common affective engagement' (2002: 180). In a discussion of the changes in fan behaviours with Hills, *Textual Poachers'* author Henry Jenkins suggests that fans have 'created a media culture that is in some degree more responsive to their interests than it was previously and where the walls between the amateur and the commercial are more permeable than they were before' (quoted in Hills 2001). Fans of *Alias* are not far removed in their community structure from other television fandoms like those of *Buffy the Vampire Slayer* and *The X-Files*. Discussion, interpretation and derivative creative work are key components in building strong – and lasting – fanbases. Jenkins believes that while fan behaviours evolved out of audience appreciation and a need to engage with the text, '[Fans] have actually created models for alternative story-telling that have fed back in a variety of ways to the commercially available text which has had to respond to their fantasies in order to stay on the air' (quoted in Hills 2001).

This view contradicts communication theorist Jan Fernbeck's insistence that online collectives, composed of 'self-seeking individuals who join together to augment individual good' (1997: 45), have contributed to the 'decline of public life'; an idea further expanded upon by Steve Jones: 'Being a part of an online community may give us a sense of connectedness, but it is an aimless connectedness, a kind which reassures that between "us" and "them" there may be some common ground after all' (1994a: 17). This idea of the 'common ground' that an online environment can create is one that is both inviting and intoxicating to fans: as their enthusiasm for the source text grows, their relationships with like-minded individuals within their community deepen, with positive side effects for the series' popularity, longevity and commercial success. The spectrum of theoretical views about fans as cultural producers and the legitimacy of the online community converge and reflect the difficulty in defining their social role in indisputable terms. Hills' concept of 'common affective engagement' is similar to Fernbeck's, and both reflect that fandom begins as a singular experience. Friendships and a social network form around the production of derivative works from the source text that Jenkins defines as the fan's primary mode of textual preservation. While most fan communities begin with the optimistic hope of serving the greater good, many invariably suffer from the effects of individual posturing and uneven social stratification.

THE VARTAN HOS AND THE SAFE HOUSE

The Vartan Hos are some of the most prolific and influential women in the *Alias* fandom, not only because of their three-year advocacy for the series, but also because of their support and collective adoration for actor Michael Vartan. The group of women met and began discussing the series on the now-closed *The X-Files* (*XF*) fansite, The Haven for The FBI's Most Unwanted, often referred to as simply 'Haven'. Haven was mostly frequented by the female fans of actor David Duchovny, offering series news, spoilers, links to fan communities, fan fiction, fan art, episode transcripts, actor news, and charity events, as well as an extensive discussion board network. Souris, one of the original members of the Vartan Hos, discusses the feelings of a new fan coming into *Alias* after long-term involvement in *XF* community: 'All of us were pretty disenchanted with *XF* at the time we started watching *Alias*, and since they happened to air opposite each other at the time, there was an even greater connection. For me, getting into *Alias* fandom helped lessen the sting somewhat of the disenchantment with *XF*.' The women, who would eventually name themselves the Vartan Hos, met on the Haven message boards in a subsection titled 'Other Shows', where they discussed the new ABC spy drama and actor Vartan. The group earned their name when a fellow poster, Kate, passed around a 'Vartan Ho' Questionnaire and signed it 'Vartan Ho #1' on the Haven boards (Ho Questions).

Once named, the group started to make plans to build a website for discussion and a fanlisting for fellow 'Hos'. The community-building process mirrored that of many fan communities, yet the Vartan Hos intentionally structured their website after that of the *The X-Files*. The original group agreed the site needed to be 'unique from other Vartan or *Alias* web pages ... with [the] intent to positively promote Michael Vartan' ('Mission Statement'). Souris discusses the creative energy that abounded during the first season of *Alias*: 'There was a lot of excitement, and a sense of creation and togetherness in the fandom as a whole. A sense of discovery. I had faith that the show would be rewarding.'

'The Safe House' (www.vartanho.com) opened on 25 April 2002 and immediately became a fan favourite. From day one, the Vartan Hos set themselves apart as no hero-worshippers of ABC, Touchstone or Bad Robot; instead, they used their influence as a powerful site to comment critically on the direction of the series. The Vartan Hos' online visibility, the quality of content, and frequency of updates made The Safe House a place that fans trusted for information and authority. In the 'Editorials' section the Vartan Hos dished on a variety of subjects, from *Alias* fashion to blunders (in a subsection called 'Run by Monkeys?'). The acerbic wit of the Vartan Hos would serve as the authoritative 'voice' of *Alias* fans through the third season. In addition, the site offered Sydney and Vaughn (S/V)-centric artwork, videos, and fan fiction created by fellow Vartan Hos, along with profiles of the original nine members, the characters of *Alias* and a fanlisting. It also included a comprehensive history of the site's founders, with excerpts from the Haven message boards and Yahoo instant messenger chat transcripts, along with a catalogue, by category, of *Alias* and Michael Vartan websites.

Within its first few weeks, The Safe House experienced visitor traffic of around 200 hits per hour. The opening of the site coincided closely with the Season One finale, and *Alias* fans, starved for information, found the site a reliable source for *Alias* spoilers and information about Vartan, as well as referrals to fan-created fiction, videos, and art. One fan, Amy, in a posting called 'Fan fic and Me'(2004), discusses finding fan fiction through the site:

> I'm not sure when I found fanfic – I think it was right after The Safe House launched. I was just peeking through links and found the fanfic linked there. It was all S/V, all the time, so it was like this epiphany and gold mine all in one! There were other people who wanted to see them together! And they wrote it!

The visibility and popularity of The Safe House helped to usher in more fans to the *Alias* fandom, either by proxy interest in Vartan or thanks to the comprehensive *Alias*-themed content the site provided. At around the time of the first anniversary of the site in April 2003, it saw regular over-usages of bandwidth, and by January 2006 the Vartan Hos had spent over $700 on web-hosting alone and dedicated several hours per day to site maintenance and updates. While this figure is relatively standard for four years of web hosting, all funding came from the Vartan Hos running the site: they have never requested visitor contributions to help with expenses. Money has never been a motivating factor, and their mission statement clarifies the reason that they started the site in a section of the 'Mission Statement' entitled 'Why We Are Here':

> For you. For us. For all the hours we spend talking about Michael and having fun. For the past two years, the Vartan Hos have gotten together on a *daily* basis simply to talk about Michael, his projects and our lives. We are a group of gals who knew *nothing* about each other and came together for a common goal: admiring Michael Vartan.

In 2003 the Vartan Hos hosted a question and answer forum for visitors, taking queries about site design, personal involvement, their love for Vartan, and the series. While they attributed their initial interest in creating the site as directly relative to *Alias* viewing, Kate reveals: 'Watching *Alias* is really the *least* time-extensive *Alias*-related thing I do. The site takes up a lot. Between coding for various sections, reading all of the mail from the site, mail from the VHo Group, and just our own personal mail . . . An hour can fly by in a heartbeat.' The other webmistresses also confess to spending more time on the website than watching and re-watching *Alias* episodes, and some, including Souris, state that their main reason for re-watching episodes – so they could write the editorials, such as 'Fashion Assassin' and the 'VSR (Vaughn/Sydney Relationship) Report' – are directly site related. Others, such as SB, confess they spent around twenty hours a week involved with *Alias*-themed content, not specifying whether or not that time included website maintenance. Out of the seven Vartan Hos who responded, most attributed the majority of their time spent on seeking or developing website content and site maintenance (in the 'Ho Questions' section).

When asked if it was worth it, the women collectively answered 'yes' – but not for their love of fandom or Vartan. Instead, the most important, positive benefit from participating in The Safe House was the friendships they had formed. Their Q&A concluded with an open 'thank you' to ABC, the cast of *Alias*, ABCMedianet.com for images, then Regina, recap writer for *Alias* on Television Without Pity, the Vartan Hos on the 'V-ho' chat system, and Michael Vartan for the 'inspiration'. These reflections confirm that the building and maintenance of fansites take more than a generalised interest in the series: they take a level of commitment and emotional involvement with other fans.

A 1998 study of fans for the series *Sentinel* conducted by Victor Costello reflected that sixty-five per cent of participants within the fandom were women, a constant in most contemporary research studies on participatory fan culture with the internet as the basis for the community environment (1998: 19). The *Alias* fandom has been consistently dominated by women (although several fansites – such as SD-6.net and ProjectAlias.com – were owned and maintained by male fans). Yet it seems that the community structure and the social hierarchy of the *Alias* fandom were formed by women, with the Vartan Hos as a key example of just how that process was completed. By creating a website complete with a listing for fans to publicly proclaim their status as Vartan Hos, a dedicated chat group for intergroup mailings, and a comprehensive index of relevant *Alias* fansites (rated from best to worst), even the new fan could find enough information to gain a footing within the community. In addition, from the first day the site opened, the Vartan Hos prided themselves on their emotional investment in Vartan and *Alias* but retained the right to revoke their emotional ties to either at any time.

That moment arrived during Season Three in February 2004, when The Safe House announced the discontinuation of updated *Alias* content in response to the creative direction of the series, with 'We no longer like or enjoy *Alias*. We think the show now, in a word, sucks. Therefore, we have decided to cut back drastically on the amount of *Alias*-related content that we add to this site. We want to concentrate our time and energies on content that is more strictly related to Michael Vartan'. The statement, entitled 'A Note About the *Alias* Content on This Site' reflects how declining enjoyment in the series affected their level of fan engagement:

> We know that this may upset or anger some visitors, but it is the right thing to do *for us*. We no longer get any joy from *Alias*, so there is little reason to keep spending so much time and energy on the show. It only leaves a nasty taste in our mouths and a feeling of pointlessness. Where once we felt affection for the show, we now feel anger, bitterness or, at best, apathy and indifference.

This disenchantment was perhaps amplified by the frustration many of the women had once felt with *The X-Files*, but instead of becoming consumed by frustration, the women intentionally distanced themselves from *Alias*. While other fans were feeling the same frustrations, the Vartan Hos, acting as the outspoken fan voice, used their position and influence as key figures to reflect their disappointment with the series. The women took a stance against *Alias* while maintaining the status quo with the fandom itself by preserving the links to other fansites, moderating updates of *Alias*-related content (but only when involving Vartan), and maintaining previous site content in an archive.

Currently, three of the original nine Vartan Hos (Souris, Lugia and Mel TM) still run and maintain The Safe House. At the time of writing (mid-way through the fifth and final season), judging by jumps in visitor hits on 'big news days' for *Alias* – news that included Vartan's return to the series for the finale – the site still maintained a fairly constant flow of *Alias*-related traffic.

While the Vartan Hos are an exception to the fansite rule – most fansite owners do not dare to speak out against their source fandom in the way the Vartan Hos have since day one – they are remarkable because of the way they helped in the structuring process of the community while simultaneously projecting the influence of *The X-Files* and its fandom on their thoughts and opinions in regard to *Alias*. As most of the women will attest, they were never well-known within the *XF* community; their voices went unheard and unnoticed, and so it became an almost natural crusade for them to use the power and influence they created within the *Alias* fandom to make their voices heard, regardless of consequence. And despite their outspoken nature, The Safe House played an important role in the creation and direction of *Alias* fandom community; its founders are arguably the most important women in their capacity to influence, inspire and structure other women within the *Alias* online community.

FANFICTION.NET, CREDIT DAUPHINE, SERVER 5, DIARY-X AND LIVEJOURNAL: *ALIAS* FAN FICTION WRITERS.

As early as a month into the series, *Alias* fans were writing and posting fan fiction to the free archive site Fanfiction.net. This practice emerged fairly early compared to other fandoms. As Kurt Lancaster's compelling research into the fan as 'textual performer' shows, fans 'try to capture – through participation and immersion – the original cathartic moment felt during the first viewing of the text' (2001: 155). Lancaster's approach, inspired by reader responses, takes fans as the active 'readers' of the text and sees creative outputs as the direct reflection of that reading and interpretative process that is in turn performative. An excellent example of the interpretive/creative dimension of the fan experience is the writing of fan fiction. Fan fiction is, as the term implies, a fictional interpretation, based on the reading response of the fan, that proposes to illustrate the internal motivations of a character or to describe an unseen moment in the course of a film or television episode. The source text acts as foundation for these derivative creative functions, further fostering (and exemplifying) the depth of the relationship with the fan and the text.

The early stories written by and for *Alias* fans seems to reinforce trends found in other fandoms, partially due to their familiarity with writing fan fiction as a form of textual interaction and knowing where and how to post their stories online for reader access. Within months of the series launch, the first specialised archive, 'Credit Dauphine', opened its doors with the intent of recommending quality stories and acting as a general archive and writing resource. Within two months of the pilot episode, a very young but active and creative community was writing fan fiction about the show. By January of 2002, roughly fifty fan fictions had been posted at Fanfiction.net and Credit Dauphine (not to mention the countless 'drabbles' – shorter fictions of 100 words or less – posted at the SD-1.net message boards).

As the early months of 2002 stretched on, a definite division formed between 'serious' fan fiction writers – those who wanted to build a writing community, employ editing/beta reading practices, and recommend quality works of fiction to other users – and those who just wanted to express themselves creatively without being concerned about the overall quality of their writing. This separation led to an offshoot of the *Alias* fan fiction community: the writers that valued critical feedback from their peers diverged from the popular SD-1.net message boards and formed their own message board community, Server 5. To further build community – and reflect their recommendations and favourite fellow authors – they developed online blogs at Diary-X, a now-defunct free blogging community. By the winter hiatus and holidays, fan fiction was being written with greater regularity, the Server-5 discussion boards opened, and social hierarchy began to form. One fan, Vilandra, shares her thoughts about these early days of the *Alias* fandom, 'I was reading amazing fiction by amazing authors, loving an incredible show, and just feeling inspired as all hell. I started writing the first (and only) fiction I've ever posted to the net. . . . Writing that was such a fun, amazing experience' (2004). Many fans found that reading inspired their own writing, as Lauren explains: 'I read some *Alias* stuff, which was just beautifully and creatively written and I started getting inspired. I was actually so moved by the characters and the storylines on the show that I found I didn't want the story to end after an hour every week' (2004). Lauren's and Vilandra's experiences mirror those of countless other *Alias* fan fiction readers and writers.

Beyond message boards and fansites, the fan fiction community that formed and built over the first three seasons of the show was comprised of some of the most tight-knit activists within the entire *Alias* fandom and was the first truly organised community experience. Many were first inspired to write their own fiction after reading, and all were acutely aware of 'community'. Amy (2004) shares how she became indoctrinated into the fan fiction community of *Alias*, which she facilitated by peripherally participating in order to learn the social structure:

> My participation in and knowledge of fandom increased – Who's who, the different factions, how to behave etc. – As I started to understand the dynamics of community and of fanfic, I thought I'd try my hand at writing something. Just really to see if I could. I'd never done any creative writing, and I thought it would be interesting to play with it.

By midwinter 2002, the Server 5 message board had well over 100 members and was a location for writers to make recommendations on what they were reading, refer information about writing resources, or form relationships with potential readers or betas. It was on this site that the first, and only, fan fiction awards, The Festival o' Fic, was conceived. *Alias* fanfic writer, Labyrinthine (2004), discusses the importance of fan fiction awards in writing communities:

> A lot of it goes back to validation – for those in the 'real world' who are not involved in fan fiction – most people scoff at the very notion of spending time writing stories that center about TV characters. I

know many people in the fandom who keep their online activities under wraps from their real life family and friends

The Festival o' Fic was held for three years: two hosted by the Credit Dauphine archive and the third by an independent site. Stories were nominated by readers and went through a multi-step judging process. As Labyrinthine suggests, the awards were part of the validation process with which fan fiction writers often grapple: while they want recognition for their hard work and dedication, they do not want to risk the exposure and humiliation of misunderstanding from outsiders. As a tip of the hat to the 'best' writers within the fandom, the awards also serve as another form of hierarchical social networking.

As the best-known writers in the fandom – that is, those that made the recommendations for fiction that were heeded by site visitors, those that posted the most prolifically, won awards and writing challenges and the like – gained popularity on message boards and Diary-X, the fandom exploded. In the run up to the third season, Credit Dauphine was receiving between 6,000 and 10,000 hits per day. The fan fiction community, and fandom as a whole, was reaching a critical mass: as more and more people wrote fan fiction, more divisions appeared within the social structuring and hierarchies within the communities. Long-running archives closed, and message boards buckled under the strain of constant postings. Credit Dauphine finally closed before the third season launched, primarily due to the amplified cost – both financial and personal – of site maintenance.

The third season seemed to mark a shift in the production of fan writings and fan art – presumably in direct response to the creative direction. Sydney's missing two years, Vaughn's marriage to Lauren, and the convoluted plot points of Sydney's life as Julia Thorne, resulted in a decreased need for the interpretive role of fan fiction. Since fan fiction's subject matter often revolves around interpreting unanswered, unseen plot points, or exploring relationships between key characters, the proliferation of multiple storylines starring secondary characters reduced the interest in writing. The majority of works focused on secondary characters, such as Julian Sark, or the relationship between Jack Bristow and Irina Derevko.

All areas of the fandom suffered from the impacts of critical mass between the second and third seasons. As more and more fans existed, the social network crumpled under the strain. Fan fiction, message board postings and fansites proliferated on the internet, and the fans that had been involved in the community since day one took offence at the demanding 'newbies'. This is a natural process in every fandom: these are formed by the emotions of enthusiasm and mutual love, the 'greater good' ideal that Fernbeck identifies, but once the novelty wears off the relationship between fans and fandom begins to suffer. Developed fandom communities rely on the active engagement of 'Big Name Fans' (BNFs) who set guidelines and establish social 'norms.' When these fans feel the pressures of their social status, stemming from the demands of newcomers requesting information, the BNFs are the first to leave, succumbing to the stress from increased need for their involvement. Labyrinthine (writing between the second and third seasons of *Alias*) provides some insight into the process of community building and growth:

> We're still a young group. There's been a big shift between Season One and Season Two in terms of the community exploding with people, and that's had both good and bad ramifications . . . I think we're a very supportive community, but still fall under the same traps and pitfalls as any fandom.

These 'traps and pitfalls' are further explored by Amy, who, once she started posting her writing to various fandom communities, learned that, as she kept writing, disillusionment set in: 'Some of those friends turned out to be not-such-good-friends. The camps and various factions of fans began to bother me. And frankly, fandom had become way too big a part of my life: it dictated too many of my moods and it was out of control' (2004). These social hierarchies – and the tendency for fandom to spin out of control – are what, invariably, led to some of the social divisions within the *Alias* fan fiction community.

Fan fiction was a very viable and lasting part of the fan community as a whole, but it was also the first community activity in the *Alias* fandom to fracture and disintegrate due to internal and external pressures. Fan fiction took the greatest hit during the fourth season: most of the better-known authors had ceased writing stories completely, and the community lost its level of intense activity.

The once happy-go-lucky mentality of easy and fast friendship in the earliest days of the fandom had to deal directly with reduced fan interaction. The well-known BNFs ceased their vigilant interactions on message boards, ceased writing, and disappeared from public view. The fans that remained active dealt with a rapidly dissolving community environment as the *Alias* fandom became less stratified and disorganised.

Many of the pre-eminent *Alias* fansites have closed in the course of the five-year series, leaving abandoned domains and memories from the fans that frequented once-popular message boards and news sites. These sites began as a way to 'feed' the fan obsession for more information about a text they connected with emotionally, fulfilling a need during hiatuses between seasons or even a stretch between new episodes. Yet, by the end of the series, these sites were first to reflect the dissolution of the fandom as a whole. In a sense, there is a degree of departure and absence that occurs when a series puts a storyline, character, or even an entire universe to rest. Concurrently, the longer the series exists and these invariable endings ensue, the more fractured and disenfranchised the fanbase becomes. Any social hierarchy suffers under the conditions of longevity: power struggles rip at the foundations of the love and emotion that once brought a collective whole of individuals together. However idealistic this sounds, the truth remains: once a series begins to suffer creatively – either in the writing, or the acting, or cinematography or quality of plot points and presentation of ideas – as judged by audiences and critics, the fandom suffers a blow. Fandoms split when members are forced to take sides, when one faction must argue against another, when one fan elects to defend while another attacks, and invariably, all of the once abundant goodwill fades into animosity and accusatory glances.

Despite this, *Alias* fans appear to reflect that the most important aspect of their involvement has been the relationships and friendships they have built on the journey. While many *Alias* fans might look at the final two seasons with less than fully appreciative eyes, they do know that their interaction with the series was based on love: for the show, the characters, and the relationships it inspired. Long-term fan Erica further conveys this sentiment:

> What always made this show work for me, and why I touted it to so many people, was Sydney, Jack, Dixon, Vaughn, Marshall, Weiss, Will. ... Even when the most bizarre, most outlandish things occurred, even when the good guys themselves didn't believe it, they still fought the good fight. Or tried to. Or fought the good fight through manipulation and subversion.   (Erica 2006)

While fans may cite the situations involving Season Three and the inclusion of Lauren and Sydney's conveniently missing two years as the start of internal fracturing and the eventual fandom breakdown, others will claim that the problems started when the series became too unbelievable as Sydney lost her close friends and stopped going to graduate school, while the Rambaldi prophecies became implausible, SD-6 dissolved too fast, the pacing became inopportune and the character development inadequate. But, before the discussions about what went wrong and why, there was a very general and widespread love affair among the fans and the show – a love affair that prompted the development of countless fansites, message board communities, and original creative works. That love helped to build and sustain the *Alias* franchise for the five years that it aired on ABC Primetime, helped it to spread to international markets, and to continue mass-market merchandising sales after syndication. This chapter tells the story of those fans, from their own perspectives and from the evolutionary history of the fandom, and it documents that the journey that every *Alias* fan took along with the show was not only worth it but had meaning and significance beyond a weekly appointment with Sydney Bristow and the blue light of a television screen.

11 (Re)Writing *Alias*?
An Examination of the Series' Fan Fiction and Media Tie-Ins

Tricia Jenkins

Kevin Weisman, the actor who plays Marshall Flinkman on *Alias*, argues that while his series has never been a top ten show in the ratings, it has produced a loyal, discerning, and invested set of fans. In fact, Weisman asserts that the fans he meets often know more about the series than the actors themselves and that it is viewers' investment in the show that has helped place *Alias* in the 'cultish "lore" of television history' (2005: 3). *Alias*, undoubtedly, has a devoted following – an argument supported not only by Weisman's interactions with fans but also by the show's active fiction communities. For instance, many viewers engage in the authorship or readership of *Alias* fan fiction, a practice that can require dozens if not hundreds of hours. Likewise, numerous viewers have consumed some or all of the eighteen *Alias* media tie-in books, helping place the debut novel, *Recruited*, on the *New York Times'* bestseller list and investing nearly $6 per book in the series. Given the time, effort and money that *Alias* viewers devote to both fan fiction and media tie-ins, this chapter seeks to understand better the fans' attraction to these works. Ultimately, I will demonstrate that while each narrative structure employs the *Alias* broadcast material as its source of inspiration, fan fiction and media tie-ins afford fans a distinct set of pleasures from their transgressive potential and narrative authority.

THE PLEASURES OF *ALIAS* FAN FICTION

For those unfamiliar with the concept of 'fic', it can be generally defined as fiction that employs the characters and/or world of a television series, video game, cartoon, comic, novel, anime, and more. Fic authors are usually amateur writers who use these characters and environments to create original stories that can vary anywhere between 100-word 'drabbles' to novel-length works. In previous decades, fic was primarily circulated at fan conventions or made available through special-order fanzines. However, today's authors most commonly host their pieces on the internet where their stories can be accessed by readers for free; thus, the internet has transformed the fan fiction community from a 'hidden' subculture into a more public and inclusive one.

The amount and location of *Alias* fan fiction currently hosted on the internet is substantial. Sometimes these pieces appear on websites solely devoted to the writing and reading of fan fiction, such as fanfiction.net, while others appear on sites devoted to *Alias* itself, such as SD-1.net or AllAlias.com. Additionally, fan fiction appears on smaller or personal websites devoted to particular characters, including Nocturnal Activities, a site that hosts fan fiction about Jack Bristow, and Allies, which solely features stories about Sydney Bristow and Michael Vaughn. Several international websites also exist: Inthemoonlight.com, for instance, hosts the series' French fan fiction, while Alias Italia: Il Dossier Sydney Bristow hosts roughly eighty stories written in Italian.[1]

Of course, one of the questions that arise when examining any kind of fan fiction is why do so many people engage in the practice, given that authors do not receive any financial rewards for their creative efforts? Part of the answer lies in the fact that while fic authors are unpaid, good ones can obtain national and even international recognition. As Henry Jenkins explains, 'fan publishing constitutes an alternative source of status, unacknowledged by the dominant social and economic systems but personally rewarding nonetheless' (1992: 159). However, as he later points out, the practice is about more than obtaining a large readership. Since fans' relationship to their favourite television series is not always one of celebration and appreciation, fans' viewing experiences are also marked by frustration and antagonism when a show's creators refuse or are unable to tell the kinds of stories viewers want to see (Jenkins 1992: 23). As a result, fan fiction is one of the primary ways that television viewers appropriate characters in order to re-tell unsatisfying aspects of a series or develop ideas insufficiently explored by it.

Emily Higgins, the moderator of the S/V (Sydney/Vaughn) fan fiction forum on SD-1.net, concurs with Jenkins' assertion when examining it within the context of *Alias* fic. When asked to comment on the general themes that appear in S/V stories, Higgins notes that they largely depend on the state of the broadcast series. 'When the show offered a lot of angst', she replied, 'the board abounded with romance or "fluff" as it's called in the fan fiction world. Likewise, when the show gave us the romance we were looking for, the stories mostly consisted of angst or torture or even character death. Generally speaking, whatever we, as fans, felt was missing from the show could be found in a story somewhere on the internet.' Both Higgins and Jenkins, then, get at one of the primary pleasures that fan fiction affords *Alias* viewers: it allows them to appropriate the show's characters to tell the kinds of stories *they* wish to see. And because *Alias* fan fiction is not usually restricted by censorship, authors can tell a multitude of stories that transgress both the rules of the broadcast narrative as well as dominant cultural values.

Before illustrating exactly how fan fiction accomplishes these goals, however, it is important to outline some of the basic strategies fic writers employ. According to Jenkins, one of the most common is 'recontextualisation', a method writers use to fill in the gaps left in the broadcast material in order to provide additional explanations for a character's conduct. Others include 'refocalisation', which refers to stories that shift the attention away from the programme's central figures to explore more thoroughly secondary ones who receive limited screen time, while 'moral realignment' is a strategy fans use when they invert or question the moral universe of the primary text, taking the show's villains and transforming them into the protagonists of their own narratives. 'Emotional intensification' and 'eroticisation' are also frequently used tools, and, respectively, centre on moments of crisis to get at a character's psychology and explore the sexual lives of characters (1992: 162–77).

Alias writers, like all fan fiction authors, often employ these strategies in their stories. For instance, several works use refocalisation to explore the characters of Eric Weiss and Katya Derevko precisely because these characters receive significantly less screentime than others. Also, *Alias* stories seek to fill in the gaps in plot lines or characters' histories (recontexualisation), including 'A Son's Journey' by

Icyfire, which explores Jack Bristow's relationship to his father as a young man in order to explain how Jack developed into an emotionally stoic adult, and 'Fragments of Truth' by Melanie-Anne, which explores the early marriage of Laura and Jack Bristow, in order to help explain their love for each other even after her betrayal is exposed.

Examples of eroticisation are easily located in the large body of 'Sarkney' stories available on the internet, which not only illustrate the common authorial tool, but also demonstrate the aforementioned transgressive potential of fan fiction. Sarkney fiction derives its name from the pairing of popular *Alias* villain, Sark, in stories with the heroine, Sydney Bristow. These stories usually use the eroticisation strategy to explore an explicit sexual relationship between the characters in response to the tension evident between them on the television series but not explicitly explored by it. This sexual subtext, for instance, is evident in several episodes, including 'Dead Drop' (2:4), where Sark compliments Sydney while holding her at gunpoint, assuring her that 'Whatever Arvin Sloane pays [her], it can't be enough'. He then goes on to slightly, but seductively, eye Sydney's body, while asking her to come and work for him instead. Sydney, who subtly eyes Sark in return, replies, 'You're cute, but I'll pass', before knocking his gun from his hand. Later, when Sydney recounts the incident to Vaughn, she remarks that 'Sark is like the good-looking guy in high school who knows how cute he is and won't take no for an answer'.

Exchanges like this suggest that Sydney and Sark find each other sexually attractive and respect each other's skills, but because they are pitted on opposite sides of good and evil they cannot make whatever desire they possess for one another manifest. In Season Four, however, it seems as though the writers of the show were aware of many viewers' desires to see the two paired together in more suggestive scenarios, for in 'A Man of his Word' (4:9) Sydney poses as Lauren Reed, Sark's now-dead lover, in order to stop a bomb from entering the black market. When Sark and Sydney enter a nightclub to meet their contact Ushek Sanko, he demands that the agents display Lauren and Sark's infamous public acts of affection before he aids them. As a result, Sydney inserts a lime into Sark's mouth, chugs the remains of her cocktail, and kisses Sark so forcefully to regain the lime that his lip begins to bleed.

While these episodes have both generated and catered to *Alias* fans' desires for the show to explore the sexual tension between Sark and Sydney, as a prime-time series on a Disney-owned network the show cannot display overtly sexual content, nor can it go beyond the types of aforementioned plots without disrupting the basic rules of the storyline that pit the two as enemies and construct Michael Vaughn as Sydney's true love. However, because fan fiction is not restricted in this manner, it *can* produce stories that explicitly explore these characters' sexuality and challenge the constructions of the broadcast material.

'In a Frame', for instance, is an approximately 46,000-word Sark-ney story hosted on fanfiction.net, written by Teresa Hebron, or TheAfterglow, as she is known online. Posted in November of 2005, 'In a Frame' took Hebron two months to write and explores Sydney's marriage to Michael Vaughn, their attempts to start a family, her subsequent miscarriage, and later, her sexual affairs with Sark. Hebron notes that the idea for 'In a Frame' occurred to her slightly before the end of *Alias'* fourth season, when it was clear that the story was moving towards Sydney and Vaughn getting married. 'I started thinking about what it would be like for two agents to be married with kids,' she remarks, and 'I decided that it was pretty ridiculous to think they could carry on a normal life, and that was when I had the idea for the beginning of the story.' She also notes that 'In a Frame' plays off two 'vibes' from the show – namely the sexual subtext between Sark and Sydney and the subtle thread running throughout the series which suggests that Sydney likes rough sex.[2]

To get at these subtexts, 'In a Frame' begins with Sydney silently criticising Vaughn for his gentle and caring lovemaking after her miscarriage. 'He had been so . . . tender lately', the story reads, 'It was not their way; she longed to slap him, have him bite her nipples, to claw at his back.' And later in the story, Sydney reflects that 'The violence in their bed – that was her doing, not [Vaughn's] – his gentleness held no currency in her world. Everything around her was brutal. How did he expect her to enjoy him when his touch was so light she could barely feel it?' However, before she is able to artic-ulate to Vaughn her dissatisfaction with their sex life, as well as their new focus on establishing a family, Sydney is sent to conduct sur-veillance on Sark and is eventually captured by him. While in his custody, Sark belittles Sydney's new life as a wife and want-to-be-mother, a move that both enrages her and suggests that Sark knows her better than Vaughn. As the tension between Sark and Sydney escalates over the chapters, the work culminates in the two characters engaging in explicit oral sex and intercourse complete with orgasms, bruising, rug burns and scratches.

'In a Frame', then, works to rewrite the broadcast narrative and even challenge dominant cultural values. For example, viewers of the show often fall into two camps regarding the pairing of Michael Vaughn and Sydney Bristow. Some feel that the two are well-matched, helping to explain the large body of S/V fiction, while others feel Vaughn is too 'soft' for the heroine, and thus Sarkney fiction challenges this pairing. According to Hebron, however, 'In a Frame' is not just about challenging the show's romantic relationships, rather it primarily seeks to reclaim some of Sydney's strength, which the author felt had been lacking in the later episodes that feature Sydney being rescued by male colleagues rather than depicting the heroine as capable of saving herself. In other words, by creating a Sydney who is aggressive in bed and desires to walk away from her conventional marriage and gentle husband, Hebron attempts to reclaim that toughness, again challenging the choices of the televised series.

The fact that 'In a Frame' employs eroticisation to achieve this goal, however, is culturally significant, especially when the story is examined in the context of the larger body of *Alias* fan fiction. More specifically, *Alias* fic – including 'In a Frame' – often employs explicit sexual content regardless of the characters it explores and, according to Higgins, the majority of *Alias* fic authors are female. This connection suggests that women may use sexually explicit fan fiction, not just to explore underdeveloped or unsatisfactory themes located within the broadcast narrative, but also to challenge dominant cultural ideas. Put another way, these women may use erotic fan fiction as a tool for sexual liberation, as it allows them to publicly voice their own fantasies, avoid or criticise what displeases them, and subvert the cultural associations between women and sexual passivity.

Of course, this act is not without risk, nor is it unique to *Alias* fan fiction. As Camille Bacon-Smith's exploration of women who write *Star Trek* fic concludes, fan fiction allows women to 'construct a safe discourse with which to explore the dangerous subject of their own lives', but for those who tackle sexually explicit themes, writers always risk the 'potential for personal revelation' (1992: 203, 204).

Thus, some women have gravitated towards writing slash fiction, rather than heterosexual fic, in order to work with stories that require a higher level of abstraction, thereby allowing for a greater distance to exist between the writer and the story itself (Bacon-Smith 1992: 204).[3] Interestingly, however, most *Alias* fan fiction is heterosexual in nature, suggesting that the (heterosexual) women who write fan fiction for this show are more willing to risk 'personal revelation' than their predecessors. However, it is also possible that the fan fiction community's move from fan-based conventions to the internet has provided women with a greater sense of anonymity, and thus these writers feel that the risk of personal exposure is limited or even insignificant.

THE PLEASURE OF *ALIAS* MEDIA TIE-INS

While *Alias* fan fiction may help writers challenge cultural norms in addition to the broadcast material, it is not the only type of writing that *Alias* viewers can turn to in order to explore the series' characters in new environments. Media tie-in novels are also readily available and provide fans of the show with a unique set of pleasures that fan fiction cannot offer. These works, for instance, are primarily motivated by profit, written by paid professionals, most commonly published in paperback form, and sold by independent distributors and mass merchandisers. In general, studios charge a media tie-in publisher to license their TV series (or film) in order to create original stories that employ the show's characters and world. While the price for a licence primarily depends on the film or show's perceived value, media tie-in editor Greg Cox (2005a) suggests that an average price for four media tie-in books would approximate $80,000, but notes that the price would most likely be renegotiated after those four books concluded.

While information regarding the cost of the *Alias* licence is currently unavailable, eighteen tie-ins have been published under it thus far, with the debut novel, *Recruited*, demanding an initial print run of 100,000 (Bantam Books: 2002).[4] The first twelve novels in the series are prequels set roughly seven years before the television series begins and, separately, explore Sydney Bristow and Michael Vaughn's young adult lives as college undergraduates and new SD-6/CIA employees. These prequel novels have been primarily marketed at a teenaged female demographic, although Random

House editor Wendy Loggia notes that the publishing firm specifically designed the series to 'look adult' so 'twenty-five-year-olds can
pick them up without feeling like they're reading a book for kids'
(quoted in Maas 2002: 18). The last six *Alias* tie-ins have been published under *The APO Series* banner and have thus replaced the
earlier prequels in order to target the show's older demographic by
creating self-contained adventures taking place in conjunction with
the television series. Altogether, thirteen different writers have
authored the *Alias* tie-ins and boast a wide range of experience and
expertise. For instance, prequel authors Lynn Mason and Laura
Peyton-Roberts write mostly young adult fiction; Greg Cox, a three-
time APO author, works as a professional media tie-in writer; while
Christopher Hollier and Rudy Gaborno, authors of the APO tie-in
Fania, both work as writers' assistants for the *Alias* television series.

Because of the unprecedented popularity of the *Star Trek* media
tie-in series, many people believe tie-ins are most popular with
adult, male, science-fiction readers and are thus surprised that the
Alias prequels are aimed at a young, female audience. However,
Karen Raugust reveals that the number of television media tie-ins
aimed at teen and preteen girls has exploded since 1993, as licensors
have more aggressively sought publishing partners for their properties (1998: 243). For instance, girls aged ten and older can currently
choose media tie-ins based on several series, including *Alias*, *Buffy
the Vampire Slayer*, *Clueless*, *Moesha*, *Party of Five*, *Sabrina*, *The Teenage
Witch*, *Saved by the Bell* and *Charmed*.

As a result of the growing popularity of tie-ins amongst girls, creating a series of *Alias* prequel novels was a reasonable step,
especially given that the female-centred show ranked second
amongst teens during its Sunday night time-slot in its debut season
(Bantam Books 2002). In fact, by choosing to set its prequel novels
seven years before the series takes place, Random House created a
tie-in concept that could easily tackle young adult themes such as
Sydney's awkward romantic encounters, getting fired from a job,
joining a sorority, and balancing school, spying, and friends. Indeed,
the young Sydney of these novels is just finding her own feet and is
somewhat removed from the strong female character she represents
in the television series. In Laura Peyton-Roberts' *A Secret Life*, for
instance, Sydney is given her first major assignment as an SD-6
trainee and is partnered with Noah Hicks, a full-status agent on
whom she has a crush. Eager to impress, Sydney decides to conduct

some early reconnaissance on her target while out for a jog and witnesses something strange. When Sydney rushes back to tell Noah of
her discovery, she is sure he will be proud of her, but instead he is
angry that she risked her cover and furiously chastises Sydney for
her naivety, causing her to press 'her lips together to keep them from
quivering'. As Noah continues to yell, Sydney feels 'her eyes filling
with tears' and begins shifting 'back and forth in her jogging shoes,
pulling her jacket tightly around her waist and wishing she were
anywhere else in the world'. When Sydney is able to leave the room,
Noah's disappointment causes the trainee's tears to finally break
'like a storm, shaking her whole body' (Peyton-Roberts 2003: 55–6).
According to Loggia, it is passages like this that make the tie-ins so
exciting because 'on the show, Sydney is already a seasoned spy, but
with us, she's still green, more of an every girl going into a crazy situation' (quoted in Maas 2002: 16). As a result, Sydney's emotional
vulnerability in the novels is appreciated by young readers because
as viewers of the television show, they know Sydney as a confident
and competent adult. Thus, the tie-in series offers readers hope that
awkward and unsure girls can and do grow up to be strong women
comfortable in their own skin.

Regardless of whether readers are consuming the *Alias* prequel
novels or the adult APO tie-ins, part of the pleasure that readers
derive from the books involve experiencing familiar characters in
brand-new environments while also getting inside characters' private thoughts through the books' first- or third-person narratives.
These works, like fan fiction, also flesh out characters that do not
receive prominent screentime and fill in the gaps of the broadcast
material. For example, the APO tie-in *Replaced* by Emma Harrison
revolves around Sydney's relationship with her half-sister Nadia
and explores issues of jealousy and sibling rivalry. The novel also
helps viewers better understand Sydney's feelings about taking
Nadia on as a roommate and family member, which the broadcast
narrative explores less directly.

Perhaps the greatest pleasure media tie-in readers derive from
these works, however, rests in the authority of the narratives.
Because all of the *Alias* media tie-ins are officially associated with the
television series and often approved by the series' creators, these
novels are able to offer readers an 'official' version of the television
characters' lives in a way that fan fiction cannot. For instance, while
'In a Frame' suggests that Sark reads Booker Prize-winning novels,

readers do not believe this detail is part of the 'official' construction of the character. However, because the media tie-ins are officially associated with the show, readers are more apt to believe that the events that unfold during these stories are part of the 'real' *Alias* narrative and thus afford readers a way to acquire an expanded knowledge of the characters' histories and psychologies, far beyond what the broadcast material allows. For readers of the prequel novels, this authoritative narrative also leads to an additional pleasure, for consumers often feel that they know more about the characters they are reading about than the characters know about themselves at the time. To cite just one example, many of the prequel novels revolve around Sydney's romantic relationship with Noah Hicks, and readers take pleasure in reading about their budding romance, all the while knowing that their story eventually ends with Noah becoming Sydney's nemesis whom she must later eliminate. Likewise, the books help further explain why Sydney is tempted to rekindle her relationship with the hardened Noah on the television series when the character makes a short reappearance.

One drawback to media tie-ins, however, is that *because* they are officially associated with the television series, authors are limited by what they can do with their characters. As *Two of a Kind?* and *The Road Not Taken* author Greg Cox explained in an email interview (2005b), one of the minor frustrations he experiences when writing the *Alias* tie-ins is that he has to stay away from some of the more 'arc-centric elements of the show, just to avoid any continuity problems'. 'I would *love* to play with Irina, Sark and Rambaldi,' he notes, 'but that's just asking for trouble; it's easier just to invent my own villains and keep my plots separate from any of the show's ongoing storylines.' While he notes that ABC has never told him that he can't write about Irina or Sark, he says he still stays clear of them, so he 'won't be tripped up by any future episodes'.

Cox's comments also hint at the fact that media tie-series cannot transgress the basic elements of the broadcast narrative. For instance, it is unlikely that the novels could explore a romantic relationship between Sark and Sydney unless the story was set before Sark became an evil villain, but even this would be problematic since the televised series does not suggest that the two knew each other prior to their interactions through SD-6.

CONCLUSION

When a series stops airing on television, the future of a show's fan fiction and media tie-in series is always threatened. Given that *Alias* ended in 2006, it is unclear if the tie-in series will continue to be published, but a show's cancellation does not always mean the death of a series. Although *Murder She Wrote* went off the air in 1996, Penguin published its twenty-fifth original novel in 2005. Likewise, publishers have launched tie-ins *after* a show has been cancelled, including Del Rey's *Dark Angel* series, which debuted in October of 2002 after Fox ended the show the previous spring. A survey of fanfiction.net also reveals that new stories are posted by a show's fans well after its cancellation, although the volume of stories undoubtedly declines. Emily Higgins, however, believes that because *Alias* is now in syndication on several channels and still airing as new in other countries around the globe, SD-1.net will continue to host stories for several years after the show stops airing in the United States and possibly gain new members in the process, although participation will surely dwindle over time. Syndication may also prove to boost interest in media tie-ins since *Alias* re-runs are now airing in the United States on TNT in the after-school time slot of 4pm. This second airing of the series is attracting younger viewers who missed the show when it aired in its previous 9pm time slot four years ago, and as these younger viewers are one of the demographics likely to buy media tie-ins, it is possible that the series will continue to sell well after the series' cancellation.

Regardless of the future of *Alias* fan fiction and media tie-ins, it is clear that the two types of works offer readers (and writers) separate pleasures. Fan fiction, because it is authored by fans outside the parameters of studio and network controls, allows for the construction of stories that function in transgressive ways. More specifically, they provide fans with an outlet to tell the types of stories *they* want to see, regardless of whether these stories follow the rules of the broadcast narrative or even the dominant culture's value system. Because media tie-ins are officially part of the *Alias* media conglomerate, they must follow the rules of the television series and are, thus, unable to function for fans on this level. Rather, the primary pleasure of these stories rests in experiencing familiar characters in new environments and expanding one's knowledge of the show's characters through an authorized, or official, narrative work. But regardless of media tie-ins' official relationship with the series or fan fiction's lack of narrative authority, both types of works ultimately influence fans' experience with the television series. According to Henry Jenkins, the cumulative effect of reading these types of works is that it alters one's perceptions of the series. In other words, readers of both fan fiction and media tie-ins will return to the television series 'with alternative conceptions of the characters and their motivations, repositioning the events into a greatly expanded narrative and a more fully elaborated world' (1992: 177).

12 Slashing *Alias*
Viewer Appropriation of Lauren Reed as Commentary on Female/Female Desire

Michaela D.E. Meyer and Linda Baughman

> Sydney Bristow wouldn't do this with Lauren Reed. She couldn't. And it didn't matter what happened in a dream, right? Lauren's breath hitched as Sydney grabbed at her, pushing and pulling and doing everything to make her scream.
>
> (Hold-That-Thought 2005)

Scholars like Radway and Jenkins argue that women utilise resistant reading practices as a way to subvert patriarchy and that slash fandom provides one context through which women can articulate alternative constructions of mediated reality. Slash fiction is a form of fan fiction that rewrites media narratives by pairing same-sex characters together in sexual and romantic relationships. In many ways, slash fiction represents viewers' desire to extend sexual content to their favourite media narratives. Interestingly, Madsen argues, those writing slash fiction are college-educated heterosexual women in their late twenties or early thirties (2002: 32), and Leveugle notes that these women are usually employed in jobs that do not reflect their education level (2003: 4). In fact, Penely's ground-breaking work claims the slash phenomenon has been defined as one of the most radical and intriguing appropriations of popular culture by women, as slash is almost exclusively about male–male relationships (1992: 483). Thus, most slash community members are straight women, writing about gay male relationships *for* straight women.

Alias presents a fascinating case study for the study of slash fiction. While male–male parings are typically the norm for nearly all slash communities, *Alias* launched a plot line that extended slash pairings to women. With the introduction of the character Lauren Reed in Season Three, viewers began slashing Sydney and Lauren rather than male characters on the series (Jack/Sloane, Sark/Sloane, Will/Vaughn, Vaughn/Weiss). This trend, although not unique to *Alias*, marks a distinct turn in slash fiction writing, one that warrants scholarly investigation – why have women moved into writing sexual narratives about female–female media pairings? In this essay, we examine *Alias* slash communities as a case study in this phenomenon, specifically focusing on the trend of Sydney/Lauren slash fiction. We are less concerned with the oppositional or emancipatory nature of slash than we are with a specific reading of the Sydney/Lauren pairing and what that means for the nature of slash fiction. For the purpose of this essay, we utilised narrative texts from the Alias Slash Archive, thus, all quoted narrative material is from this particular website. This site was appropriate for study since its creators compiled a number of Sydney/Lauren slash writings in a centralised location.

The Sydney and Lauren pairing presents several implications about women's use of popular culture and media production practices that over-sexualise women's desires. When women authors turn their attention to female/female pairings, slash communities move from the erotic male body to one more closely allied with the writers themselves (female), but still solidly in the world of 'other' (lesbian rather than heterosexual). Moreover, given the narrative arc of Season Three and Lauren's marriage to Vaughn, slash fiction serves as a foray for fans to reconstitute a heterosexual narrative of their liking: Lauren becomes Sydney's avenue to express her feelings for Vaughn. The complexity surrounding this change in fan practices presents important implications about how media proscribes sexual desire for women and also how media narratives themselves become opportunities for a more complicated vision of relationships.

A BRIEF HISTORY OF SLASH FICTION

Slash fandoms (from 'fan' and 'kingdom') originated in the science-fiction genre, particularly around the works of Isaac Asimov and Jules Verne (Verba 1996: 1). As science fiction moved into televisual representation, slash communities followed. Slash fandoms became visible through the *Star Trek* television series when fans identified the relationship between Kirk and Spock as homoerotic (Jenkins 1988: 90). The term slash originated from the '/' mark placed between the names of the characters (e.g. Kirk/Spock) to signify to readers that the story contained a romantic and/or sexual relationship between the two characters (Kustritz 2003: 372). Slash fiction about *Star Trek* was circulated through a variety of mimographic mailings, as early as 1976. In the original slashing of Kirk/Spock, both men go to a desolate planet and Scotty is unable to beam them back to the ship. While trapped on the planet, Spock goes into *Pon Far*, the Vulcan mating period which occurs only once every seven years. Kirk is faced with a serious decision – if Spock is not allowed to mate with someone he loves, he could potentially die. Thus, Kirk offers himself as a mate based on their longstanding friendship, which both Kirk and Spock come to realise is deeper than they had ever imagined. As a result, the story surpasses typical pornographic representations, which focus mainly on the physical act of sex, and delves deeply into the romantic, interpersonal connection shared by the two men.

Star Trek slash set the stage for other fan communities to write more deeply about interpersonal romantic connections in their stories. Scholars such as Kustritz and Penely argue that slash allows women to provide emotional depth to male characters often absent in media representation. In mediated texts, 'real men' are typically self-sufficient, emotionless and independent. Moreover, they are continually paired with 'sidekicks' or 'buddies' for whom they are allowed to express little emotion, despite mediated circumstances that are often incredibly traumatic and emotionally draining (Kustritz 2003: 376). By exploring men's emotional responses to each other in writing, women construct male representations in mediated texts as complex rather than one-dimensional. In many ways, most slash mimics the form and structure of contemporary romance novels (Salmon and Symons 2004: 97). Although critics often assume that romance novels are devoid of cultural value, Crane finds that romance readers often crave a union '(or perhaps reunion) of the masculine and feminine within their men; but they do not see this notion reflected in feminist thought and understand feminism (as it relates to relationships) primarily in terms of pressure to absorb masculine traits at the expense of traditional feminine ones' (1994: 266). In other words, romantic fiction often produces complex cultural values for women. In the same sense, slash writing provides women an outlet for expressing their desire for more complex male romantic subject positions in fiction.

Throughout the 1970s and 1980s, slash circulated in an underground fashion where women would order stories directly from the authors. According to Penely, although slash does mimic the genre conventions of romantic fiction, it originated from untrained writers and was typically ignored by mainstream publishers (1992: 480). Thus, women who wrote slash organised fan conventions and conferences where they could trade story lists and place orders for particular series or pairings. For the most part, early slash dealt with narratives in the science-fiction genre as the hyper-masculine characters typical of this genre were as unrealistic to women as the spaceships they inhabited. Until the 1990s, slash culture remained hidden within the larger subculture of science fiction. However, with the introduction of the internet, slash became more accessible and grew into a mainstream phenomenon, as well as allowing women to begin appropriating narratives outside the science-fiction genre. Leveugle argues that the internet provides opportunities for individuals to connect and form communities around slash interpretations. It is also a way for authors to distribute and archive their work for others to access (Kustritz 2003: 372). These changes also brought to light the fact that slash is not distinctively American, as communities from the UK, Germany, Australia, Canada and Japan sprang up all over the internet simultaneously (Salmon and Symons 2004: 94).

As the popularity of slash increased, media industries began claiming that slash stories were never intended by their original production, and that slash writers were simply reading 'too deeply' into televisual representations. As a result, scholars also often claim that these women are simply misreading or misinterpreting the text. Scholars like Grossberg and Hall argue that audiences produce oppositional meanings from texts rather than finding the original meaning behind them. Grossberg in particular argues that when one becomes a 'fan', the way in which one reads dramatically changes –

the individual looks for their own content rather than uncovering the intended content of the narrative's creator (1992: 63). Slash writers acknowledge, however, that slash interpretations were never intended by the original production. Women slash writers argue that the academic location of their (mis)interpretation as the construction of a deficient fantasy world is simply untrue:

> Most television shows are not big gay romances, and most slash fans know that the story the show is telling is not a big gay romance. Whatever final image Chris Carter intended us to walk away from *The X-Files* with, it's not a meditation on the deep, abiding love between Reyes and Scully. *Star Trek: Voyager* was not, in the final analysis, the Love Song of Tom & Harry, or an epic concerning the seduction of Seven of Nine by Captain Janeway. We understand this fundamental television truth.   (Queen 2004)

This quotation encapsulates the recognition of creative control by the media producers, but also demonstrates a willingness to ignore this original intent. Slash writers actively realise that the writers/directors/producers did not intend homoerotic interpretations of the televisual content. Thus, the practice of slashing media narratives is one that participants in slash communities recognise as distinctly *their* creation. In that sense, as Jones, Lee and other female scholars argue, slash is actually an empowering practice where women are allowed to subvert male control of the media industry by writing their own narratives regardless of the intent of the predominantly male creators in media production.

On the other hand, several scholars also argue that slash writing is not an emancipatory practice because women are still confining their narrative reality to that proscribed by the male-dominated media industry. Shugart claims that the continued use of appropriative strategies for subversion will result only in the further marginalisation of women and other non-dominant groups, because when women use the terms of patriarchy to produce 'subversion' they merely reinforce the existing social power structure (1997). With specific reference to slash communities, Scodari argues slash writing actually reproduces hegemony because slash writers often appropriate resistive rhetoric in defence of hegemonic practices in the media (2003: 111). In other words, media industries are largely controlled by men, and thus narratives that appear on regular television programming are often a result of male-centred narrative fantasy. As a result, the fact that women are writing slash in response to male-centred narratives, co-opting their characters and terminology rather than working to create their own original narratives, actually reproduces hegemonic power relationships between men and women. Thus, academics seem to have two positions related to slash fiction: one emphasises the reclaiming of power by women from the entertainment industry, and one claims that participating in slash as 'subversion' only further marginalises and criminalises women's sexual fantasy.

SYDNEY/LAUREN SLASH FAN FICTION

Sydney/Lauren slash stories on the internet concentrate on the relational dynamics between the two women. At the end of Season Two, Sydney goes missing and is presumed dead. When Season Three begins, Vaughn has moved on with his life by starting a relationship with Lauren. Vaughn and Lauren were married just before Sydney resurfaced after two years of being missing. The women are written into the series as oppositional characters – Sydney is represented as emotionally driven and nurturing to the men in her life, while Lauren is represented as heartless, career oriented and possessive, particularly after it is revealed that she is a member of the Covenant. Therefore, *Alias* slash writing deliberately draws upon existing characteristics within the series, working within the narrative parameters set by the series even though what it does with those characteristics seems oppositional. Much of the slash written about Sydney/Lauren teases out these oppositional dynamics. For example:

> Sydney ran her fingers through Lauren's hair. Feeling the texture, the weight, memorizing everything about it. She soon found herself running her fingertips down the bridge of Lauren's nose. She traced her lips with her index finger before tilting her lips towards hers. And softly, their lips met. Once. Twice. Until the need to taste each other arose. (Agent Riss)

In this passage, the author explores the Sydney/Lauren pairing writing from Sydney's perspective. The focus is on Sydney's tactile sense of Lauren, but it conveys an emotional component. In contrast, passages written from Lauren's point of view often focus on Lauren as the aggressor:

The kiss was hard and deep and real and harsh with the slightest taste of blood mixing as their tongues entangled. Soon it became evident that Lauren wasn't the only one who was taking what she wanted, although on Sydney's part perhaps it was more punishment than pleasure. Not that it mattered very much to Lauren.   (Dreiser)

In contrast to the previous section, this excerpt illustrates how Lauren cares little for emotions and far more about the physical conquest and eventual domination of Sydney. Several of the stories that slash Sydney and Lauren explore issues of dominance and submission – Lauren comes to Sydney's rescue during a mission, Sydney is broken and frail from the encounter, and Lauren uses the opportunity to dominate her sexually. For example:

The next thing she knew, Lauren was unzipping her torn pants. Sydney met her gaze. The logical thing would be to tell her to stop, but Sydney couldn't. And she didn't know why. She found herself on the edge of the bed, Lauren pulling her pants off her legs, then sliding off her panties. Lauren wasted no time, and plunged two fingers into Sydney.   (Edele Lane)

Obviously, the focus in this section is on the physical domination of Sydney by Lauren. In fact, the way that Lauren approaches sex with Sydney mimics typical heterosexual romance narratives where men with 'bulging packages' take the women, who are 'weak and waiting for it'. In some instances, Sydney fights back, but this resistance only serves to feed Lauren's intrigue with Sydney:

Using her two free hands, Sydney walloped her. Lauren hit the ground hard, stunned that her captive had knocked the breath out of her. Winded, she could only watch as Sydney tucked in her shirt and zipped up her pants. 'You played me,' Lauren mumbled angrily. Though winded, she tried to stand up, but Sydney kicked her to the ground again. Their eyes met, a tacit acknowledgement that Sydney had glimpsed her true agenda. The question of how much she had given away and how much Sydney had deduced would be left for another day.   (Elise-2)

Thus, the consistent theme of dominance and submission – one that occurs in most male/male slash as well – dictates the way the women interact in these stories. They are not same-sex lovers, intrigued by and physically attracted to the other, they are acting out common heterosexual fantasy patterns of dominance (Arcand 1993: 35).

The blatantly heterosexual nature of most slash sex scenes is obviously reproduced in Sydney/Lauren stories. In fact, while the pairing of two women seems to be a progressive move for the slash community – women are writing about sex with and between women rather than with and between men – the narratives all reinforce that the male gaze is the object of desire. Simply put, both women are having sex with each other to get to Vaughn. For example:

> Lauren obviously symbolized ... something. Sydney's jealousy. Wanting to be the one who held Vaughn at night. Or a representation of everything she'd lost in those two years. But it wasn't anything that would help recover her missing memories. Sydney had to ... to exorcise that weird dream. Find a way to get it out of her system so she could get on with her life. That night, Sydney lit the patchouli candles and swore this would be the last time she dreamed of Lauren.
> (Hold-That-Thought)

The writer acknowledges that Sydney's motivation for sexual interest in Lauren is really only that Lauren is now married to Vaughn. As such, Vaughn is unavailable and Lauren becomes the conduit through which Sydney can emotionally capture Vaughn's physical essence. Although he is never physically in the stories, there are always pieces of him tied into the writing. One story recounts, 'It wasn't long before every article of clothing they had been wearing were discarded and forgotten on the floor beside the bed. Their hair ties lay one on top of the other on the bedside table. *Michael's* bedside table' (Agent Riss). Although Vaughn is not physically in the story, his presence is suggested by the table. Similarly, Vaughn's presence is felt in a story narrated from Sydney's perspective: 'And afterwards, when they were lying on the bed, there would be a look of self-loathing in Sydney's eyes as she realized again she had just had sex with Lauren when it was really Vaughn she wanted' (Bartley). Throughout these passages, the message is clear – the women are sleeping with each other to fill a real or perceived emotional void from Vaughn: Lauren believes she does not fully capture Vaughn's heart, and Sydney believes she is now relegated to the 'other woman' status. Thus, the only way both women are able to fulfill their desire for Vaughn is to be with each other, in a very real, physical sense.

CRITICAL IMPLICATIONS FOR THE FEMALE/ FEMALE SLASH PAIRING

On the surface Sydney/Lauren slash looks new and full of potential. It is about women engaging in lesbian sex, but written by heterosexual women, for heterosexual women. In male/male slash there is an easy displacement between the readers, writers and the narrative of the sexual fantasy. Heterosexual women writing about gay male sexual, and romantic, relationships creates a space for sexual safety. Neither the writers, nor the readers, could occupy a straightforward relationship to the sexual behaviour occurring inside the text because at a very base level, heterosexual women can never be gay men. Therefore, although the relationship between author, reader and text may have been fraught with complication, there was a plausible deniability for women writing slash to make about their identities: we are not gay, we just write/read gay.

At first glance, the Sydney/Lauren pairing offers no such protection. The gendered identity of the writer, and reader, is fully implicated in *Alias* lesbian slash. With Sydney/Lauren, we see heterosexual women writing lesbian pornography, which significantly diminishes the distance between reader, writer and text. The potential for involvement in the narrative fantasy escalates. In male/male slash, the writers often observe the relationship in third person, thus allowing the readers to construe the relationship through a heterosexual lens even though the sex acts are explicitly homosexual. The reader, or writer, identifies with one of the men represented in the narrative, and thus becomes a woman having sex with a man in the terms of the fantasy narrative from the reader's point of view. Often, the sex acts depicted in male/male slash mimic heterosexual behaviour. For example, in these narratives the men tend to have sex like heterosexual couples – face to face, without the benefit of lubrication. Therefore, it makes sense that the reader enjoys the narrative text because the sex acts are familiar enough to her own experiences that she can fantasise about emotionally available and sensitive men, without being over-exposed to actual gay sex.

On the other hand, the Sydney/Lauren pairing puts readers in the position of occupying the space of a woman having sex with another woman, but yet again in a heterosexual manner. The pairing is in fact lesbian pornography written by and for heterosexual women, who are then implicated firmly inside the lesbian fantasy. Where does this leave us? Perhaps Sydney/Lauren slash might be a space for heteroflexibility, the idea that heterosexual women can comfortably, and confidently, experiment with same sex behaviour (Diamond 2005: 104). If Madonna can kiss both Britney Spears and Christina Aguilera on MTV, the average woman can read lesbian pornography while still feeling comfortable with her own basic, heterosexual desire. Lesbian slash might complicate heterosexual desire, but it could also free women from traditional gendered binaries related to their sexual fantasies. So, in one sense, this slash could be read as a progressive trend in fan cultures and society as a whole. Women are more liberated to express freely through their television viewing, writing and reading practices the content and context of their own latent desires – whether or not they include same-sex or opposite-sex pairings.

However, we are wary of interpreting Sydney/Lauren slash as the new treatise for the sexually liberated woman, because at the core of all of these stories is a silent partner: Michael Vaughn. He is omnipresent during nearly every sex act in Sydney/Lauren slash: they have sex on Vaughn and Lauren's marriage bed, or Lauren imagines she is getting a bit of Vaughn back from Sydney by having sex with her, or Sydney holds onto Vaughn's love by having sex with Lauren, or in some instances he is sleeping in the next room while they have sex. The women are never completely alone in this slash material – never completely fulfilling a lesbian desire or fantasy. They remember loving Vaughn, having sex with Vaughn. They contemplate how Vaughn matters to them, or conversely they contemplate how Vaughn has nothing to do with their sexual behaviour, bringing him into their performance though the backdoor. Sydney/Lauren slash is merely mediated heterosexual sex. There is little heteroflexibility here, as there is no lesbian behaviour here. Inside this pornography each woman desires Vaughn, although she has sex with another woman, which is an incredibly heterosexual understanding of lesbian behaviour. In fact, the key element in these narratives is desire – and that desire is not lesbian, a woman for a woman, it is heterosexual: two women for one man.

The reading of this material as being more of the same old thing, more heterosexual desire wrapped in homosexual packaging is supported by the utter absence of Sydney/Lauren slash after the third season of *Alias*. At the end of the third season, Vaughn discovers that Lauren is a traitor and eventually kills her. He is then able to return

to his real love, Sydney. If the desire between Sydney and Lauren
had been about lesbian romance, their slash should have continued
to surface on the internet. But with Lauren's demise there is a corre-
lating demise of Sydney/Lauren slash stories. This is *not* the case
with other slash forms. Spock died in an early *Star Trek* film, yet he
and Kirk are continually paired in the world of slash pornography.
Mulder still appeared in slash pairings long after David Duchovny
left *The X-Files*. So, writing a character out of a series by death or
other means does not necessarily forfeit a slash pairing in these communities; however, Lauren's death does because she is no longer
needed to mediate the desire between Sydney and Vaughn. After
her death, Sydney and Vaughn are free to explore their heterosexual
desire on their own, and Lauren's presence is rendered obsolete.

Slash pornography is still interesting if only because it is fundamentally different from other forms of pornography. Slash fiction is,
first and foremost, romantic fiction. Slash is not typical pornography
where sex is the primary goal, and romance is thrown in only to
render it intelligible as a narrative. Slash is the new *old fashioned
romance* – reminiscent of Jane Austin and Harlequin romance novels,
it is about unrequited love, desire unfulfilled, longing that finally
finds its point. In male/male slash the focus is on the taboo nature of
love between men. Men are not allowed to love. Spock cannot love
Kirk. Starsky cannot love Hutch. So when Spock does love Kirk and
Starsky does love Hutch, it is necessarily tortured and unrequited,
right up until the moment of embarrassed discovery and consummation. There is danger, fear and desire in this love: this is the love
of romance novels. When Sydney and Lauren have sex the love is
also unrequited: it is the love for Vaughn. In a sense, Vaughn
becomes the alibi for the desire of both Sydney and Lauren – if they
truly *did* want each other sexually, it would be socially unacceptable,
and thus, through Vaughn this becomes possible. Slash fiction then
becomes a safe space for both writer *and* reader to explore lesbian
desire under the guise of romance written through a heteronorma-
tive framework.

It is important to recognise that these complexities arise because
slash is operating in a cultural landscape where lesbian sex is fetishised. Are these women exploring lesbian sex as a means of releasing
their own desire, or as a means of exploring the desire produced for
them by media narratives? Diamond argues that instances of
female–female kissing in television produce and reproduce this

desire among young women (2005: 105), but Zylbergold (n.d.) notes that women often explain these desires in relationship to men – their same-sex kissing behaviour, or same-sex sexual behaviour is a byproduct of their inherent desire for men who often lack feminine traits they also desire. Stern (n.d.) further argues that when women are objectified through sexual acts in mediated narrative, it can often produce a sense of identification for women – that in some sense women are numb to their sexual desires because they have been continually commercialised and commodified. In other words, when women are presented with mediated representations of women seeking sexual gratification through other women as a means to get to men, they internalise these representations as part of the narrative landscape of female sexuality.

By writing these narratives in a manner that is solely about sexual acts between women, these stories could be read as functioning in two separate ways – as empowering narratives of women exploring their desire for other women, or as constraining narratives that simply use sex between the characters to repair the narrative break in the romantic relationship between Sydney and Vaughn. One interpretation suggests that women are still finding ways to resist male-dominated media structures, while the other suggests that patriarchy controls the means and production of women's desire. At the heart of this paradox is the fact that sexual desire between women, whether genuine or not, has also been commodified by the media. Slash pairings continue to offer us the opportunity to examine the nature of sexual desire as it is wrapped inside a thick layer of longing and romance; but this sexual agency is questionable at best – particularly when we consider the fetishised nature of lesbian sex. Slash may offer a welcome alternative to both the naive, oversimplified ever-growing mountain of romance novels and the world of pornography dominated by straightforward, uncomplicated, mechanical metaphors of sexual behaviour premised on heterosexual sex. On the other hand, slash may simply reproduce these pornographic narratives under a thinly veiled guise of subversion. The case of Sydney and Lauren thus becomes a complex popular culture site where women fight for sexual agency, desire and romance through mediated experience.

13 *Alias* DVD
Re-packaging American 'Quality' and 'Cult' Television Series

Denzell Richards

Since its official US roll-out in March 1997, Digital Versatile (or Video) Disc (DVD) has surpassed compact disc in becoming the most rapidly adopted media entertainment format ever (Hight 2005: 4; Kendrick 2005: 58). While most associated with domestic viewing of films and the proliferation of home cinema systems, it has also proved popular as a format for the re-packaging and re-presentation of television programmes as well. In March 2006, nine years after its debut, the website TVShowsOnDVD.com lists 5,635 different television properties as being available on DVD in North America.

Watching a television series on DVD represents a qualitatively different experience from watching the same series on television itself, one that affects viewer reception and ultimate meaning-interpretation of the media text. Re-packaged on DVD, viewers encounter particular primary texts (in this case episodes from a television series) in a context divorced from their original placement within the flow of television programming, and instead presented as unified (albeit episodic) in order to capitalise on the high-quality audio and visual (A/V) reproduction offered by DVD and other connected home cinema technologies. DVD titles of television series also frequently include secondary textual materials including audio commentaries, documentary and promotional materials, and deleted and alternative footage. Legitimised and rendered as 'official accounts' by their inclusion alongside the series in the same package, and typically presented from an authorial standpoint employing cast members and production personnel (see Brookey and Westerfelhaus 2002: 23–4), these secondary texts possess a strong rhetorical force and operate intertextually to create the impression of a dialogue between the series, its authors and the DVD viewers. This dialogue creates particular interpretative frames through which the series is discursively examined (Hight 2005: 8–9, 11–12), which may in turn influence particular 'reading formations' or reading positions adopted by viewers regarding the series (see Bennett and Woollacott 1987: 64–5) and therefore their ultimate meaning-interpretation of it (see Austin 2002: 22–7).

The DVD releases of the first four seasons of *Alias* (2001–6) provide excellent examples of the ways in which the re-packaging of a series for its re-presentation on DVD can potentially mediate, influence and affect reception of that series by viewers.

RE-SELLING TELEVISION SERIES ON DVD

The widespread proliferation of television series and serials on DVD was inevitable, given that vertically integrated media conglomerates like AOL TimeWarner, Disney and News Corporation have come to dominate US television broadcasting since the mid-1990s, with a vested interest not only in production but also distribution and exhibition of their properties globally across multiple media (Holt 2003: 11–12). A series like *Alias* is an example of such synergistic practices, being produced, broadcast and distributed on DVD all by different wholly owned subsidiaries of Disney (Touchstone, ABC and Buena Vista respectively). Exploitation of a television property through its release on DVD might therefore be considered as a form of spin-off merchandising similar to soundtrack CDs, episode guides and other paraphernalia, principally targeted at fans of the series as media consumers and serving similar synergistic self- and cross-promotional purposes (Jones 2003: 167–8). Crucially, where the DVD release of a property differs from such official secondary or satellite texts is that here it is the primary texts, the episodes themselves, which are re-packaged and sold to consumers on a new media format, both to those who have already viewed some or all of the series (and may consider themselves fans) and to those with no prior knowledge of, or little interest in, the original programme as broadcast. Such re-selling has previously occurred to some extent on video, however the re-presentation of series on DVD is significantly different in a number of respects.

Effectively re-selling a series involves re-packaging it on DVD to provide incentives for consumers to purchase text that they may have already viewed, were most likely originally free-to-air, and may still be being broadcast in syndication. Fans are also likely to have recorded their own off-air copies as well and subsequently re-viewed these several times. It becomes necessary, therefore, for distributors to differentiate the series on DVD from that as originally broadcast, and through the rhetoric of advertising to suggest the DVD version is of greater quality and more definitive than that originally shown on television, representing 'value-for-money' despite having been 'recycled'. This is accomplished through three principal means. Firstly, episodes are collectively presented in broadcast order, unexpurgated and unabridged, typically in season-by-season collections. Secondly, there is a reorientation of the A/V presentation of the series towards modes of reception and spectatorship associated with home cinematic rather than televisual methods of presentation. Thirdly, additional secondary textual materials are included, which serve as extra incentives for consumers to purchase the title (especially fan consumers who are likely to actively seek 'official' secondary texts related to a particular series; see Jones 2003: 165–6).

RE-PACKAGING *ALIAS* ON DVD

Alias is available on DVD in four individual releases (at the time of writing), each including all twenty-two episodes of a particular season together with varying amounts of additional secondary material spread across six discs, and identified on the releases' packaging as *The Complete First Season*, *The Complete Second Season*, and so forth.[1] Besides representing 'value-for-money', the release of season-by-season box-sets connotes a sense of 'definitiveness' and appeals to an archivist or collector mentality amongst consumers, which might be considered especially prevalent amongst television fan viewers (see Bjarkman 2004). They also appeal to consumers who were unable to follow, or put-off by, the serialised nature of the series on broadcast, who might be persuaded to purchase the DVD once the series is collected together. What this strategy also achieves is to divorce the series from its original broadcast context, and to present instead each entire season as unified texts. In part this is a continuation of the distributor's intention to establish the re-presentation of episodes on DVD as more 'definitive' than on their original or subsequent broadcast. Thus 'Truth Be Told' (1:1) is presented on DVD in its original uncut broadcast duration of sixty-five minutes, rather than the edited version of it prepared for subsequent syndicated repeat broadcasts (S1:D1), and likewise 'Nocturne' (4:6), which was cut for content upon its original ABC broadcast, has the excised footage restored (S4:D2). Other televisual interruptions including commercials, network and studio promotions, and continuity voiceovers that would have been present during each episode's original broadcast have also been removed, presenting each episode as complete and unified in a manner more associated with cinematic rather than televisual modes of presentation.

Sara Gwenllian Jones argues that for avid or fan viewers, 'quality' or 'cult' series such as *Alias* constitute '"appointment viewing" where viewers schedule the programme into their weekly routine and make every effort to ensure that they watch it' (2003: 165). *Alias'* position as 'appointment viewing' is ultimately, however, dependent upon its periodic broadcast within the television flow; its status as a 'special event' confirmed by its distinctiveness compared to other programmes around it. It is precisely these contextual televisual aspects, however, that are altered as a result of the re-packaging of the series on DVD. Specifically, the periodic aspects of television broadcasting are elided to present not only each episode but effectively each season as unified narratives. Structuring elements within the disc menu systems appear to anticipate viewer desire for an uninterrupted, non-fragmented and continuous playback of all of the episodes on any given disc. The continuation and resolution of the series' narrative strands, normally presented weeks apart in their original context, are here rendered as continuous. This form of presentation may particularly encourage viewer reading positions associated with what Matt Hills refers to as 'teleological seriality', where viewers '[analyse] serial narratives as if earlier events already presupposed later incidents and were thus inevitably moving towards them', rather than considering them more appropriately as '*ad hoc* [sic] or pragmatic/contingent sequences of production decisions' (2005: 199, 193).

Interestingly enough, where they engage with the series' narrative construction the various secondary texts included on the *Alias* DVD releases as 'bonus material' or 'features' both support and discourage such a teleological reading at different times. Within the

'KROQ's Kevin & Bean Radio Show interviews' (S2:D6) and 'The Museum of Television and Radio: Creating Characters' video extract (S3: D5), for example, J.J. Abrams argues that the series is a complete narrative ('the big picture') divided into various 'chapters' or 'phases'. He appears to confirm this reading position on the audio commentary for 'Authorized Personnel Only, Part 2' (4:2, S4:D1) where he says 'I think what's going to be interesting, watching this on DVD as opposed to over a season, is actually tracking the story and seeing how that piece of information [Jack Bristow believing that Irina Derevko had taken out a contract on Sydney Bristow's life] relates to what he learns later in the season, which is what really did happen.'

Comments in other secondary texts would seem to mitigate against such straightforward unified storytelling, however, and position the narrative instead within the media-industrial context of its production as an unfolding television series. In the audio commentary for 'Full Disclosure' (3:11, S3: D3) for example, writer/co-executive producer Jesse Alexander mentions both the effects of industrial (studio and network) pressures on the series' narrative, as well as processes of retrospective writing:

> This episode . . . was a story that we had initially planned on revealing in stages but there was pressure from outside to really kind of wrap it up as quickly as possible and let people know what had happened to Sydney. So it was a real challenge to come up with the explanations for what had happened to her and . . . why characters had done things in the past and who they were, and . . . who the arm belonged to, and all that kind of stuff.

Here it is clear there are contradictions and fractures between the various interpretative frames offered by the re-presentation of the episodes on DVD, which suggest a teleological reading position appropriate to cinematic rather than televisual modes of reception and spectatorship, supported by some secondary texts, juxtaposed with a consideration of the wider production and industrial contexts affecting the series' origins as intended for broadcast.

RE-PRESENTING *ALIAS* ON DVD FOR THE HOME CINEMA VIEWER

The re-packaging and re-presentation of *Alias* on DVD as a unified text also removes much of the 'special event' or 'appointment viewing' status it enjoyed on its original broadcast, which has to be recovered in other ways. On DVD, *Alias* substitutes its 'appointment viewing' status with different 'special event' criteria based on the adoption of cinematic modes of presentation, designed to take advantage of home cinema technologies. In particular, the A/V presentation of *Alias* episodes on DVD differs markedly from how most North American households would have received them upon original broadcast. While always filmed in the 16:9 image ratio of high-definition (HD) television, the series was mostly broadcast in the 4:3 image ratio of standard definition (SD) television, missing approximately one-third of the image to either side of the screen (Oppenheimer 2002: 88). In its re-presentation on DVD all the episodes are presented letterboxed in a 16:9 frame, thus preserving the integrity of their filmed original aspect ratio (OAR). Similarly, the series' sound-mix was initially made in AC-3 Dolby Digital 5.1 format (five discrete sound channels with speakers to the centre, front and rear left and right, plus a subwoofer), also in anticipation of HD presentation, but 'down mixed' to stereo for SD broadcast. As with the OAR, the original 5.1 sound-mix is retained for the episodes' re-presentation on DVD. This 'enhanced' A/V presentation is a continuation of the distributor's efforts to present the release as a 'definitive' version, superior to how it had been previously encountered by viewers. Indeed, the accompanying secondary texts included on the *Alias* DVDs serve to continually remind viewers of the differences between its original SD television broadcast and its re-presentation on DVD. With only a few exceptions in the Season Three release, all clips taken from actual episodes of the series included within the 'bonus material' or 'features' are presented in SD 4:3 ratio with stereo sound, unfavourably comparing with their 'enhanced' presentation elsewhere on the release.

The episodes on DVD are therefore rhetorically positioned as 'definitive', 'superior' and more 'cinematic' according to media-industrial and consumer discourses associated with home cinema technologies (see Klinger 1998; Kendrick 2005). Combined with its re-packaging as a singular, coherent and unified narrative, this re-presentation of *Alias* re-orientates the series more towards the modes of reception and spectatorship that Uma Dinsmore-Tuli (2000) has found to be associated with the domestic consumption of films by 'cinephiliacs', and away from those Kim Bjarkman (2004) suggests are associated with the domestic and personalised recording and re-viewing of television programmes.

DVD 'BONUS FEATURES': CREATING THE IMPRESSION OF PRODUCER/VIEWER DIALOGUE

Given their role as incentives to consumers to purchase a text they may have already viewed and possibly possess their own recordings of, it is unsurprising that secondary texts included on DVDs are often labelled as 'bonus' or 'special features', associating them with the same 'definitiveness' as the episodes themselves due to their 'enhanced' A/V presentation. This may be explicit and direct; for example, on the *Alias* DVDs the inclusion of 'deleted scenes' (all releases) and 'The Animated *Alias*' (S3:D6) provide a 'fuller' re-telling of the series' narrative compared to its original broadcast. Alternatively, more implicitly and indirectly, this may be through the inclusion of documentary materials that give the impression of providing privileged 'behind-the-scenes' access to viewers (connoting both exclusivity and viewer inclusiveness), allowing them to view the 'bigger picture' of how the series was produced. Such documentary materials typically originate from an authorial position, in the case of *Alias* this includes cast members (principally Jennifer Garner) and key production personnel including writers, producers and directors, but especially the series' auteur figure J.J. Abrams. Materials which would previously therefore have been released as official secondary or satellite texts are instead utilised on the series' DVD release, forming a 'localised', highly selective and manufactured version of a 'discursive surround' (see Klinger 1997) contained within a single product, a phenomenon leading Robert Alan Brookey and Robert Westerfelhaus to argue that 'DVD is perhaps the ultimate example of media-industry synergy, in which the promotion of a media product is collapsed into the product itself' (2002: 23).

Such strategies are evident within the choice of secondary texts frequently included on DVD releases, which often recycle, re-edit and/or re-present previously existing materials. This may be overt, as with the inclusion of materials originally broadcast on television to promote the series such as '*Alias* TV Spots' (S1:D6; and S2:D6) and 'Team *Alias*' (S3:D6), which appeal to an archivist-collector mentality. Alternatively, pre-existing promotional materials may be integrated into and presented within a documentary-style format, essentially eliding their origins while still serving the same purpose. John Thornton Caldwell (2005) has illustrated, for example, how electronic press kit (EPK) materials are exploited by studios and distributors, who in a form of 'viral marketing' facilitate their presentation as documentary materials through news channels and other media outlets.

This is not so much the case with the *Alias* DVDs, where the use of recycled EPK footage is very rare (the Vivica A. Fox interview in the '*Alias* Up-Close: The Guest Stars' documentary (S3:D6) being the only apparent example), and while there are exceptions,[2] the majority of the *Alias* 'bonus features' instead consist of original documentary materials produced specifically for the DVD releases rather than recycled or 'found' materials, which exploit both their originality (hence 'exclusivity') and the involvement of the series' authors to create an inclusive sense of dialogue between the producers of the programme and its audience. This is especially pronounced where cast and crew members appear to address the viewer directly, as when actor Kevin Weisman leads the 'I-camera' on a guided tour of the set in 'Marshall's World' (S4:D6), and can sometimes be particularly explicit such as in 'Agent Weiss' Spy Cam' (S4:D6), where actor Greg Grunberg says 'if you're a fan, and I know you are, thank you for buying the DVD'. This impression of dialogue is most evident within the various audio commentaries, however, typically beginning with participants introducing themselves by name and role in the series' production and end with them thanking the viewer for watching. These commentaries occasionally even directly respond to fan concerns about aspects of the series raised during its television broadcast, as with J.J. Abrams' comments about the destruction of SD-6 in the commentary for 'Phase One' (2:13, S2:D4), and problems with Season Three's narrative arc more generally in commentaries for 'Façade' (3:15, S3:D4) and 'Authorized Personnel Only, Parts 1 and 2' (4:1, 4:2, S4:D1). The inclusion of an audio commentary conducted by self-identified *Alias* fans for the episode 'The Two' (3:1) on the region 1 North American release of *The Complete Third Season* (S3:D1) provides further evidence of the reciprocal nature of the author/viewer dialogue model that these secondary texts attempt to establish.

Audio commentaries aside, however, the documentary materials included within these releases nonetheless still operate to an extent in a style associated and identifiable with EPK material as defined by Craig Hight (2005). Specifically, praise for cast and crew members is consistently and repeatedly voiced, and creative tensions, where mentioned at all, are played down (Hight 2005: 6–7). Moreover, such documentary materials tend to be relatively short, frequently subdivided into distinct 'chapters' identified through captions, and concentrate on specific aspects of, or periods in, the context of the series' production from which they do not deviate. While each is constructed along clear narrative lines ('telling the story' of a particular aspect of the series' production in 'Inside Stunts' (S1:D6) for example; or a specific episode in 'The Making of "The Telling"' (S2:D6)), there is, however, no attempt at constructing an over-arching narrative of the series' production, leaving the impression that such materials 'are in fact more like incomplete chapters from some larger, unfinished documentary' (Hight 2005: 11). To what extent these texts present a thorough account of the production of the series and are a genuine attempt at dialogue between the series' producers and audience is therefore debatable.

INTERPRETATIVE FRAMES AND *ALIAS* ON DVD

Developing Brookey and Westerfelhaus (2002), Hight contends that the secondary texts included on DVDs impose particular interpretative frames on the primary text, the cumulative effect of which is to suggest the most 'appropriate' contexts within which viewers should come to an understanding of it (2005: 8–9). So what specific interpretations are proposed and supported by the cumulative secondary texts (especially audio commentaries and documentary materials) on the *Alias* DVD releases,[3] and do these firmly establish the 'appropriate' context for understanding the series or are they relatively open to a variety of possible viewer reading positions?

In his analysis of the making-of documentaries included as secondary texts on *The Lord of the Rings* (Peter Jackson 2001, 2002 and 2003 NZ/US) DVD releases, Hight comments that this material is consistently 'self-contained' and '[invites] us into the closed and artificial world of the production in a manner that closely parallels our entry into the fictional realm of the films themselves' (2005: 12). He argues that the interpretative frames supported by the secondary texts on these DVDs prioritise the context of actual production processes and filmmaking practices, and that viewers are not 'encouraged to explore, for example, tangents into broader modes of film production, comparisons with other film texts, or debates over the trilogy's resonance with its social, political, and cultural context' (Hight 2005: 14). A similar concentration on the production context at the expense of other approaches is also evident in the documentary materials on the *Alias* DVDs, emphasised by titles such as '*Alias* Pilot Production Diary' (S1:D6), 'The Look of *Alias*' (S2:D6) and 'Anatomy of a Scene' (S4:D6). In addition to video interviews and clips from finished episodes, these texts tend to heavily utilise 'behind-the-scenes' footage of production meetings, on-set rehearsals and actual recording. Furthermore, cast and crew members are often interviewed while on-set during the actual production process and are sometimes distracted or called away mid-interview, further emphasising their role within the production context.

Production processes are therefore emphasised at the expense of other contexts affecting the series, as can be seen for example in 'The Making of "The Telling"' documentary (S2:D6). This is divided into multiple 'chapters', each of which is identified by captions providing the date the footage originates ('March 21' to 'April 17') or the stage of production ('Post Production'), subdivided by further captions providing details of the shooting location and/or script (for 'April 7', for example: 'Stage 3, Disney Studios ǀ Scene 25'). This narrative structure mirrors and emphasises the actual structure of the production schedule for an episode, which the viewer is granted privileged access to and invited to participate in through frequent use of the 'I-camera', which cast and crew often directly address, juxtaposed with an objective camera style reminiscent of 'fly-on-the-wall' documentary during periods of rehearsal or actual shooting. Where the media-industrial context surrounding the series is referenced it is only in direct relation to how it affects actual production. The tight schedule and need for broadcast on a pre-determined date, for example, is utilised principally to generate tension regarding the production process, resulting in a countdown delivered by captions such as '3 days to air,' and comments by co-producer Nicole Carrasco including 'I would love to deliver [the episode] by 2am tonight if I can.'

A further key aspect of this production-centric context, recurring across the secondary texts on the *Alias* DVDs, is the presentation of J.J. Abrams as series auteur; if not actually controlling all aspects of production, at the very least, positioned as exerting a guiding hand on them. Aside from being identified as 'series creator' by captions in the documentary materials, cast and production personnel routinely refer to Abrams as being in overall control and the instigator of multiple facets of the programme. He appears seemingly omnipresent throughout the documentary materials, appearing in virtually all of them and still mentioned where he does not. While he does not feature on the majority of audio commentaries, it is notable that where he does these include the most critical discussions of production decisions and the way the series has developed, as though Abrams' presence legitimises particular topics of discussion that cannot be raised without him to provide an authoritative view.

Despite this positioning of J.J. Abrams as auteur, however, the secondary texts, particularly the documentary materials, also stress the importance of the contribution of a wide variety of production personnel to the series' success. This does not merely detail 'the usual suspects' for the action-adventure genre (although both fight/stunt and visual effects departments are well covered) but also includes materials such as '*Alias* Up Close: Creating Props' (S3:D6) and '*Alias* Up Close: The Assistant Directors' (S3:D6). These materials frequently stress the compressed and difficult shooting schedule of television production, which is framed as being a highly collaborative yet difficult pursuit, although at the same time the cast and crew are depicted enjoying their work. At times, however, the *Alias* DVD documentary materials can become somewhat excessive in their drive to acknowledge all contributors to the production process; 'The Making of "The Telling"' (S2:D6) goes so far as to have a short on-set piece-to-camera (albeit light-hearted) by payroll accountant James Avelar.

Concurrent with this is the depiction of a particular kind of friendly and gregarious rapport amongst the cast and crew, which through being shared with the viewer further facilitates the impression of inclusiveness and dialogue between producers and audience. The establishment of this interpretative frame is particularly evident in the presentation of Jennifer Garner by the various documentary materials and audio commentaries. Garner is repeatedly praised throughout for her abilities, professionalism, hard work and dedication to the series. It is repeatedly established that she does many of her own stunts and fight sequences, and much rehearsal and 'behind-the-scenes' documentary footage of her concentrates on these aspects. However, there is also a significant amount of on-set footage in which Garner is shown, for lack of a better expression, to be 'goofing around' between takes, playing-up for the camera, and generally giving the impression of being a fun-loving klutz. This is particularly evident in the 'blooper reels' included on all the *Alias* releases, which often concentrate on Garner's antics, with some of the rehearsal footage of her apparently used because it inadvertently makes her appear slightly ridiculous, such as her rehearsals of gunfights in both 'The Making of "The Telling"' (S2:D6) and '*Alias* Up Close: The Assistant Directors' (S3:D6) where she says 'bang bang' in lieu of firing her gun. By establishing this multifaceted and essentially approachable image of its series' star (arguably the most identifiable aspect of the *Alias* franchise), these secondary texts personalise Jennifer Garner and make her seem accessible to viewers, facilitating a sense of viewer investment in the programme and its continuation.

The production-centric emphasis within these documentary materials is tempered, however, by the audio commentaries on these releases, which while still privileging production contexts sometimes incorporate others as well, although as with the documentary materials this tends to be in relation to their effect on actual production processes. Participants will, for example, often refer to other television series, films or texts which have influenced particular production decisions, including frequent references to other series created and produced by J.J. Abrams including *Felicity* (1998–2002) and *Lost* (2004–), positioning the series within a wider media landscape instead of a closed and isolated text unto itself. Discussion of the media-industrial context is also widened to refer to network and studio censorship (see the commentary for 'Nocturne' (S4:D2)) and active interference in the series' narrative content to foster audience growth (see the commentary for 'Full Disclosure' (S3:D3)).

The most prominent omission in the documentary materials, given *Alias*' subject matter, is a dearth of references to real-world political and historical contexts related to espionage and international relations. This is partly addressed by writer/producers John Eisendrath, Alex Kurtzman-Counter and Roberto Orci in the audio commentary for 'Q and A' (1:17, S1:D5), who say that having begun broadcast shortly after 11 September 2001, J.J. Abrams instigated a policy that the series would not do 'ripped from the headlines' stories and would instead be effectively constituted as a 'parallel universe'. This is only one of a number of references to 9/11 made throughout the various *Alias* DVD commentaries, and it is the one historical sociopolitical or cultural event that is incorporated into the context of the series' development, albeit principally due to its effect on the programme's production. Producer Sarah Caplan, in the commentary for 'So it Begins' (1:2, S1:D1), for example, mentions that it was subsequently impossible for the series to film in real airport locations due to security considerations. What is particularly interesting is her subsequent comment, barely audible underneath a simultaneous conversation between the other commentary participants, that '9/11 changed everything on the show'. On the only occasion where a post-9/11 context is explicitly evoked, in the commentary for 'Façade' (3:15, S3:D4), it is clearly not presented as an appropriate interpretative frame for the series to be understood by. The subject is raised by episode director Jack Bender, who references footage of 9/11 as providing inspiration for the opening scene, and there is an audible sigh from J.J. Abrams, who gently rebukes him for raising it, but who briefly addresses the issue before changing the subject back to a production context in short order.

The precise reasons for such greater openness in the audio commentaries compared to the documentary materials is unclear, but I would suggest it is due to a number of factors including: less rigorous editorial control over content (illustrated by the disclaimer from the distributor which precedes each); a more relaxed environment for the participants compared with the production of video documentary materials, where instead of talking to a camera they are discussing the series amongst themselves as contemporaries; and finally a possibly enhanced sense of the creation of a dialogue between producer and viewer, facilitated by the synchronously running primary text, which the participants are directly responding to with their commentary. In any case it is evident with the DVD releases of *Alias* that it is the audio commentaries that establish the most open interpretative frames and the widest contexts – albeit with a heavy bias towards production processes – for understanding the primary text, from which a variety of viewer reading positions might be informed.

CONCLUSION

I have examined a variety of ways in which it is possible to observe how the re-packaging and re-presentation of a 'quality' or 'cult' television series on the DVD format affects viewer reception and processes of meaning-interpretation differently to its original broadcast. Utilising the various DVD releases of *Alias* as case studies, I hope to have demonstrated how the unified presentation of the series, its reorientation within the discourse of home cinema as a more cinematic rather than televisual text, and the provision of additional secondary textual materials that endeavour to create the impression of a dialogue between producers, viewers and text, all cumulatively act to create, suggest and attempt to impose particular interpretative frames on the primary text. Ultimately it is the paradox of DVD that the greater the viewer interactivity and provision of textual information provided by it, the more it is that 'authoritative' and 'correct' interpretations of the material are directed at viewers and the variety of possible reading positions which may be adopted by them in relation to the text are closed down. This seems especially appropriate here given the analysis of *Alias*, a television series that lists technology, duplicity and determinism amongst its major thematic concerns.

Notes

Preface

1 In Season Four, *Alias* had been paired on US television with its fellow Bad Robot production, the phenomenonally successful *Lost*, resulting in an upturn in its ratings. In Season Five, ABC perversely severed the two J.J. Abrams series, and *Alias'* rating dipped.

2 It is the writers that Television Without Pity's exasperated critic, by the end incapable of suspending her disbelief, cannot forgive:

> After more commercials (yay!), Irina finally opens up the case and fondles The Sphere. 'So that's it,' says Syd, entering the room. 'That's The Horizon, isn't it?' Well, sure, Syd. It's The Horizon. Except that The Horizon that Irina stole back in 'Maternal Instinct' seemed to be about the size of a book and about as flat, so unless The Horizon started out deflated and had to be inflated in order to receive the Red Juice of Rambaldi, I'd say that the writers had NO IDEA what The Horizon was supposed to be and had to just retrofit it into this plot line so that previous episodes wouldn't be totally moot. Also? Rambaldi's really fond of spheres because there was already a Sphere of Life back in Season Four and now there's another Sphere that may have been a Horizon but only if it's made of beach ball material and, honestly? I could give two fucks because obviously the writers don't.

3 I trust I am not alone in detecting similarities between the final episodes of *Alias* and Warner Brothers' *Angel*, 2004's 'Not Fade Away'. After all, Jeffrey Bell, co-author and director of the *Angel* finale had become an executive producer on *Alias*, and Drew Goddard, co-author of 'All the Time in the World' had been story editor on *Angel*'s last season. And, of course, Amy Acker appeared in both: as *Angel*'s Illyria and *Alias'* Peyton.

4 Abrams would, of course, 'come in from the cold' – returning, an unhappy creator, for a visit to *Alias* after a Season Three that pleased him not ('We weren't as true to the characters', he would tell *USA Today*'s Bill Kaveney. 'They became pawns in a plot-driven story'.). And he would leave *Lost* to 'spy again' in his first assignment as a feature film director: 2006's *Mission Impossible III*, starring Tom Cruise, who had sought out Abrams as the franchise's saviour after watching *Alias* on DVD. Asked by *GQ* to compare making *Mission Impossible III* and *Alias*, Abrams would

identify one basic difference: 'Instead of saying "We're in Rome" and shooting in Burbank, we're actually shooting in Rome' (Rapkin 2005: 201).

5   *Taking Care of Business* (1990), *Regarding Henry* (1991), *Forever Young* (1992), *Gone Fishin'* (1997), *Armageddon* (1998), and *Joy Ride* (2001).

6   It should be noted that, like Felicity Porter, Sydney Bristow was, at least in the first two seasons, still a college student (at UCLA), but the dual life of superspy and coed always seemed forced. In 'A Free Agent' (2:15), her school days would end as she earned her MA in English. Fascinating, is it not, that contemporary American television's two most badass secret agents, Sydney and *24*'s Jack Bauer (see Cerasini 2003: 7), are both English majors?

7   'There's always a place in my heart for the genre stuff that is more pulpy storytelling,' says Abrams, 'Look at *Jaws, Alien, Die Hard, Tootsie, Back to the Future*. They're all movies that if you pitched the story [to studio executives], you'd probably get a little, polite smile. But done as well as they were and with the commitment with which they were executed, they become as good as anything' (Dilmore 2005: 24).

8   '[I]n the pilot of *Alias* we had Sydney going after this antique Rambaldi device and not just a disc of information. It's just my tendency. It's just what interests me' (Gross 2005: 36).

9   For more on Abrams' genre aesthetics and on the creation of *Alias*, see Porter and Lavery's *Unlocking the Meaning of* Lost (2006), pp. 9–12 and 108–10.

Introduction

1   'Serious Spy Stuff' is a quote from Michael Vartan from the Season Two blooper reel on *Alias: The Complete Second Series DVD* (S2:D6). Before a take he asks Jennifer Garner not to laugh because this is 'serious spy stuff'.

2   For referencing purposes, individual episodes and secondary texts on DVD will be described by season release followed by disc number. For example, 'Truth Be Told' (1:1), which appears on Disc 1 of *Alias: The Complete First Season*, is referred to as S1:D1, while 'The Making of "The Telling"' documentary is S2:D6.

3   Under the heading of '47 Ways in which the Finale sucked' three fans, Mo, Bri and Lodi, complained about various inconsistencies with the ending that ruined their enjoyment. As far as they were concerned 'the fans knew a lot about the show's intricacies and it feels as if few were left with a half-written, thrown together ending ... JJ, you did a major disservice to your fans'

(Sydneybristow77 2006). One source of complaint was the fact that Irina suddenly tries to kill Sydney after spending years protecting her. 'Suddenly she's willing to KILL SYDNEY for a red ball? No. Way. Nuh-uh. It doesn't fit with her character' (Sydneybristow77 2006).

1 The Show Must Go On . . . And On

1   Editors' Note: See Brown and Abbott, 'Can't Live With 'Em, Can Shoot 'Em: *Alias* and the (Thermo) Nuclear Family' in this volume for a discussion of the Bristow family backstory.

2 Endoscopic Spies

1   Garner and her husband Ben Affleck celebrated the birth of their daughter Violet Anne on 1 December 2005.

4 The New Hero

1   Whedon succeeded. In *Entertainment Weekly* alone, 'Buffy' appeared on twelve covers and showed up in fifty-three features and reviews. The day before and after the series' final episode, *Buffy the Vampire Slayer* was the subject of feature articles in newspapers all across the USA.

2   Buffy first confesses this to Spike in the episode 'All the Way' (6:6), then to her friends in 'Once More with Feeling' (6:7).

3   As others have noted, the series itself was 'killed' by the Fox Network at the end of Season Five, only to be reborn on UPN.

4   Romance novels and soap operas, for example.

5   Editors' Note: For more on doubling, see Dyrk Ashton, 'Reflections of Deleuze: An *Alias*-ed Critique of Truth' in this volume.

6   Arvin Sloane feigns his assassination of his wife, Emily; she is later killed while attempting to escape with him. In one of the final episodes, Sloane kills his daughter, Nadia. Jack Bristow requests permission to kill his wife, Irina, who is a terrorist agent, although he doesn't go through with it; she later attempts to kill her daughter, Sydney. After Michael Vaughn discovers that his wife Lauren is a double agent, he is forced to kill her. Marcus Dixon's wife is murdered in retribution for his actions.

7   In *Buffy*, internalised pain manifests itself in the main character's deathwish – a desire for stasis that she consistently yearns for and struggles against. In *Alias*, Sydney Bristow's masquerades represent the attempt to differentiate between the protagonist's fresh-faced 'authentic' self and the spy who kills for the government

(and sometimes, mistakenly, for the bad guys). When this fails, Sydney literally removes the memories that constitute her identity in order to be reborn, or rather, in order to return, paradoxically, to her 'self'.

6 Can't Live With 'Em, Can Shoot 'Em

1   These include of course Jack Bauer's wife in Season One and the computer technician Edgar's mother and CTU director Erin's daughter in Season Four.
2   This is another example of the blurring between work and home life, as Elena is both aunt and nemesis to Sydney and Nadia.
3   That Danny dies in the same episode after having been welcomed into the Bristow family and thus into their web of secrets is also telling.
4   The nature of fatherhood is a theme of the series that extends beyond Jack Bristow as the show is replete with conflicting images of fathers, including Dixon, responsible and loving father; Marshall, a doting father to young Mitchell; Sloane, an emotionally ambiguous father to Nadia and an abusive father-figure to Sydney; and Vaughn, who both has and becomes himself an idealised absent father.

7 *Alias*' Inversion of White Heroes and Brown Foes

1   In this same work (chapter 5) Gray also discusses 'the discourse of assimilation' and 'the discourse of invisibility'.
2   Bogle and Gray credit *The Cosby Show* for starting a new direction of programming, advertising and marketing.
3   Herman Gray also discusses hegemony as it relates to popular culture. See Gray 1995: 5.
4   Editors' Note: See also Deborah Finding and Alice MacLachlan, 'Aliases, Agency and Alienation: The Physical Integrity of Sydney Bristow' for a discussion of Sydney Bristow's aliases.
5   Dixon has some positive images while in the field. In 'The Getaway' (2:12), it is Sydney who portrays a crazy-looking punk; Dixon gets to play the priest. In 'Doppelgänger' (1:5), Dixon surgically extracts a bomb from an unsuspecting patient. He performs this surgery in an ambulance while Sydney tries to out-drive the bad guys who have the remote bomb detonator.
6   It is important to note that in Season Four Nadia takes on the role of friend and family offered by Francie. In keeping with the cultural diversity of the show, Nadia is of Latin American heritage and as such represents a very different ethnic socioeconomic background

from the other characters. Unfortunately constraints of space prevent a more detailed discussion of Nadia's role here.

8 The Good, the Bad and the Justified

1. See Sutherland and Swan 2007.
2. Kate Austen of *Lost* is an exception, as discussed later.
3. One of J.J. Abrams other female lead characters, Felicity (Keri Russell) of the eponymous series, also continually vocalises her decision-making processes.
4. Shakespeare's *Hamlet* and Charles Bronson's series of *Death Wish* films provide both classical and modern examples.
5. Uniting and Strengthening America by Providing Appropriate Tools Required to Intercept and Obstruct Terrorism (USA Patriot) Act of 2001, HR 3162.
6. The government's relationship with the bad guys is complex, and contributes to the moral ambiguity of the government. While the relationship between Sark, Irina, Sloane and the government is particularly interesting, it is unfortunately beyond the scope of this chapter.

9 Reflections of Deleuze

1. It is important here to qualify that, for Deleuze, the truth

   is not opposed to the false as its opposite or negation; rather, the powers of the false are a measure of truth in its temporal, and therefore fragile and embattled, forms . . . 'The idea that truth is not preexistent', writes Deleuze, 'something to be discovered, but instead, must be created in every field, is easily seen in the sciences. Even in physics, all truths presuppose symbolic systems, even if only coordinates. All truths "falsify" pre-established ideas. To say "the truth is a creation" implies that truth is produced by a series of processes that shape its substance; literally, a series of falsifications' (Rodowick 1997: 16).

2. The world for Hegel 'progresses' through a constant process of thesis, antithesis and synthesis, where the thesis is an existent state of affairs, an antithesis comes along to challenge or oppose it, and through this clash a synthesis of the two is born. This is Hegel's 'dialectic'. For Hegel this progression is toward a unity of world and humankind with God, and therefore the Ideal is God's vision of the world. Marx also believed the dialectic to be the way of the world, but for him the Ideal was not God's vision of the world, but unity and equality of all humankind brought about by humankind alone.

3 Deleuze's conceptualisation of time draws primarily from Bergson, but the influences of a number of philosophers on both Deleuze and Bergson are apparent. These include Kant, Sartre, Leibniz, St Augustine, and (for Deleuze, at least) Nietzsche, among others.

4 Neither Bergson nor Deleuze actually discusses the future at any great length, and Bogue (2003: 203) points out that Milic Capek deduces for Bergson that the future simply does not exist. I proffer that the future exists in thought, intention and attentive human consciousness, much as the past exists in memory, in every present moment.

11 (Re)Writing *Alias*

1 It is also important to note that since many fan fiction sites are run by individuals in their free time and with their own money, they are not always able to survive over the long run. Many modest sites hosting *Alias* fan fiction disappeared within the first few seasons of the show, while even larger, more popular sites have struggled financially. For example, SD-1.net, one of the most popular places to find *Alias* fan fiction and discussion boards, asks its members to subscribe to its community for $10 a year to help pay for server space and has had to step up its campaign for further subscriptions in the last few years due to recent drops in membership and advertising revenue.

2 Editors' Note: See also Deborah Finding and Alice MacLachlan, 'Aliases, Alienation and Agency: The Physical Integrity of Sydney Bristow' in this volume for a further discussion of Sydney's sexual attitudes.

3 Editors' Note: See Michaela D.E. Meyer and Linda Baughman, 'Slashing *Alias*: Viewer Appropriation of Lauren Reed as Commentary on Female/Female Desire' in this volume for a further discussion of slash fiction.

4 At the time this chapter was written, eighteen Alias tie-ins had been released. Since then a further seven have been published, bringing the total to twenty-five.

13 *Alias* DVD

1 I am utilising the region 2 British DVDs of *Alias* for the basis of this chapter; however, aside from some minor language differences, these are identical with only one exception (the fan audio commentary on Disc 1 of *Alias: The Complete Third Season* region 1

North American release) in all respects with other international DVD releases of the series.

2 The 'KROQ's Kevin & Bean Radio Show interviews' (S2:D6), 'The Museum of Television and Radio: Creating Characters' video extract (S3:D5) and the interview with Ricky Gervais included in the '*Alias* Up-Close: The Guest Stars' documentary (S3:D6) present 'found' interview materials from alternative sources to the production. While these pre-exist the DVD release, however, they do not generally conform to a typical EPK presentation style, and indeed represent some of the few occasions where authorial interpretation and intent is explicitly challenged.

3 Lack of space precludes its thorough discussion here, but following Isaac Mace-Tessler (2005) this should also include how the visually presented disc menu systems on these DVDs act to frame the series' narrative in an extra-diegetic process of 'world expansion'. Concentration on particular visual aspects of the series facilitates viewer expectations regarding the series' narrative and themes, notably the Rambaldi narrative-arc but also elements of subterfuge and espionage, the use of 'hi-tech' gadgets and hyperrealistic action sequences. Such viewer expectations might in turn affect reading positions adopted by them in relation to the series, and therefore their ultimate meaning-interpretation of various aspects of it.

Episode Guide

In North America *Alias* aired on ABC.
In the UK, Seasons One and Two first aired on Sky One, Seasons Three to
Five on Bravo.

Episode	*Title*	*Original Airdate*
	Season One	

1:1   **'Truth Be Told'**   (US) 30.9.2001
Writer (w.) J.J. Abrams.   (UK) 23.1.2002
Director (d.) J.J. Abrams.

1:2   **'So it Begins'**   (US) 7.10.2001
w. J.J. Abrams   (UK) 30.1.2002
d. Ken Olin

1:3   **'Parity'**   (US) 14.10.2001
w. Alex Kurtzman and Roberto Orci   (UK) 6.2.2002
d. Mikael Salomon
Guest Star: Gina Torres

1:4   **'A Broken Heart'**   (US) 21.10.2001
w. Vanessa Taylor   (UK) 15.2.2002
d. Harry Winer
Guest Star: Gina Torres

1:5   **'Doppelgänger'**   (US) 28.10.2001
w. Daniel Arkin   (UK) 20.2.2002
d. Ken Olin

1:6   **'Reckoning'**   (US) 18.11.2001
w. Jesse Alexander   (UK) 27.2.2002
d. Daniel Attias
Guest Star: John Hannah

1:7   **'Colour Blind'**   (US) 25.11.2001
w. Roberto Orci and Alex Kurtzman   (UK) 6.3.2002
d. Jack Bender
Guest Star: John Hannah

| 1:8 | **'Time Will Tell'** | (US) 2.12.2001 |
| | w. Jeff Pinkner | (UK) 13.3.2002 |

1:8   **'Time Will Tell'**   (US) 2.12.2001
w. Jeff Pinkner   (UK) 13.3.2002
d. Perry Lang
Guest Star: Gina Torres

1:9   **'Mea Culpa'**   (US) 9.12.2001
w. Debra J. Fisher and Erica Messer   (UK) 20.3.2002
d. Ken Olin

1:10   **'Spirit'**   (US) 16.12.2001
w. J.J. Abrams and Vanessa Taylor   (UK) 27.3.2002
d. Jack Bender

1:11   **'The Confession'**   (US) 6.1.2002
w. J.J. Abrams and Daniel Arkin   (UK) 3.4.2002
d. Harry Winer

1:12   **'The Box, Part One'**   (US) 20.1.2002
w. Jesse Alexander and John Eisendrath   (UK) 10.4.2002
d. Jack Bender
Guest Star: Quentin Tarantino

1:13   **'The Box: Part Two'**   (US) 10.2.2002
w. Jesse Alexander and John Eisendrath   (UK) 17.4.2002
d. Jack Bender
Guest Star: Quentin Tarantino

1:14   **'The Coup'**   (US) 24.2.2002
w. Alex Kurtzman and Roberto Orci   (UK) 24.4.2002
d. Tom Wright
Guest Star: David Anders

1:15   **'Page 47'**   (US) 3.3.2002
w. J.J. Abrams and Jeff Pinkner   (UK) 1.5.2002
d. Ken Olin
Guest Star: Amy Irving

1:16   **'The Prophecy'**   (US) 10.3.2002
w. John Eisendrath   (UK) 8.5.2002
d. Davis Guggenheim
Guest Stars: Roger Moore
    Lindsay Crouse
    Amy Irving

1:17   **'Q and A'**   (US) 17.3.2002
w. J.J. Abrams   (UK) 15.5.2002
d. Ken Olin
Guest Star: Terry O'Quinn

1:18   **'Masquerade'**   (US) 7.4.2002
w. Roberto Orci and Alex Kurtzman   (UK) 22.5.2002
d. Craig Zisk
Guest Star: Peter Berg

1:19   **'Snowman'**   (US) 14.4.2002
w. Jesse Alexander and Jeff Pinkner   (UK) 29.5.2002
d. Barnet Kellman
Guest Star: Peter Berg

1:20   **'The Solution'**   (US) 21.4.2002
w. John Eisendrath   (UK) 5.6.2002
d. DanielAttias
Guest Star: David Anders

1:21   **'Rendezvous'**   (US) 5.5.2002
w. Erica Messer and Debra J. Fisher   (UK) 12.6.2002
d. Ken Olin
Guest Stars: David Anders
    Amy Irving

1:22   **'Almost Thirty Years'**   (US) 12.5.2002
w. J.J. Abrams   (UK) 19.6.2002
d. J.J. Abrams
Guest Stars: David Anders
    Amy Irving

Season Two

2:1   **'The Enemy Walks In'**   (US) 29.9.2002
w. J.J. Abrams   (UK) 4.3.2003
d. Ken Olin

2:2   **'Trust Me'**   (US) 6.10.2002
w. John Eisendrath   (UK) 11.3.2003
d. Craig Zisk

2:3   **'Cipher'**   (US) 13.10.2002
w. Alex Kurtzman-Counter   (UK) 18.3.2003
    and Roberto Orci
d. Daniel Attias

2:4   **'Dead Drop'**   (US) 20.10.2002
w. Jesse Alexander   (UK) 25.3.2003
d. Guy Norman Bee

2:5	**'The Indicator'**	(US) 3.11.2002
	w. Jeff Pinkner	(UK) 1.4.2003
	d. Ken Olin	

2:6   **'Salvation'**   (US) 10.11.2002
w. Roberto Orci   (UK) 8.4.2003
     and Alex Kurtzman-Counter
d. Perry Lang
Guest Star: Amy Irving

2:7   **'The Counteragent'**   (US) 17.11.2002
w. John Eisendrath   (UK) 15.4.2003
d. Daniel Attias

2:8   **'The Passage, Part One'**   (US) 1.12.2002
w. Debra J. Fisher and Erica Messer   (UK) 28.4.2003
d. Ken Olin

2:9   **'The Passage, Part Two'**   (US) 8.12.2002
w. Crystal Nix Hines   (UK) 5.5.2003
d. Ken Olin

2:10   **'The Abduction'**   (US) 15.12.2002
w. Alex Kurtzman-Counter   (UK) 12.5.2003
     and Roberto Orci
d. Nelson McCormick
Guest Star: Faye Dunaway

2:11   **'A Higher Echelon'**   (US) 5.1.2003
w. John Eisendrath   (UK) 19.5.2003
d. Guy Norman Bee
Guest Star: Faye Dunaway

2:12   **'The Getaway'**   (US) 12.1.2003
w. Jeff Pinkner   (UK) 26.5.2003
d. Lawrence Trilling
Guest Star: Faye Dunaway

2:13   **'Phase One'**   (US) 26.1.2003
w. J.J. Abrams   (UK) 2.6.2003
d. Jack Bender
Guest Star: Rutger Hauer

2:14   **'Double Agent'**   (US) 2.2.2003
w. Roberto Orci   (UK) 9.6.2003
     and Alex Kurtzman-Counter
d. Ken Olin
Guest Star: Ethan Hawke

2:15	**'A Free Agent'**	(US) 9.2.2003

2:15   **'A Free Agent'**   (US) 9.2.2003
        w. Roberto Orci   (UK) 16.6.2003
            and Alex Kurtzman-Counter
        d. Alex Kurtzman-Counter
        Guest Star: Christian Slater

2:16   **'Firebomb'**   (US) 23.2.2003
        w. John Eisendrath   (UK) 23.6.2003
        d. Craig Zisk

2:17   **'A Dark Turn'**   (US) 2.3.2003
        w. Jesse Alexander   (UK) 30.6.2003
        d. Ken Olin

2:18   **'Truth Takes Time'**   (US) 16.3.2003
        w. J.R. Orci   (UK) 12.7.2003
        d. Nelson McCormick
        Guest Star: Amy Irving

2:19   **'Endgame'**   (US) 30.3. 2003
        w. Sean Gerace   (UK) 20.7.2003
        d. Perry Lang
        Guest Star: Christian Slater

2:20   **'Countdown'**   (US) 27.4.2003
        w. Jeff Pinkner   (UK) 27.7.2003
        Story: R.P. Gaborno
        d. Lawrence Trilling
        Guest Stars: David Carradine
            Danny Trejo

2:21   **'Second Double'**   (US) 4.5.2003
        w. Crystal Nix Hines   (UK) 3.8.2003
        Story: Breen Frazier
        d. Ken Olin

2:22   **'The Telling'**   (US) 4.5.2003
        w. J.J. Abrams   (UK) 10.8.2003
        d. J.J. Abrams

Season Three

3:1   **'The Two'**   (US) 29.9.2003
        w. J.J. Abrams   (UK) 15.3.2004
        d. Ken Olin

3:2	**'Succession'**	(US) 5.10.2003
	w. Roberto Orci	(UK) 21.3.2004
	and Alex Kurtzman-Counter	
	d. Daniel Attias	

3:3	**'Reunion'**	(US) 12.10.2003
	w. Jeff Pinkner	(UK) 28.3.2004
	d. Jack Bender	

3:4	**'A Missing Link'**	(US) 19.10.2003
	w. Monica Breen and Alison Schapker	(UK) 4.4.2004
	d. Lawrence Trilling	
	Guest Star: Justin Theroux	

3:5	**'Repercussions'**	(US) 26.10.2003
	w. Jesse Alexander	(UK) 11.4.2004
	d. Ken Olin	
	Guest Star: Justin Theroux	
	Djimon Hounsou	

3:6	**'The Nemesis'**	(US) 2.11.2003
	w. Crystal Nix Hines	(UK) 18.4.2004
	d. Lawrence Trilling	
	Guest Star: Merrin Dungey	

3:7	**'Prelude'**	(US) 9.11.2003
	w. J.R.Orci	(UK) 25.4.2004
	d. Jack Bender	

3:8	**'Breaking Point'**	(US) 23.11.2003
	w. Breen Frazier	(UK) 2.5.2004
	d. Daniel Attias	
	Guest Star: Richard Roundtree	

3:9	**'Conscious'**	(US) 20.11.2003
	w. Josh Appelbaum and André Nemec	(UK) 9.5.2004
	d. Ken Olin	
	Guest Star: David Cronenberg	

3:10	**'Remnants'**	(US) 7.12.2003
	w. Jeff Pinkner	(UK) 16.5.2004
	d. Jack Bender	
	Guest Stars: Bradley Cooper	
	Merrin Dungey	
	David Cronenberg	

3:11   **'Full Disclosure'**   (US) 11.1.2004
w. Jesse Alexander   (UK) 23.5.2004
d. Lawrence Trilling
Guest Star: Terry O'Quinn

3:12   **'Crossings'**   (US) 18.1.2004
w. Josh Appelbaum and André Nemec   (UK) 30.5.2004
d. Ken Olin
Guest Stars: Griffin Dunne
           Isabella Rossellini
           Arnold Vosloo

3:13   **'After Six'**   (US) 15.2.2004
w. Alison Schapker and Monica Breen   (UK) 6.6.2004
d. Maryann Brandon
Guest Stars: Vivica A. Fox
           Quentin Tarantino

3:14   **'Blowback'**   (US) 7.3.2004
w. Laurence Andries   (UK) 13.6.2004
d. Lawrence Trilling

3:15   **'Façade'**   (US) 14.3.2004
w. R.P. Gaborno and Christopher Hollier   (UK) 20.6.2004
d. Jack Bender
Guest Stars: Griffin Dunne
           Ricky Gervais

3:16   **'Taken'**   (US) 21.3.2004
w. J.R. Orci   (UK) 27.6.2004
d. Lawrence Trilling

3:17   **'The Frame'**   (US) 28.3.2004
w. Crystal Nix Hines   (UK) 4.7.2004
d. Max Mayer
Guest Star: Djimon Hounsou

3:18   **'Unveiled'**   (US) 11.4.2004
w. Monica Breen and Alison Schapker ›   (UK) 11.7.2004
d. Jack Bender
Guest Star: Djimon Hounsou

3:19   **'Hourglass'**   (US) 18.4.2004
w. Josh Appelbaum and André Nemec   (UK) 18.7.2004
d. Ken Olin
Guest Star: David Carradine

3:20	**'Blood Ties'**	(US) 25.4.2004
	w. J.R.Orci	(UK) 25.7.2004

Story: Monica Breen and Alison Schapker
d. Jack Bender
Guest Star: Richard Roundtree
    Mia Maestro

3:21   **'Legacy'**   (US) 2.5.2004
     w. Jesse Alexander   (UK) 1.8.2004
     d. Lawrence Trilling
     Guest Stars: Vivica A. Fox
         Isabella Rossellini
         Mia Maestro

3:22   **'Resurrection'**   (US) 23.5.2004
     w. Jeff Pinkner   (UK) 8.8.2004
     d. Ken Olin
     Guest Stars: Isabella Rossellini
         Mia Maestro

Season Four

4:1   **'Authorized Personnel Only, Part 1'**   (US) 5.1.2005
     J.J. Abrams and Jeff Melvoin   (UK) 3.4.2005
     d. Ken Olin
     Guest Stars: Angela Bassett

4:2   **'Authorized Personnel Only, Part 2'**   (US) 5.1.2005
     w. J.J. Abrams and Jeff Melvoin   (UK) 3.4.2005
     d. Ken Olin

4:3   **'The Awful Truth'**   (US) 12.1.2005
     w. Jesse Alexander   (UK) 10.4.2005
     d. Lawrence Trilling

4:4   **'Ice'**   (US) 19.1.2005
     w. Jeff Bell   (UK) 17.4.2005
     d. Jeff Bell
     Guest Star: Kelly MacDonald

4:5   **'Welcome to Liberty Village'**   (US) 26.1.2005
     w. Drew Goddard   (UK) 24.4.2005
     d. Kevin Hooks

4:6   **'Nocturne'**   (US) 9.2.2005
     w. Jeff Pinkner   (UK) 1.5.2005
     d. Lawrence Trilling

4:7	**'Détente'**	(US) 16.2.2005
	w. Monica Breen and Alison Schapker	(UK) 8.5.2005
	d. Craig Zisk	

4:7   **'Détente'**   (US) 16.2.2005
w. Monica Breen and Alison Schapker (UK) 8.5.2005
d. Craig Zisk

4:8   **'Echoes'**   (US) 23.2.2005
w. Josh Appelbaum and André Nemec (UK) 15.5.2005
d. Dan Attias
Guest Star: Gina Torres

4:9   **'A Man of his Word'**   (US) 2.3.2005
w. Breen Frazier (UK) 22.5.2005
d. Marita Grabiak
Guest Stars: Gina Torres
    David Anders

4:10   **'The Index'**   (US) 9.3.2005
w. Alison Shapker and J.R. Orci (UK) 29.5.2005
d. Lawrence Trilling
Guest Star: Angela Bassett

4:11   **'The Road Home'**   (US) 16.3.2005
w. Josh Appelbaum and André Nemec (UK) 5.6.2005
d. Maryann Brandon

4:12   **'The Orphan'**   (US) 23.3.2005
w. Jeff Bell and Monica Breen (UK) 12.6.2005
d. Ken Olin
Guest Star: Sonia Braga

4:13   **'Tuesday'**   (US) 30.3.2005
w. Drew Goddard and Breen Frazier (UK) 19.6.2005
d. Frederick E.O. Toye
Guest Star: Ulrich Thomsen

4:14   **'Nightingale'**   (US) 6.4.2005
w. Breen Frazier (UK) 26.6.2005
d. Lawrence Trilling

4:15   **'Pandora'**   (US) 13.4.2005
w. Jeff Pinkner and J.R. Orci (UK) 10.7.2005
d. Kevin Hooks
Guest Stars: Isabella Rossellini
    Joel Grey
    Izabella Scorupco

4:16	**'Another Mister Sloane'**	(US) 13.4.2005
	w. Luke McMullen	(UK) 17.7.2005
	d. Greg Yaitanes	
	Guest Star: Joel Grey	

4:17	**'A Clear Conscience'**	(US) 27.4.2005
	w. J.R. Orci	(UK) 24.7.2005
	d. Lawrence Trilling	
	Guest Stars: Sonia Braga	
	Michael McKean	

4:18	**'Mirage'**	(US) 4.5.2005
	w. Steven Kane	(UK) 31.7.2005
	d. Brad Turner	
	Guest Stars: Sonia Braga	
	Michael McKean	

4:19	**'In Dreams'**	(US) 11.5.2005
	w. Jon Robin Baitz	(UK) 7.8.2005
	d. Jennifer Garner	
	Guest Stars: Joel Grey	
	Amy Irving	

4:20	**'The Descent'**	(US) 18.5.2005
	w. Jeff Bell	(UK) 14.8.2005
	d. Jeff Bell	
	Guest Stars: Sonia Braga	
	Isabella Rossellini	
	Angela Bassett	

4:21	**'Search and Rescue'**	(US) 25.5.2005
	w. Monica Breen and Alison Schapker	(UK) 21.8.2005
	d. Lawrence Trilling	
	Guest Stars: Lena Olin	
	Angela Bassett	

4:22	**'Before the Flood'**	(US) 25.5.2005
	w. Josh Appelbaum and André Nemec	(UK) 29.8.2005
	d. Lawrence Trilling	
	Guest Stars: Lena Olin	
	Sonia Braga	

Season Five

5:1	**'Prophet Five'**	(US) 29.9.2005
	w. Alison Shapker and Monica Breen	(UK) 26.3.2006
	d. Ken Olin	

| 5:2 | '...1...'
w. J.R. Orci
d. Frederick E.O. Toye | (US) 6.10.2005
(UK) 2.04.2006 |

5:2   '...1...'   (US) 6.10.2005
w. J.R. Orci   (UK) 2.04.2006
d. Frederick E.O. Toye

5:3   **'The Shed'**   (US) 13.10.2005
w. Breen Frazier   (UK) 9.04.2006
d. Tucker Gates

5:4   **'Mockingbird'**   (US) 20.10.2005
w. Drew Goddard   (UK) 16.04.2006
d. Frederick E.O. Toye

5:5   **'Out of the Box'**   (US) 27.10.2005
w. Jesse Alexander   (UK) 23.04.2006
d. Jay Torres

5:6   **'Solo'**   (US) 10.11.2005
w. Jeff Bell   (UK) 30.04.2006
d. Jeff Bell

5:7   **'Fait Accompli'**   (US) 17.11.2005
w. Andi Bushell   (UK) 7.05.2006
d. Richard Coad
Guest Stars: Mia Maestro
   Angus MacFadyen

5:8   **'Bob'**   (US) 7.12.2005
w. Monica Breen and Alison Schapker   (UK) 15.05.2006
d. Donald Thorin Jnr
Guest Star: David Anders

5:9   **'The Horizon'**   (US) 14.12.2005
w. Josh Appelbaum and André Nemec   (UK) 21.05.2006
d. Tucker Gates

5:10   **'SOS'**   (US) 19.4.2006
w. J.R. Orci   (UK) 28.05.2006
d. Karen Gaviola
Guest Star: Greg Grunberg

5:11   **'Maternal Instinct'**   (US) 19.4.2006
w. Breen Frazier   (UK) 4.6.2006
d. Tucker Gates
Guest Stars: Lena Olin
   Michael Vartan

5:12	'There's Only One Sydney Bristow'	(US) 26.4.2006
	w. Drew Goddard	(UK) 11.6.2006

'There's Only One Sydney Bristow'   (US) 26.4.2006
w. Drew Goddard   (UK) 11.6.2006
d. Robert M. Williams Jnr
Guest Stars: Bradley Cooper
    Gina Torres
    Angus MacFadyen

5:13   '30 Seconds'   (US) 3.5.2006
w. Alison Shapker and Monica Breen   (UK) 18.6.2006
d. Frederick E.O. Toye
Guest Stars: Mia Maestro
    Angus MacFadyen

5:14   'I See Dead People'   (US) 10.5.2006
w. Andi Bushell and J.R. Orci   (UK) 25.6.2006
d. Jamie Babbit
Guest Stars: Michael Vartan
    Mia Maestro
    David Anders

5:15   'No Hard Feelings'   (US) 17.5.2006
w. Samantha Humphry   (UK) 2.7.2006
d. Tucker Gates
Guest Stars: David Anders
    Michael Vartan

5:16   'Reprisal'   (US) 22.5.2006
w. Alison Schnapker and Monica Breen   (UK) 9.7.2006
d. Frederick E.O. Toye
Guest Stars: Lena Olin
    Michael Vartan
    David Anders
    Mia Maestro
    Amanda Foreman

5:17   'All the Time in the World'   (US) 22.5.2006
w. Jeff Pinkner and Drew Goddard   (UK) 9.7.2006
d. Tucker Gates
Guest Stars: Lena Olin
    Michael Vartan
    Mia Maestro
    David Anders
    Merrin Dungay

Bibliography

ABC Television Network. Press release, ABC Media.net, 26 February 2003. http://www.abcmedianet.com/pressrel/dispDNR.html?id= 022603_08. Accessed 6 April 2006.

Adder, Plaid. 'Join Us on the Dark Side: A Critical Introduction to the Sith Academy Corpus', Welcome to the Sith Academy. http://www.siubhan.com/sithacademy/ criticalintro.html. Accessed 10 November 2005.

Addyawesome. 'The Worst Season?', 22 May 2006. http://forums.go.com/abc/primetime/alias/thread?ID=1089834#13616974. Accessed 11 June 2006.

TheAfterglow. 'In a Frame', Fanfiction.net, 24 November 2005. http://www.fanfiction.net/s/2654849/1/. Accessed 29 November 2005.

Agent Riss. 'The Ex, The Wife', Alias Slash Archive. http://www.imjust-sayin.net/aliasslash/. Accessed 6 March 2006.

Agha-Jaffar, Tamara. *Demeter and Persephone: Lessons from a Myth*. Jefferson, NC: McFarland and Company, 2002.

Alias: The Complete First Season. UK: Buena Vista Home Entertainment Inc., region 2, PAL, 2003.

Alias: The Complete Second Season. UK: Buena Vista Home Entertainment Inc., region 2, PAL, 2004.

Alias: The Complete Third Season. UK: Buena Vista Home Entertainment Inc., region 2, PAL, 2005.

Alias: The Complete Fourth Season. UK: Buena Vista Home Entertainment Inc., region 2, PAL, 2005.

Alias Italia: Il Dossier Sydney Bristow. http:www.antoniogenna.net/alias/alias.htm. Accessed 30 November 2005.

Alias Slash Archive. http://www.imjustsayin.net/aliasslash/. Accessed 26 March 2006.

Aliasmycrack. 'The Worst Season?', 22 May 2006. http://forums.go.com/abc/primetime/alias/thread?ID=1089834#13616974. Accessed 11 June 2006

Allies: Syd/Vaughn Fan Fic. http://www.alias-media.com/allies/. Accessed 12 December 2005.

AllAlias.com. http:www.allalias.com. Accessed 30 November 2005.

Allrath, Gaby, Marion Gymnich and Carola Surkamp. 'Towards a Narratology of TV Series', in Gaby Allrath and Marion Gymnich, eds,

Narrative Strategies in Television Series. Basingstoke: Palgrave Macmillan, 2005: 1–43.

Amy. 'Fanfic and Me: A (Sort of) Love Story', 26 May 2004, personal email.

Angelini, Sergio. 'TV Spies: 1970s and Beyond'. http://www.screenonline.org.uk/tv/id/1008415/. Accessed 26 March 2006.

Angvau57. 'The Iceman Cometh'. Allies: Syd/Vaughn Fan Fic. http://alias-media.com/allies/viewstory.php?sid=1174. Accessed 10 December 2005.

Anonymous. 'Black Love in Movies and on Television', *Ebony*, 46:4 (February 1991): 162–9.

Anonymous. 'Spy Games', *TV Guide*, 50:38 (21 September 2002): 18–22, 24.

Arcand, Bernard. *The Jaguar and the Anteater: Pornography Degree Zero*, trans. Wayne Grady. New York: Verso, 1993.

Austin, Thomas. *Hollywood, Hype and Audiences: Selling and Watching Popular Film in the 1990s.* Manchester: Manchester University Press, 2002.

Bacon-Smith, Camille. *Enterprising Women: Television Fandom and the Creation of Popular Myth.* Philadelphia: University of Pennsylvania Press, 1992.

Bantam Books. 'Bantam Books to Publish Official Companion and Fiction Series', press release, 11 June 2002. http://www.teenlit.com/bookreviews/press_releases.htm. Accessed 28 April 2006.

Bartley, Jena. 'Afternoon Delight', Alias Slash Archive. http://www.imjustsayin.net/aliasslash/. Accessed 18 April 2006.

Battis, Jes. *Blood Relations: Chosen Families in Buffy the Vampire Slayer and Angel.* Jefferson, NC and London: McFarland & Company, 2005.

Bennett, Tony, and Janet Woollacott. *Bond and Beyond: The Political Career of a Popular Hero.* London: Macmillan, 1987.

bitterbyrden. 23 May 2006. http:// ramdonomo.livejournal.com/462773.html. Accessed 11 June 2006.

Bjarkman, Kim. 'To Have and to Hold: The Video Collector's Relationship with an Ethereal Medium', *Television & New Media*, 5:3 (2004): 217–46.

Blake. 'Home', September, 2005. http://www.sd-6.com/. Accessed 5 January 2006.

Bogle, Donald. *Prime Time Blues: African Americans on Network Television.* New York: Farrar, Straus and Giroux, 2001.

Bogue, Ronald. *Deleuze on Cinema.* New York: Routledge, 2003.

Brison, Susan J. *Aftermath: Violence and the Remaking of a Self.* Princeton, NJ: Princeton University Press, 2002.

Britton, Wesley. *Spy Television.* Westport, CT: Praeger, 2004.

Brookey, Robert Alan, and Robert Westerfelhaus. 'Hiding Homoeroticism in Plain View: The *Fight Club* DVD as Digital Closet', *Critical Studies in Media Communication*, 19:1 (2002): 21–43.

Brown, Mary Ellen, ed. *Television and Women's Culture: The Politics of the Popular*. London: Sage Publications, 1990.

Bruzzi, Stella. *Bringing Up Daddy: Fatherhood and Masculinity in Post-War Hollywood*. London: BFI, 2005.

Bundy, Bill. '"*Alias*" Over in May', zap2it.com, 23 November 2005. http://tv.zap2it.com/tveditorial/tve_main/1,1002,271I98775I11,00.html. Accessed 12 February 2006.

Burkert, Walter. *Greek Religion*. Cambridge, MA: Harvard University Press, 1985.

Butler, Judith. *Precarious Life: The Powers of Mourning and Violence*. London and New York: Verso, 2004.

Calabrese, Omar. *Neo-Baroque: A Sign of the Times*. Princeton, NJ: Princeton University Press, 1992.

Caldwell, John Thornton, 'Prefiguring DVD Bonus Tracks: Making-Ofs and Behind-The-Scenes as Historic Television Programming Strategies', paper presented at conference Some People are Disappointed to Only Get the Film . . . What is a DVD?, Humanities Research Centre, University of Warwick, 23 April 2005, see conference report by James Walters in *Screen*. 46:4 (2005): 503–7.

Campbell, Joseph. *The Hero with a Thousand Faces*. Princeton, NJ: Princeton University Press, 1973.

Cerasini, Marc. *24: The House Special Subcommittee's Findings at CTU*. New York: HarperEntertainment, 2003.

Chatman, Seymour. *Story and Discourse: Narrative Structure in Fiction and Film*. Ithaca, NY: Cornell University Press, 1978.

Clute, John. 'Davies L(eslie) P(urnell) (1914–)', in John Clute and Peter Nicholls, eds, *The Encyclopedia of Science Fiction*, 2nd edition. London: Orbit, 1999: 303.

Costello, Victor. 'Interactivity and the "Cyber-Fan": An Exploration of Audience Involvement Within the Electronic Fan Culture of the Internet', unpublished PhD dissertation, University of Tennessee, 1998: 1–25.

Cox, Greg. 'The Business of Novelization & Tie-Ins Part One: The Deal', The International Association of Media Tie-in Writers. http://www.iamtw.org/art_business_deal.html. Accessed 12 December 2005a.

——. Email interview, 7 November 2005b.

Crane, Lynda. 'Romance Novel Readers: In Search of Feminist Change?', *Women's Studies*, 23 (1994): 257–69.

Creeber, Glen. *Serial Television: Big Drama on the Small Screen*. London: BFI Publishing, 2004.

Deleuze, Gilles. *Cinema 2: The Time-Image*, trans. Hugh Tomlinson, Robert Galeta. Minneapolis: University of Minnesota Press, 1989.

Diamond, Lisa. 'I'm Straight But I Kissed a Girl: The Trouble with American Media Representations of Female-Female Sexuality', *Feminism and Psychology*, 15:1 (2005): 104–10.

Dilmore, Kevin. 'Of Spies and Survivors', *Amazing Stories*, 74:3 (February 2005): 20–4.

di Mattia, Joanna. 'Fisher's Sons: Brotherly Love and the Spaces of Male Intimacy in *Six Feet Under*', in Kim Akass and Janet McCabe, eds, *Reading Six Feet Under: TV to Die For*. London: I.B.Tauris, 2005: 150–60.

Dinsmore-Tuli, Uma, 'The Pleasures of "Home Cinema", or Watching Movies on Telly: An Audience Study of Cinephiliac VCR Use', *Screen*, 41:3 (2000): 315–27.

Dreiser. 'Clever Girl', Alias Slash Archive. http://www.imjustsayin.net/aliasslash/. Accessed 26 March 2006.

'Duress', in *Wikipedia, the Free Encyclopedia*. http://en.wikipedia.org/wiki/Duress. Accessed 2 February 2006.

Early, Frances, and Kathleen Kennedy. 'Introduction: Athena's Daughters', in Frances Early and Kathleen Kennedy, eds, *Athena's Daughters: Television's New Women Warriors*. Syracuse, NY: Syracuse University Press, 2003: 1–10.

Edinger, Edward F. *The Bible and the Psyche: Individuation Symbolism in the Old Testament*. Toronto: Inner City Books, 1986.

——. *The Christian Archetype: A Jungian Commentary on the Life of Christ*. Toronto: Inner City Books, 1987.

——. *Ego and Archetype*. Baltimore: Penguin Books, 1973.

——. *The Eternal Drama: The Inner Meaning of Greek Mythology*. Boston: Shambhala Publications, 1994.

Elise-2. 'Know Thy Enemy', Alias Slash Archive. http://www.imjustsayin.net/aliasslash/. Accessed 26 March 2006.

Ellis, John. *Visible Fictions: Cinema, Television, Video*. London and New York: Routledge, 1992.

Erica. '*Alias* Fan Essay', 26 March 2006, personal email.

Fanfiction.net. http:www.fanfiction.net. Accessed 30 November 2005.

Ferguson, George. *Signs and Symbols in Christian Art*. New York: Oxford University Press, 1961.

Fernbeck, Jan. 'The Individual within the Collective: Virtual Ideology and the Realization of Collective Principles', in Steven G. Jones, ed., *Virtual Culture: Identity and Communication in Cyberspace*. London: Sage, 1997: 36–54.

Feuer, Jane. *MTM Quality Television*. London: BFI, 1984.

Fudge, Rachel. 'The Buffy Effect; or, a Tale of Cleavage and Marketing', *Bitch*, 10 (Summer 1999). www.bitchmagazine/archives/ 08_01buffy/buffy1.shtml. Accessed 10 March 2006.

Gertie Beth. 'Site Statistics', Alias-Media.com, 2002–6. http://alias-media.com/modules.php?name=Statistics. Accessed 31 March 2006.

Gillers, Stephen. 'Taking *L.A. Law* More Seriously', *Yale Law Journal*, 98:8 (June 1989) Symposium: Popular Legal Culture: 1607–23.

Gitlin, Todd. *Inside Prime Time*, 2nd edition. London: Routledge, 1994.

Gray, Herman. *Watching Race – Television and the Struggle for Blackness*. Minneapolis and London: University of Minnesota Press, 1995.

Gross, Edward. '*Alias*: Turning Spy Genre and Television on its Head, a College Student Turned Secret Agent Takes no Prisoners', *Cinefantastique*, 34: 6 (October/November, 2002): 32–43.

——. 'Agent Provocateur', *Cinefantastique*, 35:5 (October/November 2003): 46–52, 75.

——. 'Man on a Mission', *Cinefantastique*, 36:1 (February/March 2005): 34–6 (Interview with J.J. Abrams).

Grossberg, Lawrence. 'Is There a Fan in the House?: The Affective Sensibility of Fandom', in Lisa Lewis, ed., *The Adoring Audience: Fan Culture and Popular Media*. New York: Routledge, 1992: 50–65.

Hagedorn, Roger. 'Technology and Economic Exploitation: The Serial as a Form of Narrative Presentation', *Wide Angle*, 10:4 (1988): 4–12.

Hall, Stuart. 'Encoding/Decoding', in Stuart Hall, Dortoy Hobson, Andrew Lowe and Paul Willis, eds, *Culture, Media, Language*. London: Hutchinson, 1980: 128–38.

Hammond, Michael. 'Introduction' [to section 'The series/serial form'], in Michael Hammond and Lucy Mazdon, eds, *The Contemporary Television Series*. Edinburgh: Edinburgh University Press, 2005: 75–82.

Hard, Robin. *Apollodorus: The Library of Greek Mythology*. Oxford: Oxford University Press, 1997.

Harolovich, Mary Beth. 'Sitcoms and Suburbs: Positioning the 1950s Homemaker', *Quarterly Review of Film and Video*, 11:1 (1989): 61–83.

Harris, Stephen L., and Gloria Platzner. *Classical Mythology: Images and Insights*. Mountain View: Mayfield Publishing Company, 2001.

Heidegger, Martin. *Nietzsche, Volumes Three and Four*. San Francisco: Harper Collins, 1991.

Hebron, Teresa. Email interview, 22 November 2005.

Herman, Judith Lewis. *Trauma and Recovery*. London: Pandora, 1994.

Higgins, Emily. Email interview, 12 December 2005.

Hight, Craig. 'Making-of Documentaries on DVD: *The Lord of the Rings* Trilogy and Special Editions', *The Velvet Light Trap*, 56:3 (2005): 4–17.

Hills, Matt. 'Interview with Henry Jenkins', *Intensities*, 2 (2001). http://www.cult-media.com/issue2/CMRjenk.htm. Accessed 10 April 2005.

——. *Fan Cultures*. London: Routledge, 2002.

——. 'Cult TV, Quality and the Role of the Episode/Programme Guide', in Michael Hammond and Lucy Mazdon, eds, *The Contemporary Television Series*. Edinburgh: Edinburgh University Press, 2005: 190–206.

hold-that-thought. 'Need to Destroy', Alias Slash Archive. http://www.imjustsayin.net/aliasslash/. Accessed 10 November 2005.

Holt, Jennifer. 'Vertical Vision: Deregulation, Industrial Economy and Prime-time Design', in Mark Jancovich and James Lyons, eds, *Quality Popular Television*. London: BFI, 2003: 11–31.

The Holy Bible: Translated from the Latin Vulgate, Dr Challoner and Dr H.J. Ganss, gen. eds. Detroit: E.J. McDevitt Co., 1912.

Icyfire. 'A Son's Journey', Fanfiction.net, 8 December 2002. http://www.fanfiction.net/s/1110856/1/. Accessed 30 November 2005.

In the Moonlight. http:www.inthemoonlight.com. Accessed 30 November 2005.

Jancovich, Mark, and James Lyons. 'Introduction', in Mark Jancovich and James Lyons, eds, *Quality Popular Television*. London: BFI, 2003: 1–8.

Jeffords, Susan. 'The Big Switch: Hollywood Masculinity in the Nineties', in Jim Collins, Hilary Radner and Ava Preacher Collins, eds, *Film Theory Goes to the Movies*. New York and London: Routledge, 1993: 196–208.

Jenkins, III, Henry. 'Star Trek Rerun, Reread, Rewritten: Fan Writing as Textual Poaching', *Critical Studies in Mass Communication*, 5 (1988): 85–105.

——. *Textual Poachers: Television Fans and Participatory Fan Culture*. New York: Routledge, 1992.

Jensen, Jeff. 'Going. Going. Going. Gone', *Entertainment Weekly*, 873 (2006): 18–19.

Johnson, Catherine. *Telefantasy*. London: BFI, 2005.

Jones, Sara Gwenllian. 'The Sex Lives of Cult Television Characters', *Screen*, 43:1 (Spring 2002): 79–90.

——. 'Web Wars: Resistance, Online Fandom and Studio Censorship', in Mark Jancovich and James Lyons, eds, *Quality Popular Television*, London: BFI, 2003: 163–77.

——, and Roberta E. Pearson. 'Introduction', in Sara Gwenllian Jones and Roberta E. Pearson, eds, *Cult Television*. Minneapolis: University of Minnesota Press, 2004: ix–xx.

Jones, Steve. *Cybersociety: Computer Mediated Communication and Community*. London: Sage, 1994a.

——. 'Virtual Culture', in Steve Jones, ed., *Cybersociety: Computer Mediated Communication and Community*. London: Sage, 1994b: 20–36.

——. *Cybersociety 2.0: Revisiting Computer Mediated Community and Technology*. London: Sage, 1998.

Joshi, S.T. 'Powers of the Mind', *The Armchair Detective*, 24:2 (1991): 174–85.

Jung, Carl G. *Man and His Symbols*. New York: Dell Publishing, 1968.

Karras, Irene. 'The Third Wave's Final Girl: *Buffy the Vampire Slayer*', *thirdspace*, 1:2 (March 2002). www.iiav.nl/ezines/web/Thirdspace/2002Vol1(March)/thirdspace/karras.htm. Accessed 18 June 2006.

Kendrick, James. 'Aspect Ratios and Joe Six-Packs: Home Theatre Enthusiasts' Battle to Legitimize the DVD Experience', *The Velvet Light Trap*, 56 (2005): 58–70.

Keveney, Bill. 'The Many Aliases of J.J. Abrams', *USA Today*, 1 April 2005, 10:19.

Klinger, Barbara. 'Film History Terminable and Interminable: Recovering the Past in Reception Studies', *Screen*, 38:2 (1997): 107–28.

——. 'The New Media Aristocrats: Home Theatre and the Domestic Film Experience', *The Velvet Light Trap*, 42 (1998): 4–19.

Kozloff, Sarah. 'Narrative Theory and Television', in Robert C. Allen, ed., *Channels of Discourse, Reassembled*. London: Routledge, 1992: 67–100.

Kustritz, Ann. 'Slashing the Romance Narrative', *Journal of American Culture*, 26 (2003): 371–85.

Labi, Nadya. 'Girl Power', *Time Magazine*, 29 June 1998: 28.

Labyrinthine. 'Fanfiction', 15 January 2006, personal email.

Lancaster, Kurt. *Interacting with Babylon 5: Fan Performances in a Media Universe*. Austin: University of Texas Press, 2001.

Lane, Edele. 'Bare', Alias Slash Archive. http://www.imjustsayin.net/aliasslash/. Accessed 26 March 2006.

Lane, Philip J. 'The Existential Condition of Television Crime Drama', *Journal of Popular Culture* (March 2001): 137–51.

Lauren. '*Alias* Fandom', 28 May 2004, personal email.

——. 'The *Alias* Fandom', We're Almost There, 26 March 2006. http://ciachick711.livejournal.com/179337.html#cutid1. Accessed 26 March 2006.

Lavery, David. 'The Soul of Andy Sipowicz: Depth of Character and the Depth of Television', Culture Clash online journal, 5: Crime, 6 November 2001. http://www.poppolitics.com/articles/2001-06-11-sipowicz.shtml.

——. 'Afterword', in Steven Peacock, ed., *Reading 24: TV Against the Clock*. London: I.B. Tauris, 2007.

Lee, Kylie. 'Confronting Enterprise Slash Fan Fiction', *Extrapolation*, 44 (2003): 69–83.

Leibman, Nina A. *Living Room Lectures: The Fifties Family in Film and Television*. Austin: University of Texas Press, 1995.

Leveugle, L. 'People, Observations, Curiosities: The Plot Thickens', *Guardian*, 9 December 2003: 4.

Luna_Sky. 'The Chains of Self'. http://www.perchance-to-dream.net/luna/chains.htm. Accessed 6 December 2005.

Maas, John-Michael. 'Breaking Out of the Box: Original Novels Based on Popular TV Series are Finding a Ready Market', *Publishers' Weekly*, 249:51 (23 December 2002): 16–18.

MacDonald, Fred. *Black and White TV: African Americans in Television Since 1948*, 2nd edition. Chicago: Nelson Hall, 1992.

Mace-Tessler, Isaac. '"Have You Got the Look?": How DVD Extras and Interactive Menus Expand the Experience of Cinematic Visual Design', paper presented at conference Some People are Disappointed to Only Get the Film . . . What is a DVD?, Humanities Research Centre, University of Warwick, 23 April 2005, see conference report by James Walters in *Screen*, 46:4 (2005): 503–7.

Madsen, Julie. '"Kirk, Honey. It's Me, Spock!"', *Utne Reader*, 113 (2002): 32.

Mahan, Colin. 'ABC Buries *Alias* Finale: Last Episode of Spy Series Gets Lost in a Sea of Season Finales', TV.com, 23 May 2006. http://www.tv.com/story/story.html&story_id=4651&q=ALIAS?tag=search_results;additional_links;0.

Melanie-Anne. 'Fragments of Truth', Fanfiction.net, 10 November 2005. http://www.fanfiction.net/s/2654185/1/. Accessed 30 November 2005.

Morreale, Joanne. 'Sitcoms Say Goodbye: The Cultural Spectacle of *Seinfeld*'s Last Episode', in Joanne Morreale, ed., *Critiquing the Sitcom: A Reader*, The Television Series. Syracuse, NY: Syracuse University Press, 2003: 274–85.

Murphy, Robert. *Sixties British Cinema*. London: BFI, 1992.

Ndalianis, Angela. 'Television and the Neo-baroque', in Michael Hammond and Lucy Mazdon, eds, *The Contemporary Television Series*. Edinburgh: Edinburgh University Press, 2005: 83–101.

Nelson, Robin. *TV Drama in Transition: Forms, Values and Cultural Change*. Basingstoke: Macmillan, 1997.

Nietzsche, Friedrich. *The Birth of Tragedy and The Case of Wagner*, trans. Walter Kaufman. New York: Vintage Books, 1967.

Nocturnal Activities: A Jack Bristow Fanfic Archive. http:www.nocturnalactivities.net. Accessed 30 November 2005.

Nova88. 'Amsterdam', LiveJournal. http://www.livejournal.com/community/clandestine_ops/2775.html. Accessed 1 December 2005.

Oppenheimer, Jean, 'Espionage 101', *American Cinematographer*, 83:11 (2002): 80–9.

Penely, Constance. 'Feminism, Psychoanalysis, and the Study of Popular Culture', in Lawrence Grossberg, Cary Nelson, Paula Treichler, Linda Baughman and Greg Wise, eds, *Cultural Studies*. New York: Routledge, 1992: 479–500.

Peyton-Roberts, Laura. *A Secret Life*. New York: Bantam Books, 2003.

Phriendly11. 'Credit Dauphine', 22 May 2004, personal email.

Porter, Lynnette, and David Lavery. *Unlocking the Meaning of Lost: An Unauthorized Guide*. Napierville, IL: Sourcebooks, 2006.

Porter, Rick. '"Alias" Creator Explains Why SD-6 Had To Go', 18 February 2003. http://tv.zap2it.com/tveditorial/tve_main/ 1,1002,271 | 80232 | 11 |,00.html. Accessed 3 May 2006.

Queen, Witch (n.d.). 'The gayness of Smallville', May 20, 2004. http:// www.somedistantgalaxy.com/heroes/gayness.htm.

Radway, Janice. *Reading the Romance: Women, Patriarchy, and Popular Culture*. Chapel Hill: University of North Carolina Press, 1984.

Rapkin, Mickey. 'Drama King', *GQ*, December 2005: 196, 201.

Raugust, Karen. 'TV Tie-ins Target Teen and Preteen Girls', *Publishers' Weekly*, 245:3 (19 January 1998): 243–4.

Rimmon-Kenan, Shlomith. *Narrative Fiction*, 2nd edition. London: Routledge, 2002.

Rodowick, D.N. *Gilles Deleuze's Time Machine*. Durham, NC: Duke University Press, 1997.

Rosen, Lisa. 'R.I.P. "Buffy": You drove a stake through convention', *Los Angeles Times*, 20 May 2003: Section E: 1.

Rporche. 'The Worst Season?'. 22 May 2006. http://forums.go.com/abc/ primetime/alias/thread?ID=1089834#13616974. Accessed 11 June 2006.

Salmon, Catherine, and Don Symons. 'Slash Fiction and Human Mating Psychology', *Journal of Sex Research*, 41 (2004): 94–101.

Scarry, Elaine. *The Body in Pain : The Making and Unmaking of the World*. New York: Oxford University Press, 1985.

Schneider, Karen. 'With Violence if Necessary: Rearticulating the Family in the Contemporary Action Thriller', *Journal of Popular Film and Television*, 27:1 (1999): 2–11.

Scodari, Christine. 'Resistance Re-examined: Gender, Fan Practices, and Science Fiction Television', *Popular Communication*, 1:2 (2003): 111–31.

SD-1.net. 'Alias Discussion'. http://www.SD-1.net. Accessed 30 November 2005.

'Series 2005–6 Primetime Wrap'. www.hollywoodreporter.com/thr/ television/feature-display.jsp?vnu_content_id=1002576393. Accessed 11 June 2006.

Shugart, Helene A. 'Counterhegemonic Acts: Appropriation as a Feminist Rhetorical Strategy', *Quarterly Journal of Speech*, 83 (1997): 210–29.

Simon, William H. 'Moral Pluck: Legal Ethics in Popular Culture', *Columbia Law Review*, 101:3 (April 2001): 421–47.

Sivi. 'The Acts of Gods', Alias Slash Archive. http://www.imjustsayin.net/aliasslash/. Accessed 26 March 2006.

Smith, Greg. 'Serial Narrative and Guest Stars: Ally McBeal's Eccentrics', in Michael Hammond and Lucy Mazdon, eds, *The Contemporary Television Series*. Edinburgh: Edinburgh University Press, 2005: 102–22.

Souris. 'Fandom', 12 December 2005, personal email.

Stern, Danielle M. 'Real World Commodities: MTV and the Selling of Sexuality on Reality Television', *American Sexuality Magazine*, 3:4, Online Version. http://nsrc.sfsu.edu/MagArticle.cfm?&Article =600. Accessed 27 April 2006.

Sumser, John. *Morality and Social Order in Television Crime Drama*. Jefferson, NC: McFarland, 1996.

Suro, Xiomara. 'A Pregnant Action Hero: What a Concept', *Whoosh*, 57 (2001). http://www.whoosh.org/issue58/suro2.html. Accessed 9 June 2006.

Sutherland, Sharon, and Sarah Swan, '"Tell Me Where the Bomb Is, Or I Will Kill Your Son": Situational Morality on *24*', in S. Peacock, ed., *Reading 24: TV Against the Clock*. London and New York: I.B.Tauris, 2007.

Sydneybristow77. '47 Ways in which the Finale Sucked . . .', 25 May 2006. http://forums.go.com/abc/primetime/alias/thread?ID=1101992&forumStart=0. Accessed 11 June 2006.

Tallerico, Brian. 'For Alias on the High Wire w/o a Net', 4 January 2005. http://www.medlialifemagazine.com/News2005/jan05/jan03/2_tues/news2tuesday.html. Accessed 11 June 2006.

Terr, Lenore. *Unchained Memories: True Stories of Traumatic Memories, Lost and Found*. New York: Harper Collins, 1994.

Thompson, Kristin. *Storytelling in Film and Television*. Cambridge, MA: Harvard University Press, 2003.

Thompson, Robert J. *From Hill Street Blues to ER: Television's Second Golden Age*. Syracuse: Syracuse University Press, 1996.

Thorne. 'No Subject,' This Time is Whatever I want it to Be, 22 May 2006 http://akathorne/livejournal.com.

Tonkin, Boyd. 'Farewell Buffy, and Fangs for the Memories', 21 May 2003. www.independent.co.uk/Media/article105509.ece. Accessed 10 March 2006

TVShowsOnDVD.com. www.tvshowsondvd.com. Accessed 13 March 2006.

Vartan Hos, The. 'Ho Questions', The Safe House, 25 April 2003. http://
www.vartanho.com/faq/askthehos3.html. Accessed 10 December
2005.

——. 'Thank You', The Safe House, 25 April 2003. http://www.
vartanho.com/faq/thanks.html. Accessed 10 December 2005.

——. 'A Note About the *Alias* Content on this Site', The Safe House, 28
February 2004. http://www.vartanho.com/news/Aliasbye.html.
Accessed 12 January 2006.

——. 'Mission Statement', The Safe House. http://www.vartanho.com/
faq/index.html. Accessed December 2005.

Verba, Joan. *Boldly Writing: A Trekker Fan & Zine History, 1967–1987*.
Minneapolis, MN: FTL Publications, 1996.

Vilandra. 'Fandom-ness', 28 May 2004, personal email.

Vogler, Christopher. *The Writer's Journey: Mythic Structures for Storytell-
ers and Screenwriters*. London: Pan Books, 1998.

Weisman, Kevin. 'Introduction', in Kevin Weisman, ed., *Alias Assumed:
Sex, Lies, and SD-6*. Dallas: Benbella Books, 2005: 1–3.

Wilcox, Rhonda V. '"Who Died and Made Her the Boss?": Patterns of
Mortality in *Buffy*', in Rhonda V. Wilcox and David Lavery, eds,
Fighting the Forces: What's at Stake in Buffy the Vampire Slayer. Lan-
ham, MD: Rowman & Littlefield, 2002: 3–17.

——. 'Foreword: Out Far or In Deep', in Frances Early and Kathleen
Kennedy, eds, *Athena's Daughters: Television's New Women Warriors*. Syracuse, NY: Syracuse University Press: 2003: ix–xii.

Zylbergold, Bonnie. 'No Strings Attached: Women Discover Lesbian
Pleasures but Say No to Relationships', *American Sexuality Maga-
zine*, 3:4, Online Version. http://nsrc.sfsu.edu/MagArticle.cfm?
SID=9FF23290769930AA3ECA3E101E96034 F&DSN=nsrc_dsn
&Mode=EDIT&Article=544&ReturnURL=1. Accessed 27 April
2006.

Television Guide

21 Jump Street (Fox, 1987–91)
24 (Fox, 2001–)
Adventures of Ozzie & Harriet, The (ABC, 1952–66)
Agency, The (CBS, 2001–3)
All in the Family (CBS, 1971–9)
Ally McBeal (Fox, 1997–2002)
Amos'n' Andy (CBS, 1951–3)
Andy Griffith Show, The (CBS, 1960–8)
Angel (WB, 1999–2004)
Avengers, The (ITV, 1961–9)
Bernie Mac Show, The (Fox, 2001–)
Bionic Woman, The (ABC/NBC, 1976–8)
Buffy the Vampire Slayer (WB/UPN, 1997–2003)
Charmed (WB, 1998–2006)
City of Angels (CBS, 2000)
Clueless (ABC, 1996–9)
Commander in Chief (ABC, 2005–6)
The Cosby Show (NBC, 1984–92)
Danger Man (aka *Secret Agent*) (ITV, 1964–6)
Dark Angel (Fox, 2000–2)
Desperate Housewives (ABC, 2004–)
Donna Reed Show, The (ABC, 1958–66)
ER (NBC, 1994–)
Everybody Hates Chris (UPN/CW Television Network, 2005–)
Everybody Loves Raymond (CBS, 1996–2005)
Family Ties (NBC, 1982–9)
Father Knows Best (CBS/NBC, 1954–60)
Felicity (WB, 1998–2002)
Femme Nikita, La (CTV, 1997–2001)
Frank's Place (CBS, 1987–8)
Freddie (ABC, 2005–)
Fresh Prince of Bel-Air (NBC, 1990–6)
Friends (NBC, 1994–2004)
George Lopez (ABC, 2002–)
Girl from U.N.C.L.E, The (NBC, 1966–7)
Girlfriends (UPN/CW Television Network, 2000–)
Grey's Anatomy (ABC, 2005–)
Growing Pains (ABC, 1985–92)
Homicide: Life on the Streets (NBC, 1993–9)
Honeymooners, The (CBS, 1955–6)
I Love Lucy (CBS, 1951–7)

I, Spy (NBC, 1965–8)
I'll Fly Away (NBC, 1991–3)
In the Heat of the Night (NBC/CBS, 1988–94)
Jeffersons, The (CBS, 1975–85)
Julia (NBC, 1968–71)
L.A. Law (NBC, 1986–94)
Law & Order (Universal Network Television/NBC, 1990–)
Leave it to Beaver (ABC, 1959–63)
Living Single (Fox, 1993–8)
Lost (ABC, 2004–)
Malcolm in the Middle (Fox, 2000–6)
Man from U.N.C.L.E., The (NBC, 1964–8)
Martin (Fox, 1992–7)
Medium (NBC, 2005–)
Mission: Impossible (CBS, 1966–73)
Moesha (UPN, 1996–2001)
Murder She Wrote (CBS, 1984–96)
My Three Sons (ABC/CBS, 1960–72)
NYPD Blue (ABC, 1993–2005)
New York Undercover (Fox, 1994–8)
Party of Five (Fox, 1994–2000)
Prisoner, The (ITV, 1967–8)
Sabrina, The Teenage Witch (ABC/WB, 1996–2003)
Saved by the Bell (NBC, 1989–93)
Scarecrow and Mrs. King (CBS, 1983–7)
Seinfeld (NBC, 1990–8)
Sex and the City (HBO, 1998–2004)
Shield, The (FX Network, 2002–)
Sister Sister (ABC/WB, 1994–8)
Six Feet Under (HBO, 2001–5)
Six Million Dollar Man, The (ABC, 1974–8)
Sopranos, The (HBO, 1999–2007)
Spooks (BBC, 2002–)
Star Trek (NBC, 1966–9)
Star Trek: The Next Generation (1987–94)
Star Trek: Voyager (UPN, 1995–2001)
Starsky and Hutch (ABC, 1975–9)
Sweet Justice (NBC, 1994–5)
That Seventies Show (Fox, 1998–2006)
Toast of the Town (CBS, 1948–71)
VR-5 (Fox, 1995)
West Wing, The (John Wells Production/NBC, 1999–2006)
Without a Trace (CBS, 2002–)
Xena, Warrior Princess (1995–2001)
X-Files, The (Fox, 1993–2002)

Index